Lydia Lopokova

All joys go with you: let sweet peace attend
You on the way, and wait your journey's end.
But let your discontents and sourer fate
Remain with me, born off in my retreat.

And think not, Dearest, 'cause this parting knell
Is run in verses that at your farewell
I only mourn in Poetry and ink:
No, my pen's melancholy plummets sink
So low, they dive where th' hid affections sit,
Blotting that Paper where my mirth was writ.

From 'The Departure: An Elegy' by Henry
    King (1592–1669) sent by John Maynard
Keynes to Lydia Lopokova in a letter from
King's College, Cambridge, 10 June 1927

Lydia Lopokova

edited by

Milo Keynes

Weidenfeld and Nicolson

London

Printed in Great Britain by Butler & Tanner Ltd, Frome
and London

Contents

The Contributors

Dennis Arundell
Sir Frederick Ashton, OM, CH
Sir Cecil Beaton (1904–1980)
Cyril W. Beaumont (1891–1976)
Quentin Bell
Sir Isaiah Berlin, OM
Henrietta Couper
Sir Anton Dolin
Annabel Farjeon
Lynn Garafola
David Garnett (1892–1981)
Polly Hill
Milo Keynes
Fedor V. Lopukhov (1886–1973)
Malcolm MacDonald, OM (1901–1981)
Frank W. Ries
Sir Austin Robinson
Dame Ninette de Valois, CH
Virginia Woolf (1882–1941)

Illustrations

Unless otherwise credited, photographs are in the author's private collection.

Between pages 78 and 79
1 Constanza, Fedor and Andrei Lopukhova, St Petersburg, 1900
2 Lydia as a Polovtsian Maiden, Mariinsky Theatre, 1909
3 Chaliapine as Mephistopheles in Gounod's *Faust*, Alexandrinsky Theatre, 1901
4 Pavlova and Lydia at the San Francisco Zoo, 1910 (Pavlova Museum, London)
5 Charlie Chaplin, Nijinsky, Eric Campbell, Lydia and Olga Spesivtseva, 1916
6 Publicity photograph of Lydia, New York, 1910
7 'Diaghileff's Ballet-Russe', Chicago, 1916
8 Karsavina as Columbine, *Le Carnaval*, 1912
9 Lydia with Nijinsky, *Le Carnaval*, 1916
10 Red Cross Charity Show at the London Coliseum, 1918
11 Picasso's drawing of Lydia on the back of a menu, 1919 (Keynes family collection)
12 Picasso's drawing of Lydia and Massine in the Can-Can from *La Boutique Fantasque*, London, 1919 (Private collection; photo: Keynes family collection)
13 Picasso's drawing of Diaghilev, Lydia and Massine, Rome, 1917 (Sotheby & Co., London)
14 Lydia Lopokova by Picasso, 1919 (Private collection; photo: Christopher Dalton)
15 Lydia Lopokova in *The Good-humoured Ladies*, London, 1918 (Photo: Hana)
16 Lydia, posed, London, 1918 (Photo: Hana)
17 Lydia Lopokova and Serge Lifar in *Firebird*, His Majesty's Theatre, 1926

Between pages 110 and 111
18 Lydia Lopokova and Leonid Massine dancing the Can-Can in *La Boutique Fantasque*, Alhambra Theatre, 1919
19 Lydia Lopokova by Augustus John, 1921 (National Museum of Wales, Cardiff)

Acknowledgements

Many have helped in the preparation of this book, either by discussion, or by correspondence, or by helping with the illustrations. Particular thanks are due to Anne Olivier Bell, Quentin Bell, Constantine Brancovan, Peter Oppenheimer, David Castillejo, William Chappell, Mary Clarke, Tim Crane, Dame Ninette de Valois, Lynn Garafola, Michael Halls, Margaret Lintott, Richard Shone, Frances Spalding, and, above all, to George Rylands. Thanks must also be gratefully acknowledged to Mari Bicknell, Robert Eddison, Julian Fry, Angelica Garnett, Sir John Gielgud, Sir Robert Helpmann, Philippa Hill, Michael Holroyd, Eileen Hose, Irene Huntoon, Romilly John, the late John Laurie, John Lazzarini, Sir Henry Lintott, the late T. H. Marshall, Angelina Morhange, Oleg Palunin, the late Ian Parsons, Frances Partridge, Sir Roland Penrose, Sir Edward Playfair, Dame Marie Rambert, Margaret Rawlings, Dame Flora Robson, Lady Sainsbury (Anya Linden), Thomas Schoff, Sir Sacheverell Sitwell, David Scrase, Elizabeta Souritz, the late L. B. Sutcliffe, Hugo Vickers, Ruby Weller and Basil Wright.

The contribution by David Garnett has already appeared in *Great Friends*, Macmillan, London (1979), although it was originally written for this book. Malcolm MacDonald died before he could write again on Lydia Lopokova, and his piece first appeared in *People and Places*, published by Collins, London, in 1969. The quotation from Cecil Beaton's unpublished diaries appears by permission of Miss Eileen Hose and the Estate of Cecil Beaton, and the main part of 'A Visit to Lopokova in 1951' appeared in *The Strenuous Years, The Diaries of Cecil Beaton, 1948–55*, Weidenfeld and Nicolson, London (1973). The quotations from *Balletomania* by Arnold Haskell, originally published by Gollancz in 1934, also appear by permission of

Weidenfeld and Nicolson, London (1977). Vladimir Lopukhov provided the original Russian version of his father's 'Lydia Vasilievna Lopukhov'. I should also like to thank William Heinemann Ltd, London, for permission to quote from *Theatre Street* by Tamara Karsavina (1930), and from *Lytton Strachey* by Michael Holroyd (Vol. II 1968), and Macmillan, London, for permission to quote from *The Life of John Maynard Keynes* by Roy Harrod (1951) and from *Laughter in the Next Room* by Osbert Sitwell (1949). In the appendix, Cyril Beaumont's 'Lydia Lopokova: an appreciation' first appeared in *The Art of Lydia Lopokova*, published by C. W. Beaumont in 1920 and reprinted by kind permission of the Cecchetti Society Branch of the Imperial Society of Teachers of Dancing. The 'Obituary of Diaghilev' appears by permission of the *New Statesman*. Virginia Woolf's review, 'Twelfth Night at the Old Vic', which was originally published in the *New Statesman and Nation* in 1933, was reprinted in *The Death of the Moth and other essays* in 1942 and is here quoted by kind permission of The Hogarth Press. I am also grateful to Virginia Woolf's Literary Estate, The Hogarth Press, Anne Olivier Bell, Quentin Bell, Angelica Garnett and Nigel Nicolson for permission to quote from *The Letters of Virginia Woolf* (1976–80) and *The Diary of Virginia Woolf* (1977–83). Two letters from Vanessa Bell are quoted by permission of Quentin Bell and Angelica Garnett.

The Duke of Portland said: 'Who was the Don, who married the dancing girl?' He'd never heard of Maynard. So Ottoline said: 'He's Maynard Keynes. Very well known.' And the Duke said: 'Maynard? Any relation of the Miss Maynard who married Lord Warwick?'

From a letter from Virginia Woolf to Angelica Bell,
18 November 1935
The sixth Duke of Portland (1857–1943) was half-brother to
Lady Ottoline Morrell (1873–1938).

'What's this, I hear, about Maynard Keynes marrying a chorus girl?'

From the diary of David, twenty-seventh Earl of Crawford and Balcarres
(1871–1940)

Preface

This book pays tribute to the irrepressible wit and charm of Lydia
Lopokova, the great ballet dancer and wife of John Maynard Keynes,
the economist. Cecil Beaton describes her later in these pages as 'that
most stimulating and entertaining of all human beings', and the
economist, Lord Robbins, wrote to me at the time of her death that
'in her way she was as unique as Maynard'. Few can have had such
a marvellous aunt about whom to write, and I hope that I have
succeeded in communicating my delight in the task.

Lydia was born in St Petersburg in 1892, and joined the Imperial
Ballet School at the age of eight. She graduated in 1909, but the next
year, aged seventeen and a half, she left Russia, never to dance there
again, and joined Diaghilev in his second summer tour in Western
Europe. After this short season she went to the United States, where
she appeared in music-halls as well as on the stage for the next six
years. In 1916, when Diaghilev's Russian Ballet arrived in New
York, she joined the company and then toured with it until they
arrived in London in 1918. In the United States she had married the
company's business manager, Randolfo Barocchi, and it was the
breakdown of this marriage, described at the start of my introduc-
tory chapter, which was the cause of her abrupt disappearance in
1919. In 1921 she rejoined the Russian Ballet and appeared that year
in Diaghilev's production of *The Sleeping Princess* during the company's season at the Alhambra Theatre. She last danced for Diaghilev
in 1927, and altogether danced for him over seventeen years, during
which time she left his Company, only to rejoin it, more times than
any other dancer.

In London Lydia soon met members of the Bloomsbury group,
including Maynard Keynes, but she did not marry him until 1925

due to her difficulty in obtaining a divorce from Barocchi. Thereafter she appeared in ballet less frequently, though she became a
great force in the early days of English ballet. From 1928 she won
attention as an actress on the English dramatic stage, despite her
marked Russian accent.

During the 1930s Lydia introduced programmes of Russian ballet
music broadcast by the BBC, and from the scripts (often in Maynard's handwriting) I have taken some autobiographical fragments
and incorporated them in my chapters; I have also reconstituted
from them two pieces that appear in the Appendix, 'Pavlova' and
'Memories of the Diaghilev Ballet'. Maynard Keynes died in 1946
after a remarkable and happy association of over twenty-five years,
leaving Lydia a widow for thirty-five years. She continued to live
in London, Cambridge and Tilton in Sussex, dying near Tilton, at
the age of eighty-eight years, in 1981.

I have assembled this book in a similar way to that of my *Essays
on John Maynard Keynes* (Cambridge University Press, 1975): each
contributor was asked to write about a different aspect of Lydia's
life, so that the resulting chapters, taken together, form a rounded
appreciation. I felt that a book was needed on this extraordinarily
gifted and often astounding personality, my Russian aunt, before it
was too late and memories had faded. Dame Marie Rambert died
soon after being interviewed for this book, and other contemporaries
of Lydia's (such as Sir Cecil Beaton and David Garnett), whose
reminiscences of her are included here, have also died. The alacrity
with which the contributors agreed to write for the book was
notable, and their pleasure in it obvious. In most of the chapters the
reason for the choice of the writer will be clear. Dennis Arundell
was an actor, musician and noted stage director, now retired;
Annabel Farjeon was formerly a member of Sadler's Wells Ballet
Company and ballet critic of the *New Statesman*; Lynn Garafola
writes on the history of ballet from New York; Frank Ries is Dance
Historian at the University of California at Santa Barbara.

Diaghilev, with his St Petersburg background, spoke French, but
not English, and when his Russian dancers appeared in Western
Europe their names were transliterated into French forms of spelling.
Due to the phonetic characteristics of the French language, these
spellings may differ from the English forms of the names which are
used in the present book. In some instances, however, the familiarity
of the French form to English-speaking readers has dictated its

retention. For instance, transliterated from Russian into English, Nijinsky should be 'Nizhinsky'; Chaliapine, 'Shaliapin'; Tchaikovsky, 'Chaikovsky'; Tchernicheva, 'Chernishova'; Léonide Massine, 'Leonid Miasin', and so on. As Richard Buckle, the author of *Diaghilev* (Weidenfeld and Nicolson, 1979), has confirmed, it is difficult to standardize the spellings of Russian names, as has been attempted in this book. Lydia's own spellings (such as 'Massin' and 'Chernicheva') have been retained – as, indeed, have her eccentricities of English spelling – in all excerpts from her letters.

Diaghilev sometimes encouraged a simpler spelling for the names of the members of his company, such as 'Spessiva' for 'Spesivtseva'. This is not, however, the explanation for Lydia's decision to change 'Lopukhova' to 'Lopokova' – a change which she made in 1914, when she had been away from Diaghilev for four years. She pronounced her new legalized name in an English way, accenting the first and third syllables. Richard Buckle does not appear to have known of the official change, and wrote, '"Lopokova" does *not* give the right idea of "Lopukhova".' It was not meant to do so. I should add that in my chapter entitled 'The Lopukhov Family', which discusses Lydia's early years, and in the chapter by her brother, Fedor, her name is given as Lydia Lopukhova. As a rule, titles of ballets are given in English in all cases where the English forms have become generally accepted. The surname Keynes is pronounced 'Kaynes' and not 'Keens'.

Milo Keynes
Cambridge, 1983

Lydia Lopokova

Milo Keynes

Osbert Sitwell, writing (in *Laughter in the Next Room*, 1949) of Lydia Lopokova's performance in *The Good-humoured Ladies* in 1918, paid tribute to her supreme artistry:

> It was the grace, pathos, entrancing cleverness, the true comic genius, and liveliness of a dancer new to this country, Lydia Lopokova, which made the chief impression. ... Her face, too, was appealing, inquisitive, bird-like, that of a mask of comedy; while being an artist in everything, she comprehended exactly the span and the limits of her capacities: the personification of gaiety, of spontaneity, and of that particular pathos which is its complement, she had developed the movements of her hands and arms in a way that hitherto no dancer had attempted, thereby achieving a new step forward in technique. Her wit entered into every gesture, into everything she did.

But, besides the artistry shown in her dancing, there were other aspects of Lydia's life, equally special and always original, which together gave it a truly fascinating quality. When John Maynard Keynes died in 1946, she received a different kind of tribute – or, rather, a tribute to her artistry in a different sphere from dancing – when Patrick Hadley, the composer and Professor of Music at Cambridge, wrote to her, 'It was a most wonderful union, you two. I believe it was the most wonderful I have ever known between two humans.' And Frederick Ashton wrote to her, 'You will go down in history as the most devoted wife a great man could have had. I always thought that it was through your will, devotion and care that Maynard was spared to do the great work that he did, for your vigil was incessant both on his pleasure and his work.' This book is both an account of an entrancing and intensely vivacious prima ballerina, who spoke English with variation, amusement and wit, and a record of a devoted and supremely happy relationship that lasted for twenty-five years.

Lydia Vasilievna Lopukhova was born in St Petersburg on 21 October 1892 – the year has long been doubted as each of her three passports differed on this point. She graduated from the Imperial Ballet School in 1909, and a year later left Russia for good to join Diaghilev for his summer tour in Berlin, Paris and Brussels. In July 1910 she left for the United States, where she performed in music-halls as well as on the dramatic stage for the next six years, and married Randolfo Barocchi, the business manager of Diaghilev's company. She did not join what had now become Diaghilev's *Ballets Russes*, or Russian Ballet, until 1916, when the company arrived in New York, with Nijinsky as *premier danseur*. Working with them, she travelled in the United States, South America and Spain, where she last danced with Nijinsky in June 1917. She once told me that when Nijinsky 'came on stage he was God to all of us, but on tour he was rather tiresome, constantly playing schoolboy pranks. Diaghilev, however, knew how to manage him.' Shortly afterwards the company arrived in Rome and began rehearsals there of Massine's early ballets.

Lydia reached London for the first time in August 1918, during the closing stages of the First World War. She took part in a season of the Russian Ballet in which she won over the heart of London by her performance in Massine's *The Good-humoured Ladies*. Another ballet by Massine, *La Boutique Fantasque*, opened in June 1919 at the Alhambra Theatre (since destroyed) in Leicester Square; in this she danced the Can-Can with him, to wild acclamation. Massine later wrote,

> Lopokova knew instinctively the effect I was aiming at, and without a word from me would speed up her kicks or tilt her head coquettishly in response to my sinuous movements. Perhaps it was the contrast between the fluttering, pink-petticoated, mischievous Lopokova, taunting and being taunted, and her greasy and sinister-looking partner, which caused the can-can to be so well received.

Marie Rambert told me

> Lydia's dancing in the Can-Can was *fantasque*. She rejoiced on the
> stage, but she could be more romantic than anyone in *Les Syl-*
> *phides*. When she did a split, you felt it with her. She was so
> sensitive, and had a wonderful stage presence, a wonderful basic
> technique and belonged to the great ones. She never, however,
> underlined the technique, but just danced with an incredible,
> contagious gaiety. Besides this, she showed great poetry and
> musicality, and really she could have danced without music. She
> was a born dancer, a born mover, and such a romp.

She possessed the mysterious gift of holding an audience in the
hollow of her palm, and, as her obituary notice in *The Times* stated,
'Ovations such as greeted her at the end of the Can-Can in the
Boutique Fantasque can surely seldom have been equalled.'

The next month, on Thursday 10 July, Lopokova abruptly left
Diaghilev's company, less than three weeks before the end of the
season, amid rumours that she had eloped with a Russian officer.
Grigoriev, who was managing the company in London while
Diaghilev was in Paris, received a short note from her to say that she
had left the company that day. The newspapers printed headlines
about her disappearance, and the ballet world had grave doubts
about this most unprofessional behaviour. Meanwhile, Vera Nemchinova was given her role in *La Boutique Fantasque*, and performed
it with great success. By the Saturday it was revealed that Lydia had,
in fact, gone no further than St John's Wood, where she was staying
with friends. On 17 July Virginia Woolf asked in a letter to her
sister, Vanessa Bell, 'I wish you'd explain to me the truth about
Lopokova. Did she run away – and with whom – and why – and
where is she? Mrs Hamilton pretended to know for certain she was
ill in a villa in St John's Wood. But dear old Molly Hamilton has a
temperamental lust for the commonplace.'

In the *Observer* for 20 July, there was a report of Diaghilev's
somewhat disingenuous reply when questioned: 'Lopokova is ill. It
is hoped she will recover. But it is not to be wondered at that she is
suffering from fatigue after nearly a year of continuous dancing.
Many of the other dancers might also discover that they had the
same reason for being ill if it were not for their intense anxiety to
continue to give pleasure to the public.' The reason for Lydia's
sudden disappearance was the break-up of her marriage to Randolfo

Barocchi, though her elopement with the Russian officer has passed into ballet folklore.*

Barocchi was an Italian, who, according to Cyril Beaumont, was the owner of a marble statuary business and an amateur of music and the theatre. He became secretary to Henry Russell and the San Carlo Opera Company while it was on a tour of North America. Diaghilev discovered him in 1915 as a new backer who soon became an associate and then business manager of his company just before its American tour in 1916. Lydia met him after he had arrived in New York with the Russian Ballet for this tour, and within a short time – perhaps with Diaghilev's heavy connivance, so that she should acquire a strong link with the company – he 'married' Lydia, although, unknown to her, he had not yet completed the divorce from his first, Italian, wife. Barocchi was older than Lydia, spoke several languages and seems to have been lively and amusing; Virginia Woolf saw him at a performance of the ballet and in a letter described him as a 'little ivory figure'. But Lydia began to tire of him, and by the beginning of 1919 Cyril Beumont noticed a serious estrangement.

On 10 July, Lydia left the following note for Barocchi at the Savoy Hotel, where they had been staying: 'It is very hard for me to continue the life I led lately. I decided to go away from it. If you really want to help me you will send me the necessary papers. It is suffering for me to continue to dance also, so I informed Grigorieff and Diaghileff that I am no more in the troupe. Excuse me if I trouble you, but I can't do otherwise.' To Diaghilev, she wrote the same day in Russian,

> Recently, for reasons of a personal nature, I have had a nervous breakdown so serious that only with difficulty was I able to get through the performances at the end of last week, and of the current week, and, in particular, of yesterday. Under the circum-stances, in order not to overstrain myself irreparably, I shall literally be unable henceforward to take part in performances, not

---

* Richard Buckle, in *Diaghilev* (1979, p. 357) wrote, 'A few days later, on 10 July, Lydia Lopokova, who was bored with Barocchi, eloped (to St John's Wood) with a Russian officer', and cites as the evidence for this remark *The Memoirs of Lydia Sokolova* (Murray, 1960) which describes (pp. 139–40) a party at the Savoy Hotel which Lydia and Barocchi attended, with three Russian officers, one of whom passed out. Sokolova adds, 'I cannot think this appalling scene had anything to do with Lydia's running away, but disappear she did a few days later.'

only today, but on subsequent days generally. I very much regret that, on the basis of the final clauses of our contract, my agreement with you will be terminated by this; but I am consoled by the thought that my departure from the troupe now, only a few days before the end of the season, will pass wholly unnoticed.

Barocchi immediately left London that evening and went to Rome. From there he wrote in French to Diaghilev on 16 July,

> As far as L. is concerned, I had already been through Hell for a few weeks because she acted totally out of character, and I may confess to you that on more than one occasion I strongly felt like going away so as not to suffer any longer, but my idea was in fact that she should have at least finished the season at the Alhambra and saved both her name and mine. I had already taken all the depositions that were necessary, and we had agreed that I would help her to get her divorce very peacefully, immediately after the London season, so that we would avoid scandal and dishonour. ... All I could do then was to leave London to avoid a probably irreparable disaster. ... All my life I have never met a more sweet, charming, decent, good and generous woman than L.

The sudden breaking of her contract with Diaghilev certainly worried Lydia a great deal, and the intensity of feeling in the correspondence quoted above does imply that she left the company because of the break-up of her marriage to Randolfo Barocchi rather than because she wanted to have an affair with anyone, let alone a general (as the rank of the unknown Russian officer became in some accounts). Also, her discovery in St John's Wood within thirty-six hours of her disappearance, hardly implies a well planned escape, or anything more than a sudden impulse.

What Lydia did from July 1919, when she ran away from Barocchi and the Diaghilev company, until February 1921, when she appeared in New York dancing for seven minutes in a musical play called *The Rose Girl*, remains a mystery. In a letter she wrote that she gave up dancing for eighteen months, and when she arrived back in America is unknown. Later (on the BBC) she said of this episode,

> I was in New York out of training, for I had run away from the stage. So, I thought it would not be a bad plan to appear in musical comedy, where it is so easy to cover up your faults, which

in a real ballet is impossible. Fokine was invited to stage the number based on a Brahms waltz. It was called 'Perfume'. I *was* a flop, so much so that the management got rid of me as soon as they could. I had to borrow money from friends to reach Europe. In the ballet in the play I was a kind of female spectre de la rose, without seed or flower. It is good to be a flop sometimes, but not at the time.

The Rose Girl ran for ninety-nine performances, and so would have closed in May, but Lydia had left earlier, to rejoin the Diaghilev company.

Early in March 1921 Diaghilev, in Paris, received a telegram from Lydia's manager in New York, asking, 'Will you have Lopokova back?', to which he replied, 'Yes, if it is the same Lopokova I knew.' She accordingly rejoined the Russian Ballet in Madrid, where they were staying for a season until mid-April. Her special relationship with Diaghilev was emphasized, then and later, by the number of times over seventeen years that she left his company (in which she was always a success), only to be taken back again; she continued dancing for him, intermittently, until 1927. Once she overheard Diaghilev shouting at someone and remarked to him, 'You have never shouted at me like that.' 'No,' he replied, 'and I never shall.' On a later occasion, Lydia recalled, her shoe-lace came undone on stage as he was watching from the wings. He followed her to her dressing-room, and, in a fury, started shouting abuse at her dresser, though not at her. 'And everyone knows that a dancer does up her own shoes,' Lydia added. She once related to me how Diaghilev had told her that Pavlova and Spesivtseva were two halves of the same apple, and that Spesivtseva was the one on the sunny side.

Lydia returned to London for a short time, but rejoined the Diaghilev company on 17 May for a week at the Gaieté Lyrique, in Paris, where she opened in *The Firebird* and subsequently danced in *Les Sylphides* and *Petrushka*. On 26 May, the company opened in London at the Prince's Theatre for a season, ending on 31 July, in which Lydia danced in twelve ballets: *La Boutique Fantasque*, *Les Sylphides*, *Petrushka*, *Carnaval*, *Prince Igor*, *Papillons*, *Le Spectre de la Rose*, *Cleopatra*, *The Midnight Sun*, *Pulcinella*, *The Good-humoured Ladies* and *The Firebird*. After only one month's holiday the preparations began for the classical ballet, Tchaikovsky's *The Sleeping Princess* – the change of name from *The Sleeping Beauty* will be explained later – which finally opened on 3 November at the Alhambra Theatre.

Diaghilev had begun planning a revival of *The Sleeping Beauty* in Spain in April. Stravinsky revised the music; in particular he 'instrumented' a solo for Aurora in the vision scene and an interlude between this scene and the awakening, both of which had been omitted from Tchaikovsky's published score. For the production Diaghilev had a team of four Russian ballerinas – Trefilova, Spesivtseva, Egorova and Lopokova – though Lopokova was not a 'classical' dancer, being short and at times appearing even dumpy (as shown in the drawings of her dancing made by Picasso). Her arms and legs did not have the grace and long, flowing lines of the classical prima ballerina, and, besides, she did not take much trouble over her make-up, her costumes, or, indeed, her appearance on stage – or, for that matter, when off it! When she was dancing, it was the unconventionality, the exuberance and the happiness of her personality which were communicated to audiences, so that the others who were on stage ceased to matter. In addition, she was, as Cyril Beaumont noted, a born comédienne, and that is a rare quality in a dancer.

The production was financed by Sir Oswald Stoll, who had a reputation for putting on pantomimes in the West End of London and who did not want the Tchaikovsky ballet to appear to be another one of these. He therefore insisted that it should be called *The Sleeping Princess*, and so it was for many years. Diaghilev always disliked being told what to do, particularly by an impresario who was exerting financial pressure on him, and when he told Lopokova that the title of the ballet was to be *The Sleeping Princess*, rather than *The Sleeping Beauty*, he made a joke about it, telling her that the change was because of the shape of her nose. Lydia at first danced the part of the Lilac Fairy and stole the reviews: the *Daily Express* thought that 'Taglioni might have envied Lopokova her series of ovations', and *The Times* that Princess Aurora and the Prince Charming 'were completely outshone by Lopokova and Idzikovsky'. As she was the 'star' attraction of the show, Stoll encouraged Diaghilev to give her some performances as Princess Aurora which is, however, a particularly classical part. This he did, and though, according to Marie Rambert, she was not suited to it, she danced it beautifully and triumphed in it because of her enchanting personality.

Stravinsky gave Lydia the three pages of a piano arrangement he had made (presumably for rehearsals) of the variations of the Lilac Fairy; he had inscribed the manuscript, 'To Lopushka – the traitress' and signed it. The probable explanation is that, according to Anton Dolin, Lydia did not dance the traditional solo of the Lilac Fairy in the performances of *The Sleeping Princess*, but the more important one of the Sugar Plum Fairy from *The Nutcracker*. Later Lydia kept the manuscript, framed, on a bookcase at Tilton; it is now in the Fitzwilliam Museum, Cambridge.

Lydia had danced in *The Firebird* from its opening in 1910, taking over the title-role from Karsavina within days. Later she danced in other Stravinsky ballets: *Petrushka*, *Pulcinella*, *Les Noces* and *Ragtime* (which she created with Massine in 1922), and she was the Princess (a part said to have been created for her) in *A Soldier's Tale* when this was first performed in London in 1927 under the title of *The Tale of the Soldier*. (Earlier, in 1918, it had been given a concert performance in Switzerland under the title *L'Histoire du Soldat*.) Lydia once told me that Stravinsky seemed to have religious problems (about which she did not enlarge) which she thought had been a distinct handicap to the development of his personality. At his funeral a very elaborate and lengthy Russian Orthodox service was given. Lydia's own attitude to religion amounted, I think, to a pleasurable acknowledgement of the traditional rituals of that Church.

The production of *The Sleeping Princess* had been planned to last six months but in the event it closed after only three, on 4 February 1922. Barocchi was with Diaghilev until its end, by which time Lydia had been back with the Russian Ballet for nearly a year. He then returned to Italy. Apparently his last attempt to make contact with Lydia occurred in 1950, when he wrote to her from Rome on 27 December:

> I just happened to find out your address, and although you never answered any of my letters I sent to the old London address I still wish to write to you every happyness [sic] for the New Year. You needn't bother to reply to this letter, for, as long as I know that you are well and in good health I am perfectly content – although I don't wish to convey the thought that a few lines from you wouldn't bring me unspeakable happyness!

Lydia was back among friends in London, and there she remained. She continued to dance, and in April she performed twice daily with Massine at Covent Garden in a divertissement called *The Cockatoo's Holiday*, in which they both had blackened faces. This ballet was an adjunct to the showing at Covent Garden of a film entitled *Love* in a programme devised by the American impresario, Walter F. Wanger, to accustom the English to films – and also, perhaps, to secure the theatre for himself as a cinema. She danced with Massine at Covent Garden again later that month in the opening of Stravinsky's *Ragtime*, which they repeated in June at the London Coliseum in a programme that also featured the Marx brothers.

The Diaghilev company first arrived in London in June 1911, with Karsavina and Nijinsky as its leading dancers, and it opened a second season there later in the year. It returned in June the next year, and on this visit was particularly taken up by Lady Ottoline Morrell, who introduced her friends in the Bloomsbury circle to the company. Other seasons followed in 1913 and 1914, and when the Russian Ballet returned to London in August 1918, this time with Lopokova, the Bloomsbury group, which included Maynard Keynes, renewed its association. Although he had most probably been introduced to her earlier in her dressing-room at the London Coliseum, Maynard is said to have first met Lopokova at a party given by the Sitwell brothers on 10 October after a performance of *Schéhérazade*. At their house in Carlyle Square there were a number of many-coloured stuffed love-birds in a glass case. On seeing them, Lydia threw up her arms and asked to be given one. The gaudiest she nicknamed 'Pimp'. On Armistice night, 11 November, Montague Shearman gave a party at the Adelphi Hotel to which Diaghilev and Massine went, and at which Diaghilev was the only person not to dance. There Maynard met Lydia again. As I have related, after her disappearance Lydia returned to London in 1921, and at the performances of *The Sleeping Princess* Maynard was at the theatre night after night, almost alone in the empty stalls.

Maynard Keynes was born at 6 Harvey Road, Cambridge, on 5 June 1883, the elder son of John Neville Keynes, philosopher and for many years Registrary (senior administrator) of the University, and of Florence Ada Brown, one of the first students at Newnham College and (in 1932) the first woman Mayor of Cambridge. He had a sister, Margaret, who later married A. V. Hill, CH, FRS, a Nobel prize-winner, and a brother, Geoffrey (my father) – surgeon, writer, bibliographer and much else – who died, aged ninety-five, in 1982. (Polly Hill has written about 6 Harvey Road and Lydia's English parents-in-law – whom Lydia used to call 'F-i-l' and 'M-i-l' – in a chapter of this book.)

Maynard won scholarships to Eton and to King's College, Cambridge. In 1909, he was elected a Fellow of King's, later becoming Bursar, a position he held until his death on 21 April, 1946. He began his studies in economics in 1905 and was to work for the Treasury in both World Wars. In 1919 he resigned from the Civil Service and wrote *The Economic Consequences of the Peace*, which made him famous. Adroit transactions on the Stock Exchange resulted in financial independence, and he continued to develop his economic theories and concern himself with public affairs. In 1936 he built the Arts Theatre for the City and University of Cambridge, and from 1942 he was Chairman of the Council for the Encouragement of Music and the Arts (CEMA), which became the Arts Council – for which he had written the charter – after his death. He became Lord Keynes in 1942, and was offered and accepted a Fellowship of the Royal Society and the Order of Merit just before he died.

On entering the Civil Service in 1906, Maynard moved to London, where he joined a group of Cambridge friends who, because they lived in what was the then unfashionable district of Bloomsbury, became known as the Bloomsbury group. Clive and Vanessa Bell, Lytton Strachey, Leonard and Virginia Woolf, Duncan Grant, E. M. Forster, Roger Fry and Maynard Keynes formed its nucleus. From 1916 Maynard spent much time at Charleston, a farmhouse on the north edge of the South Downs, five miles from Lewes, in which by then the Bells and Duncan Grant lived most of the time.

On Lydia's return to London in 1921, Maynard began to pay her particular attention, and after the closing of *The Sleeping Princess* in 1922 she remained in the capital. She was living at the Waldorf Hotel in the Bloomsbury area, and used to bank her money with the head-porter, but now Maynard took over her financial affairs and became her manager. She moved into 50 Gordon Square, a few doors away from Maynard's house at no. 46. Adrian Stephen (brother of Vanessa Bell and Virginia Woolf) lived there, as did Clive and Vanessa Bell when in London. But this arrangement did not work well, and in September Lydia moved into the ground-floor flat at 41 Gordon Square, where James (the brother of Lytton) and Alix Strachey lived. According to James, the whole house used to shake when Lydia practised her entrechats. Duncan Grant had a studio round the corner at 8 Fitzroy Street, though he mainly slept at 46 Gordon Square, and Lytton was at no. 51.

In a later chapter, 'Bloomsbury and Lydia', Quentin Bell gives an intimate and detailed account of Lydia's introduction to the Blooms-bury circle (and to Vanessa Bell and Duncan Grant in particular), as well as of the *angst* which Maynard showed in his deepening rela-tionship with her. Vanessa wrote to Maynard about plans for the summer holidays:

> ... Clive says he thinks it impossible for anyone of us, you, he, I or Duncan, to introduce a new wife or husband into the existing circle for more than one week at a time. . . . Don't think however that what I say is some kind of criticism of Lydia for it isn't. We feel that no one can come into the sort of intimate society we have without altering it (she has done so perhaps less than anyone, certainly less than any other woman could have) That is inevitable isn't it? . . .

In another letter to Maynard of 1922, written before Lydia's move from no. 50 Gordon Square, Vanessa wrote about plans for her and Quentin to use no. 50 more frequently, now that Julian Bell was away at school. Vanessa could use Duncan's studio for her painting, and Angelica, their daughter, could live at no. 46, Maynard's house: 'If Angelica stayed at 46 I expect I should nearly always come round there for tea and the only time when I might want to be at 50 would be in the evenings after dinner. But I'm sure we could arrange it. This is all supposing that Lydia prefers to do this rather than leave. If she does it would suit me quite well.'

Difficulties had arisen from Lydia's living at no. 50 owing to her constant interruptions and chatter about the ballet when Vanessa was trying to paint, and Vanessa and Duncan, though they liked her, began to find her annoying – not that Duncan would ever have expressed any irritation. Lydia found it almost impossible to settle down to a serious conversation, and, when she did, would ruin it by a flippant remark. Bloomsbury found her unsound, from their standpoint, on the eternal verities: morality, religion, the soul and, particularly, politics and public affairs – matters of which she pos-

sessed only a superficial knowledge. Then Maynard began talking
about marrying her, and they were worried for him. Perhaps they
felt that if he took this step, he would become less available to them
– which in the event was true – but they had also begun to assume
that they had the right to dictate his actions. Of course, they had
quickly discovered Lydia's gaiety and infectious laughter; and appreciated her for these qualities. Virginia Woolf wrote to Vanessa
Bell on 22 December, 1922:

> Seriously, I think you ought to prevent Maynard before it is too
> late. I can't believe that he realizes what the effects would be. I can
> foresee only too well Lydia stout, charming, exacting; Maynard
> in the Cabinet; 46 Gordon Square the resort of the dukes and
> prime ministers. M. being a simple man, not analytic as we are,
> would sink beyond recall long before he realized his state. Then
> he would awake, to find 3 children, and his life entirely and for
> ever controlled.
>   That is how it appears to me, without considering my own
> grievances. If you don't put your view before him, he will have
> a case against you when the catastrophe arrives. Moreover, Lydia
> is far better as a Bohemian unattached, hungry, and expectant,
> than as a matron with nothing to hope, and all her rights secure.

Lydia's marriage to Maynard, however, was by no means imminent.
For she could not marry him until she had obtained an expensive
and long-delayed disentanglement from her first husband, both the
expense and the delay being due to her having married Barocchi
before he had obtained a full divorce from his first wife. They
married at St Pancras Central Registry Office on 25 August, 1925;
Maynard's parents and sister attended and Duncan Grant and Vera
Bowen were the witnesses. Immediately after the ceremony the
couple left for Russia, not only to meet Lydia's family but also for
Maynard to represent Cambridge University at the bicentenary
celebrations of the foundation of the Leningrad Academy of Sciences
formerly the Imperial Academy of St Petersburg. On their return
Maynard wrote 'A Short View of Russia' (in which he acknowledged, with thanks, the help of his interpreter); this first appeared
in the *Nation and Athenaeum* and was later published by Leonard and
Virginia Woolf at the Hogarth Press. Lydia and Maynard were to
revisit Russia in 1928 and 1937.

Lydia once remarked simply to me, 'Maynard gave gaiety to life.'
Once he asked her, 'What are you thinking about?' 'Nothing,' said
Lydia. 'I wish I could,' replied Maynard. Lydia always bluntly
claimed to dislike economists, but when asked by Marie Rambert
whether she had ever read *The Economic Consequences of the Peace*,
she replied, 'There is no need to understand it; for me it is just like
Bach!' She did sometimes try to read Maynard's articles and books
(as a wifely duty? – see Polly Hill's account of her correspondence
with him, 'Lydia's letters to Maynard', later in this book), but she
never read Roy Harrod's biography of him (1951) or my collection
of essays (1975). In his biography of Lytton Strachey (1968, vol.2)
Michael Holroyd wrote,

> How could Maynard, Lytton wondered, have brought himself to
> marry such 'a half-witted canary'? There was nothing to her. She
> bobbed and flitted about the furniture, chirruping away to every-
> one, and failing in every way to conceal her incomprehension of
> even the most coherent English speech. It was a disaster! What
> ever could have possessed Maynard? Why had he done it? they
> [Bloomsbury] wondered. Of course some people might cynically
> suggest that being able to show off a brilliant ballerina as his wife
> could prove an asset in his aspiring career. But it was not this. He
> actually seemed to be in love with her – and she with him.
> Extraordinary! Before long they would be taking marriage to the
> ultimate absurdity by having children – but that, on second
> thoughts, was *too* improbable.

What a different view is this from that of H. G. Wells, who said of
Lopokova in November 1925, 'She is not only clever for a dancer,
but clever for anybody – and Keynes's brain is the best in the
country.' As for the prospect of having children, a subsequent
gynaecological examination of Lydia showed that she would be
unable to have a family.

From 1925, besides living at 46 Gordon Square, Maynard and
Lydia took a lease on the farmhouse at Tilton, a hamlet under Firle
Beacon, on the South Downs in Sussex, a few hundred yards from
Charleston. Later Maynard farmed from there, with Logan Thomp-
son as the manager. Until a heart attack in 1937 Maynard's routine
was to spend the weeks in London and long weekends in Cambridge
during Term, but otherwise to be at Tilton as much as possible.
Lydia had a *barre*, with a huge mirror, fitted for her practice in the

ground-floor front room at Gordon Square. She only rarely went
to Cambridge, where Maynard had rooms in King's College, de-
corated by Duncan and Vanessa. When separated, they wrote to
each other every day, and all the letters were kept.

In May 1937, just before Maynard's illness, they moved into a flat
in Cambridge, in St Edward's Passage, close to the Arts Theatre.
The flat was King's College property, and when it was being con-
verted for them, wooden panels, with carved Tudor roses, were
discovered lining the walls of the main room. Furniture was ordered
from Heal's, and although the flat had a rather bleak and underused
air it was adequate for their visits there. Side by side with a
Gaudier-Brzeska stone carving was a board onto which they pinned
newspaper clippings. For years it had been Lydia's practice to cut
out quaint asides and photographs from newspapers, many of which
lay around her rooms, but of which some were either stuck into
albums or pinned up on this board. Two examples are 'A cow-
milking ape in Pittsburgh: farmers reported that their cows were
being milked by some unknown individual, and eight of the best
milkers were absolutely dry,' and 'Why cats have whiskers – their
uses in catching mice.' The most famous one was a photograph of
Lloyd George, in full evening dress and smothered with ribbons,
addressing a banquet in Paris, on which Maynard had written,
'Lying in state.'

In time Bloomsbury ceased to be worried by Lydia, both because
she always remained amusing on her own subjects and because she
obviously made Maynard extremely happy. But, once the pair had
married, they started to move away from the close contact that they
had formerly had with the circle. This, one presumes, was partly
because Maynard became more involved with other worlds, partly,
as Austin Robinson wrote in *Essays on John Maynard Keynes*, because
he deviated from the Bloomsbury sense of values, and partly because
of Bloomsbury's initial failure to accept and welcome Lydia. They
continued to spend evenings with their Bloomsbury friends, of
course (though far less frequently than before), and met them at the
parties which they gave, or attended, as well as on holiday visits.
Contact with them at weekends was limited because Maynard was
so often in Cambridge.

In later years I sensed that Lydia thought that Vanessa despised
her, and when I took her over from Tilton to neighbouring Charleston for a meal, I found that she was still shy of Vanessa's possible

judgements on her. Her favourite friend of Bloomsbury days was always E. M. Forster, an affection which, I think, was reciprocated. I remember being at the Cambridge Arts Theatre with Lydia for a stage adaptation of *A Room with a View*, with Forster sitting immediately behind us; his amusement at her comments, made in a fairly loud voice during the performance, was obvious. (This facility for talking unconcernedly during performances, which occurred more frequently when she was bored, caused me embarrassment on several occasions.) In his later years, Morgan Forster was aware that Bloomsbury had taken a long time to understand Lydia. 'How we all used to underrate her!' he once said. He found her constantly amusing and 'whose every word should be recorded' (commonplace book, King's College Library, p. 208). On one of her last visits to Cambridge he returned from lunching with her in her flat and told with a chuckle of how he had just written down her parting remark. She had warned him to take care and not to slip on the steep steps outside the flat – he was then nearly eighty – and had added, 'You know, I once tumbled from the stairs, and believe me I paid the price.' The other member of 'old' Bloomsbury that Lydia particularly enjoyed seeing was Leonard Woolf, whom she met usually only once a year, on Christmas Day. Another devoted friend over the years was T. S. Eliot.

I never met any member of the Bloomsbury group who seemed to me as humorous and witty as Lydia. (Admittedly, I did not meet Lytton Strachey or Virginia Woolf.) Her humour was not malicious, even though she could be outrageous. Bloomsbury may have been puzzled by this absence of malice and by the genuine happiness of her wit, which they sometimes mistook for stupidity. One day, after reading some of Virginia Woolf's letters, she said, with amazement in her eyes, 'Oh! How intelligent she was. I see now how terribly stupid she must have thought me.' On the other hand, she once wrote to Maynard (26 April 1925): 'Virginia Woolf is a bunch of sweet flowers in words.'

In the summer of 1937 Maynard suffered a massive coronary artery thrombosis while he was in Cambridge for a longer period than usual, in order 'to escape the Coronation crowds'. After a few weeks he went to recuperate at Ruthin Castle in Wales, and finally got to Tilton in the early autumn, to complete his convalescence. Unfortunately he never made a full recovery and remained partially incapacitated for the rest of his life, though he was able to make

six visits to America between 1941 and 1946, to head financial
negotiations.

From the moment of the first attack Lydia dedicated herself to
nursing Maynard and looking after him with ceaseless solicitude.
She had always been a devoted wife, and now faced a long-drawn-
out ordeal with undiminished high spirits and vigour, dedicating
her entire existence to his maintenance. In her loving care for
Maynard she embodied natural goodness and consummate tact.
She travelled with him, and once incurred the displeasure of the
wartime Lords of the Admiralty for accompanying him to America
on a naval ship without having first asked for their permission.
In his biography, Roy Harrod wrote of their visit to America in
1943:

> He was still a sick man; and she never relaxed her vigilance. 'How
> are you, Lydia?' – 'I am very well. When Maynard is well, I am
> well; when he is ill, I am ill.' She became in due course almost a
> legendary figure. Her boundless gaiety, her manifest devotion,
> her resourcefulness in providing comfort on the most unpromis-
> ing occasions with all sorts of queer contrivances, her shopping
> expeditions, her infinite sweetness with all his associates, her quips
> and sallies, unconventional and personal, but always acceptable,
> suffused with some unique quality of simplicity and thereby
> dignity, endeared her to the American hearts. To be a friend of
> the great British economist – that was something to be proud of;
> but to be a friend of Lydia – that was the supreme glory.

As my father, Geoffrey Keynes, pointed out, through her protection
of Maynard Lydia had become once again, and quite unknowingly,
a figure of international importance.

Lydia was a stern and unremitting scourge of anyone who occupied Maynard's time unnecessarily, or for too long, and a strict
guard who limited the length of meetings, though the ration was
increased with time. Luckily, as a member of the family, I was
considered outside the edict, and was included in the weekly visit to
the Cambridge Arts Theatre and in any entertainment thereafter, as
well as in the Sunday lunch party at 6 Harvey Road. Sometimes
there were stormy conflicts of will, for it was not always easy for
Lydia to enforce restraint on Maynard, who naturally could become
impatient. Nor was it necessarily easy to win the verbal battles, as
the following story, from Quentin Bell, emphasizes. Each year

Maynard used to give shooting parties on the farm at Tilton, and used to walk with the guns and watch the sport. On one of these occasions Lydia was worried that he would overtire himself, and said so, but he still insisted on going from beat to beat, until, despairingly, she besought him at least to take a long rest after lunch. 'Of course I'll lie down,' he replied, 'of course I will. Why, I'm lying now!' Lydia's devotion to Maynard was absolute, and the late Marie Rambert said that he became sacred to her. Once she lunched with Lydia when she was dancing at the London Coliseum with Idzikovsky. They got into a taxi to go to the theatre, but instead Lydia insisted on going home. 'I haven't got something of Maynard with me, and I must get it to put in my bosom.' The something was one of his handkerchiefs.

At parties, Maynard never took his eyes off her, and it was wonderful to find that he was still amused by her, laughing with her and at her, after so many years. Right up to the time of his death he was still unable to tell what she would say or do next. When he died, Lydia said it would take ten years for her to recover, and it did. At first she used to wear his clothes, but after the ten years, she said, she no longer thought of him; such was her realism. No one who had ever met Lydia would find the success of this marriage at all strange. Lady Violet Bonham Carter once wrote that it was 'one of the most perfect marriages I have ever known. ... No two human beings could have provided a greater contrast nor given each other greater happiness.'

Lydia was a child actor on the Imperial stage in St Petersburg as well as a child dancer at the Imperial Ballet School. She greatly enjoyed acting in plays, and at times, when disenchanted with ballet dancing, she became an actress, as during her stay in America from 1910 until 1916. After she had settled in England, she was determined to appear on the professional stage here, and did so both before and after her final retirement from dancing. For most people, however, Lydia's strong Russian accent ('Malwolio') was a deterrent from full enjoyment of her skills as an actress. At the opening in 1936 of Maynard's Arts Theatre, Cambridge (built partly for her to act in and of which she was a Trustee from June 1946 until the end of 1960), Lydia acted Nora in Ibsen's *A Doll's House* and Hilda Wangel in *The Master Builder*. William Chappell told me, 'Lydia didn't act. She was it. She was being herself being that person.' Robert Helpmann thought that 'she had an extraordinary talent for taking the most banal line and making it sound funny, though never grotesque. She was an extremely good actress, and would have been a wonderful screen actress with a director such as Bergman. She was, of course, lovable, and when, as Olivia in *Twelfth Night*, she put down her veil, saying, "Is't not well done?" the audience roared with laughter at the charming way she evidently believed her face "well done".'

Both in Bloomsbury and in Sussex there were theatrical evenings, at some of which there might be dancing. In 1926 Lydia and May-nard danced a variant of the Can-Can from *La Boutique Fantasque*, a dance which became known as the Keynes-Keynes and of which Vanessa Bell painted a cartoon; it was repeated on several later occasions. On 21 December 1927 an entertainment called *Interpretations* was performed at 46 Gordon Square. The programme for this was apparently printed by Lydia herself at the Hogarth Press, the press which belonged to the Woolfs. In the first number, 'Albert - so white, so whiskered and so good', Lydia danced the role of Queen Victoria and Frederick Ashton that of Prince Albert. He remembers, 'She talked and then we did some sort of dance.' The fifth and last 'interpretation' was entitled 'The Economic Consequences of the Piece'. The script of this (written by Maynard) went as follows:

> You *monsters*, why don't you slink off to your beds?
> I've told you already, you've got ougly* heads.
> (What a lov-el-y beard!) The Lord knows *who* you are!
> But I'll tell you who *I* am: I am the char.
> *That*'s what I am *now*. For the gay days are over
> When economists courted the fair Lopokova.
> Yet when Company's here, I'm still told that I must
> Try to kick up my heels, as I stir up the dust.
> So I'll do what I can with my wobbly old knees,
> Still showing myself off, still anxious to please.

As early as 1919 Virginia Woolf had stated her intention of writing a comedy about her great-aunt, Julia Margaret Cameron, the Victorian portrait photographer, and she completed a version of it (entitled *Freshwater*) by 1923. It was to be stage-managed by

* The word 'ugly' is spelt like this in Milton's autograph manuscript of *Comus* in the Library at Trinity College, Cambridge, and in some editions.

Desmond MacCarthy and Lydia was given the part of Ellen Terry and possibly the non-speaking role of Queen Victoria also. She is mentioned in the text when Mr Cameron says, 'And there was a damsel – an exquisite but not altogether ethereal nymph. Her name was Lydia. She was a dancer. She came from Muscovy. She had danced before the Tsar. She snatched me by the waist and whirled me through the currant bushes.' Later Lord Tennyson asks, 'Who is Lydia, what is she that all our swains adore her?' To which Mr Cameron replies, 'She is a Muscovite. She danced before the Tsar', and Mrs Cameron adds, 'The very person I want! A housemaid who can dance!' But in October Virginia – who was at the time deeply involved in writing her novel *The Hours*, later entitled *Mrs Dalloway* – wrote to Vanessa, saying that she must abandon the project and that she 'could write something much better, if I give a little more time to it'. An expanded version of *Freshwater* was written and duly performed in the studio at 8 Fitzroy Street in January 1935. Angelica Bell played Ellen Terry, and the references to Lydia were omitted in the new text.

There are numerous mentions of Lydia in the six volumes of *The Letters of Virginia Woolf*, as well as in Virginia Woolf's published diary. Virginia's comments on people could be most unkind at times, though on other occasions they were warm. To Vanessa Bell she wrote on 24 May 1923:

> Unfortunately, talking to Lydia, I called Maynard 'your husband' I see this is not the thing to do. Poor little parrokeet – there she sits at the window in a pink kimono awaiting him, I suppose. 'Maynār liked your article so much Leonār. What a good paper it is! Noā, noā, I cant come out to tea. I am awaiting someone!' I suppose she has to read the Nation now. What tragedies these parrokeets go through!

And on 4 November she wrote to Jacques Raverat:*

> You were saying that you would like a little gossip about Maynard and Lydia. On Sep. 7th we went to stay with them at Studland – a ducal home, in which they fared, rather uneasily I thought,

---

*Jacques Raverat, who was dying of multiple sclerosis in France, was the husband of Gwen Raverat, sister of Geoffrey Keynes's wife Margaret. He had written asking for some gossip.

because the dukes servants were in the pantry; and Lydia's habits, of course, are not ducal.... Lydia, whose father was porter in a Petersburg hotel, and whose entire life has been spent hopping from foot to foot with the daughters of publicans, did not know this perhaps most binding of all laws of female life.... Lydia has the soul of a squirrel: anything nicer you cant conceive: she sits by the hour polishing the sides of her nose with her front paws. But, poor little wretch, trapped in Bloomsbury, what can she do but learn Shakespeare by heart? I assure you its tragic to see her sitting down to King Lear. Nobody can take her seriously: every nice young man kisses her. Then she flies into a rage and says she is like Vanessa, like Virginia, ... – a seerious wooman.

On 25 April the next year, Virginia wrote to Vanessa Bell:

Its been almost too fine to be true here; and nothing has happened, except that Maynard and Lydia came over in their car, obviously unable to face even one whole day alone. 'Politics are so interesting' Lydia remarked, but gossiped to me all the time about the Courtaulds and such like. The problem of one's friends marriages is indeed insoluble. A rare bird would really suit Maynard better, I can't help thinking. However she caught a frog and was very charming about crows which she rhymes to Cows, and her armpits, which are called mouseholes in Russian; and I see I should rather like her for a mistress myself.

On 8 June she wrote to Jacques Raverat:

Maynard is very heavy and rather portentous; Maynard is passionately and pathetically in love, because he sees very well that he's dished if he marries her, and she has him by the snout. You can't argue solidly when Lydia's there, and as we set now to the decline, and prefer reason to any amount of high spirits, Lydia's pranks put us all on edge; and Bloomsbury steals off to its dens, leaving Maynard with Lydia on his knee, a sublime but heartrending spectacle.

To the same correspondent she wrote again on 4 September:

Why will Maynard be dished if he marries her? Because she has the nicest nature in the world and a very limited head-piece. She came to tea on Sunday with your brother-in-law Geoffrey, and really I had the hardest time in the world. Her contribution is one shriek, two dances; then silence, like a submissive child, with her hands crossed. At 30 this is pathetic. Soon she will be plaintive. And they say you can only talk to Maynard now in words of one syllable. This he will tire of. She will cry, and the great ladies wont ask her to their parties.

To Vanessa Bell (15 May 1927) she noted:

Lydia ripens visibly. She has her little stories and jokes; but is settling into housekeeping, and talks, religiously, of the fresh fish she gets at Selfridges, and how, by making eyes at a certain shop man, he pulls the kidneys fresh and bleeding from the sheep (or is it cow?) in her presence. I see in this the tragedy of the childless, which no doubt, will corrode her entirely.

In contrast to these critical quotations from Virginia's letters, the warmth expressed in others was somewhat less assured. The quotations, however, reveal much about Lydia, as seen through the eyes of not only one observer who was a wonderfully acute critic, but of the Bloomsbury circle as a whole. The identification of living people with Virginia Woolf's fictional characters is usually unwise, but it is interesting to find the note (in Virginia Woolf's *Diary*, 11 September 1923) that one reason why the Woolfs had stayed with Maynard and Lydia at 'The Knoll', Studland, that month, was that Virginia 'wanted to observe Lydia as a type for Rezia [Lucrezia Warren Smith, the wife of Septimus, in *Mrs Dalloway*]; & did observe one or two facts.' On 9 August 1924 she records that she called Lydia 'Rezia' by mistake. Lydia's 'Russianness' was also, no doubt, observed by Virginia to help with the portrayal of Sasha, the Russian princess, in *Orlando*. (The subject of the photograph of the princess in that book is, however, Angelica Bell, and not Lydia, as some have thought.)

Another writer with whom Lydia became friendly was J.M. Barrie; Maynard once told Frederick Ashton that Lydia used to go and sit on his knee. Barrie conceived the one-act play, *The Truth about the Russian Dancers*, for her, and she was to have a speaking part in it as Mlle Uvula. But when Lydia disappeared in 1919, the part was offered to Karsavina, whose English was far less fluent, and so the role was confined to dancing. The first performance was on 15 March 1920, with music by Arnold Bax, scenery by Paul Nash and choreography by Karsavina. On 20 January 1924, Lydia wrote to Maynard, 'Barrie tells me on telephone that Massin coached Gladys Cooper's "Peter [Pan]" in all her movements, especially on the wires! He [Barrie] is so very occupied with the rehearsals that I can't ever see him. Now it is "Alice sit by the fire".'* Ashton told me that he had heard that Barrie had Lydia in mind for *The Boy David* in 1936. In the event the part was taken by Elisabeth Bergner, who also had a foreign accent.

During the 1920s the Pathé Frères Cinema Company brought out not only newsreels but also a series, featuring theatre and fashion items, called *Eve's Film Review*. Lydia Lopokova made a slow-motion dance sequence, 'Dancing Grace', for the *Review* some time between 1922 and 1924; a copy is in the archives of the British Film Institute. She also played in a full-length, 'super-talking' film, *Dark Red Roses*, made at Wembley by British Sound Film Productions in 1929. The director was Sinclair Hill, the stars, Stewart Rome and Frances Doble. The film included a 'Russian ballet', entitled 'Jealousy', composed by George Balanchine; Lydia appeared in this, Balanchine and Anton Dolin being the other dancers. *Dark Red Roses*, first shown in October 1929, was an important early British sound film, but no copy appears to have survived and the ballet sequence has been lost. Lydia talked about the film in a broadcast given during the 1930s:

> This was the first English talkie film which was ever made. I was invited to produce a little ballet for it and, as money doesn't matter in the film industry, was offered £1000. So I said 'Yes' and invited Balanchine to be choreographer and Dolin to be my leading man. We were asked to do something oriental. It was an entertainment at a fashionable out-door party. So we chose the music of Mussorgsky from his opera *Khovanshchina*, and it seemed easiest to choose a triangle for the ballet, the husband, the wife and the lover. At first the married couple moves with slow motion (this was in the very early days of ballet for the films and we did not think it safe to dance too fast). The husband goes to hunt, the lover appears and the husband, of course, returns to kill. It is nice to be killed in the ballet, the floor is so comfortable to spread one's body in relaxation. At the end I come down off stage and joined the party in the film and was allowed to speak one word. I should have forgotten the ballet, if it had not been for the sad news which

*A play by Barrie which appeared in 1905.

came to us while we performed. You know how long you have to wait for filming. The lights are never right, the organization very queer. I waited for twelve hours, dressed in my tights and ballet shoes, sitting out of doors in the cold garden before I was called on to do my bit. Whilst Dolin and I sat there waiting and shivering, the evening paper came with the death of Diaghilev. We were shaken to the bottom of our souls, for we knew that an age in our art of the ballet, so great an age, was over.

There is a clip still extant of Lydia, in rehearsal with the Vic-Wells Ballet, as Swanilda in *Coppélia* at Covent Garden in June 1933. With her are Ninette de Valois, Ursula Moreton and Frederick Ashton. There is also a film showing her and Maynard in their box at Covent Garden at the reopening of the theatre after the war in February 1946. One curiosity to add to all this, is that Lydia appeared on skates in a charity 'Ice Festival' in March 1929. In a letter to Clive Bell Virginia Woolf reports, 'Lydia by the way has fallen and cut her lip skating.'

In 1923 Maynard Keynes became a major shareholder and chairman of the board of the *Nation and Athenaeum*, a Liberal weekly which eventually amalgamated with the *New Statesman* in 1931. Lydia wrote some book reviews and reports on ballet performances for it, as well as occasional articles for other newspapers and weeklies. In 1927 she wrote a series of eight pieces on cooking for the *Evening News*. She was billed as 'a most accomplished cook', though she had never cooked anything in her life and it once took her three telephone calls to boil an egg ('what do I do now? The water is boiling'). The articles were filled out with many asides. The first piece, entitled 'A Way of Cooking Black Game – and a very good Ragout', describes two banquets in Germany at one of which Einstein was present, looking 'like Shakespeare and like Charlie Chaplin at the same time'. The second was on a Russian cabbage soup, called 'Shee' (which was taken with sour milk and buckwheat cakes), and another soup, called 'Ooha', made from fish. The third starts off: 'An old friend once gave me the best pheasant I have ever tasted. He was a Polish count, and he must be nameless here, not because I would conceal his name, but because I cannot remember how to spell it.' In the last article she returns to cabbage. It is entitled 'Making a Cabbage Delicious the Russian Way – even Sylphs of the Ballet Must Eat!' Lydia spends nine-tenths of the space describing two vegetarians: Nijinsky (from 1916) and Isadora Duncan. Towards the end, just before giving a recipe that includes boiling cabbage slowly for an hour, she states, 'There is nothing better all the year round than a cabbage. But perhaps I am prejudiced, for Lopokova means in Russian "sea-cabbage", or, as you call it, seakale.' Later she told me that the name 'Lopukhov' means a plant, the burdock (which it does) – 'one that puffs out,' she said; but seakales cannot do that!

Mention has already been made of the broadcasts Lydia gave during the 1930s, introducing programmes of Russian ballet music. She also gave a series of broadcasts in 1938 in which she read translations from Russian authors, including Chekhov, Tolstoy, Gorky and Dostoievsky, entitled *Studies of Childhood and Adolescence from the Russian Masters, selected and presented by Lydia Lopokova.* Somewhat oddly, a passage was included from Hans Christian Andersen's story 'The Red Shoes'. She gave other talks from time to time, such as one on Andrew Marvell's poem 'The Nymph Complaining for the Death of her Faun'. Two unpublished monologues by Stevie Smith, recently found among her papers by Michael Halls and presumably written for her, do not appear to have been used.

In January 1943 Tolstoy's *War and Peace* was broadcast in eight dramatized parts, with Lydia Lopokova as a 'Woman Narrator', picking her way through the maze of personal relationships involved. Since this was in the middle of the Second World War, the aim was to give a sense of the scope and purpose of the book. This major production, with Celia Johnson, Leon Quartermaine, Francis Lister and Val Gielgud, achieved great success. It also marked Lydia's last appearances in a dramatic production.

Apart from her dancing master, Enrico Cecchetti, it was Tamara Karsavina who especially influenced Lopokova in her dancing career, over many years. Lydia regularly shared roles with Karsavina, such as those in *Petrushka*, *Pulcinella* and *Le Spectre de la Rose*, as well as *Firebird* – though not in *The Three-cornered Hat*. The exchange was reversed in *Carnaval*, *Parade* and *La Boutique Fantasque*. Karsavina wrote touchingly and affectionately of Lydia in her autobiography, *Theatre Street* (1930), and Lydia clearly revered her in return. She and Karsavina both married Englishmen as second husbands, but unfortunately Karsavina's, Henry Bruce, was not very well off as a diplomat, and she was consequently faced with financial problems in retirement. Lydia eventually organized a fund for her which she could only with great difficulty be persuaded to accept. Would Karsavina, however, allow her to provide an electric fire Lydia asked her one very cold winter? 'Because it's not right that the Firebird should be cold in winter, is it?' she told me, almost with tears in her eyes. I asked, 'Didn't you dance the Firebird, too?' 'Yes,' Lydia replied immediately, 'but I was only the fried-bird.'

Another long-lasting friendship which began in the days of the Russian Ballet was with Picasso, whom Lydia first met in 1917 in Rome, where he was planning the ballet *Parade* with Jean Cocteau. Lydia, who was to create the part of the female acrobat in this ballet, later said of it, on the BBC:

> This was the first time Diaghilev set himself really to upset the public with modern cubist art, which the general public did not know at all at that time. But there was one number in it much more usual – the number for the two acrobats. The first time I danced the girl acrobat in 1917 I remember Erik Satie, the composer and leader of modern French music, sent me flowers at the first performance with the words 'To the most graceful acrobat', for I wore white tights with designs on them, and, believe me, it was ticklish to be painted by Picasso, who amused himself doing circles on the coils on my body.

It was in Rome, too, that Picasso met another member of the Diaghilev Company, Olga Khoklova, who was also working with Massine, and during his suit of her Lydia became a friend. Of this time, Ernest Ansermet later wrote (in *Ecrits sur la musique*, 1971): 'Picasso took the opportunity of seeing me back to my hotel. Then, after a few moments, went out, saying "I'm going to see Olga." I heard Picasso in the passage knocking at her door, and Olga on the other side of it saying, "No! No! Monsieur Picasso, I'm not going to let you in."' Picasso married Olga in Paris in August 1918, and there is a letter from them to Lydia, dating from that time, thanking her for writing and sending her a thousand kisses.

While in Rome, Picasso made drawings of Lydia. He also drew her in London, where he was preparing the scenery and costumes for *The Three-cornered Hat*, in the summer of 1919, when Lydia once again saw a great deal of him and Olga. The next Picasso ballet to be done (in 1920) was *Pulcinella*, in which Lydia danced after she had rejoined Diaghilev's Company in 1921. She later wrote in *Vogue* that this ballet had

> the tenderest and most exquisite of the pale colours of Picasso. It is its own lyrical qualities which touch me – the eyes of the onlookers and of the dancers are caressed by the music and by the colours. Except for the character of Pulcinella [a part created by Massine] the dancing is not important. It is another *Carnaval* in a way – but for the modern soul.

In 1924 Lydia danced in *Les Soirées de Paris* in Paris and met the Picassos there. She created the part of Proserpine in the Picasso ballet *Mercure*, in which she appeared 'only in the 3rd tableau that lasts 2 minutes, and my part probably lasts a second....' On 19 May she wrote in a letter to Maynard,

> As Massin was tired, we luckily had no rehearsal and I asked Picassos to come for lunch, but in the end he snatched my bill so that I was struggling with him. However, quick minded V. [Vera Bowen] saved 'my honour' and while we convinced each other in the corner, she paid the bill without the bill. They were as ever charming, and of the opinion of V. and G. [Garia, or Harold, Bowen] how Massin is 'mesquin' and that he will never achieve much with his meanness. He [Picasso] is also miscontent how they treat his ideas, and although they run 'Picasso, Picasso', they do not do what he tells them about his things, but he is wise and smiles and so do I.

Two more letters from Lydia to Maynard offer glimpses of Picasso. In 1926 she was dancing with the Diaghilev Company in Paris. On Saturday, 29 May, at '2½ o'clock of night' she wrote,

> Petrushka was given as a first ballet. I was in time and eager to get it over. I thought I performed myself fairly well but one could ever improve on oneself. I saw the new ballet 'Pastorale', music [by Auric] was charming. Some dances especially done by Doubrovska (she has long lanky legs like yours) were particularly suited to her; Lifar rides bicycle like Stas at the Coliseum. One does not grumble but everything is too much of a fake. One wants meat instead of a caramel. Poor Hilda [Sokolova] is bleeding with her 'guests' [menstrual periods]. She still dances but they are cruel to her and almost force her to perform in corps de ballet. After the

performance I drove with the composer *Lambert* to the party in honour of the 'Pastorale'. Auric, Milhaud, Pruna, Picassos, Princesses and tytled Ladies were there. I drank 2 glasses of champagne and laughed so much with Lifar whom I called 'little monkey'. He prayed me to retire soon as he thought Karsavina in spite of her charm was really old. I asked if I was old already. He thought not, but I am so much influenced that I like to retire for ever after London season. Very 'swanky' audience in the theatre, who are they? Not a ticket to be had for a long time. I told big Serge how extraordinary that Russian Ballet *continued* to tickle the big public. [Comte Etienne de] Beaumont and his lady came to greet me, but I sat in close touch with Olga Picasso and Picasso. They are so easy to be with.

Years later, 20 October 1935, Lydia wrote to Maynard in Cambridge:

I am piano, and asked Fred [Ashton] and Sophie [Fedorovich] to come to lunch and cheer me. Fred had tickets offered for Romeo & Juliette, and saw it on the second night. He thought it should be called 'Mercutio & Nurse'. Gielgud was like Sarah Bernhardt, and Edith Evans so important that the whole production was upside down and out of balance. . . . The Russian ballet intrigues: Leon [Woizikovsky] came with his present wife in excellent state. It is good for his self-respect to be successful, as he was always cramped under Massin, too much cramped. His first wife is on excellent terms with the second (Sokolova), but the third hates the two. Sokolova's Tash [their daughter Natasha] says that 'Papa Leon is like a Blue Beard, with one exception, he does not murder his wives'. Leon's daughter was brought up to call Sokolova, her mother, 'the white louse', but now they are on kissing terms instead of spitting ones. Awful news about Picasso. Olga left him, the house is sealed by the police, so that he cannot get anything out of it. The report is that Olga lost her patience about 'the other women', and after all Picasso was not born respectable. There was strain in his sitting on gold Louis Phillippe chairs, and 18th century abra cadabra, which his smart friends supplied him with. However, it is all very sad.

Picasso's last visit to England occurred in November 1950, when he came to attend a Communist 'Peace Congress' which was suddenly banned. He stayed with Roland Penrose in Sussex, and there was only one other person he wanted to see before returning to France: Lydia. They arranged to lunch at 46 Gordon Square, and on arrival Picasso asked Lydia whether she still danced. Lydia said, 'Yes,' and they danced in the street in front of the house. Lydia asked, 'Why did you leave Olga?' and was told, 'Olga asked too much of me.' She also asked Picasso whether it was true that his son Paulo was a pimp. 'Yes,' he replied, 'but he is *so* charming.' He wanted to give Lydia a present, and later sent her an inscribed photograph of a drawing of her with Massine in the Can-Can from *La Boutique Fantasque*, done in 1919.

Lydia Lopokova took no interest in her past, and lived (typically, realistically) for the present; this was as true of her artistic life as of her social life. She would never help interviewers in their researches into her past achievements, or show off, or assert her greatness as a dancer. She used to say that in art only the first-rate mattered, but when she had seen a poor performance, she almost invariably tried to find something of merit in it, even if it was only a costume. As must already have been appreciated, she was entirely honest and realistic in her criticisms. Lydia Sokolova wrote in her *Memoirs* (1960), 'In all the years of my friendship with Lydia Lopokova, I have never known her say or do an unkind thing either in the theatre or out of it. She was sweet to everybody, never jealous and never coveting another dancer's roles; but she always seemed to be hopping off somewhere, and obviously valued her private life as much as life in ballet.' I, too, never heard her speak ill of any artist, and, as there was no malice in her humour, she was never spiteful about a performance and somehow always managed to give a feeling that something good had emerged. Robert Helpmann found her marvellous at spotting any falsity in a performance and at commenting on the subtleties of interpretation of a role. She was not particularly critical of technique, but recognized a dancer's technical problems. She could be moved by performances; I particularly remember her being affected by Verdi's *Otello* at Covent Garden. Robert Helpmann, too, told me how, after a performance of *Dante Sonata*, she came on stage in tears.

Dignity was not one of her attributes, and more than once she was found sitting *inside* a refrigerator during a heat-wave in North America. Once she was seen in the branches of a mulberry tree in a court in King's College, eating the fruit. She used to sunbathe naked on the verandah at Tilton, though a footpath crossed in front of it only a few yards away. I asked if this might not cause embarrassment, and Maynard replied, 'No – passers-by simply can't believe their eyes!' She once opened the front door to her sister-in-law, Margaret Hill, wearing only ballet shoes. She would wander on the Downs above Tilton, stripped to the waist, with 'udders' (that is, rubber gloves for pulling up thistles) in her pockets. When one arrived at Tilton, one might find her coats hanging on the *outside* of the front door, 'to protect them from the moth'.

Lydia's equable temperament and general happiness of outlook were noteworthy, and it is hard to find instances of any expression of irritability. In her diary for 11 September 1923 Virginia Woolf wrote, 'It was very hot at Lulworth, & we sat with the sun in our eyes on a verandah having tea. Suddenly she [Lydia] got cross, frowned, complained of the heat, seemed about to cry, precisely like a child of six. She was concerned to know what Leonard meant by coupling her with me among the "sillies".* It means that you can both be beaten, Maynard said.' In a letter to Ethel Smyth (31 July 1933) she wrote,

> I seize this moment, having put out a cake and honey and the kettle on the stove, to write: but the Keynes's will be here in a moment and wont go, God bless them and all my friends, till dinner. And then I shall be so talk weary. . . . Yes here they were the Keynes's and they stayed until 8 and the dinner was burnt, but they were very very charming. Maynard prancing all over the world and saying outrageous things, and he and L. [Leonard Woolf] quarrelled – Even I was drawn in – about the state of Europe in 50 years: imagine quarrelling about Free Trade and Fascism – still we did, and were very fond of each other too.

Quentin Bell (in an unpublished essay) can only once remember Lydia getting cross with Maynard:

> It was when Duncan Grant produced a design for a dress in which she was to dance, a kind of trapeze-shaped tabard ending suddenly about half way up the thigh – perhaps it was for *L'Ecossaise*. Lydia

---

*According to Leonard Woolf, 'sillies' were 'absurd in ordinary life and by the standards of practical men'; they were 'terribly simple and at the same time tragically complicated'.

didn't like it, it showed too much leg, and Maynard jokingly
suggested that people would not say, 'What a short small dress!'
but, 'What a large naked Lydia!' 'Oh, Maynard,' she said, in a
shocked, resentful voice, and blushed. There was a very awkward
pause. I didn't quite understand why Lydia should have been so
annoyed.

Her extravagances were not always obvious. She did not go out
and buy ten hats at one go; but she might buy ten hats over two
weeks. She wrote to Maynard (4 February 1933), 'I had my face
patted, sifted, cooled, warmed, egged and oiled, and now I can say
that vice is agreeable. Price enormous £1.' Besides hats, her chief
love was the purchase of shoes – as, she said, old dancers always have
painful feet, afflicted by bunions. On 27 April 1936 she wrote: 'Oh,
the sweetness of the soft air makes me feel how nice it is to breathe
on this earth ... Being in such a mood I found myself at Woodlands
[Woollands, the Knightsbridge store] and I gazed at a silver cape
with foxes ... but it is very expensive you would blush, so I better
tell you £95.' Once, when Maynard had had a severe reverse on the
stock market, she went out and pawned the table silver. She came
back and proudly presented the cash to him, adding that now they
would *have* to eat with wooden spoons. Unfortunately she was
made to redeem the silver forthwith, even though she said she was
tired of it. She owned no jewellery at all, and many noted her
relative inattention to her appearance.

Sokolova wrote in her *Memoirs*,

> On the stage, as well as off, Lydia Lopokova was full of surprises.
> She had not the appearance or physique of a classical dancer, but
> to one's astonishment whatever she attempted came off. Few
> dancers have performed with such assurance or flown through the
> air as she did. Lydia had tiny strong feet, little hands and short
> arms. She had no idea of hairdressing and wore very little make-
> up on the stage – what there was was usually still there next
> morning – but when she stood looking up at Big Serge (which
> was what she called Diaghilev), with her screwed-up little bun of
> hair, the tip of her nose quivering, and an expression between
> laughter and tears, I defy anybody to say she wasn't worth her
> weight in gold.

(I remember my delight when, as a six-year-old, I was told by

Maynard that the reason that Lydia wore her hair in a bun was so that I could undo it.) In a letter written to Maynard on 28 April 1924 from Paris, where she was dancing in *Les Soirées de Paris*, Lydia wrote with amusement,

> I rehearse like a Geraclus [Hercules], but to-night as Flory [Grenfell] goes away tomorrow I consented to go to the theatre to see a farce, but what an air of congestion in the theatre. Behind us sat the daughter of Baroness Erlanger who married the French Marquis who sat behind Vera [Bowen] with an American lady, who in her turn told him that I was a famous dancer. The Marquis said, looking at my plover-egg head, 'Impossible. I can't believe it. Look what kind of hair pins she wears.' He was almost disgusted with my appearance; I was amused.

John Gielgud remembers (in a letter to me) 'seeing her during the war years, trudging up Shaftesbury Avenue in a strange balaclava helmet, very thick stockings and oddly bundled up'. She was completely unselfconscious about her appearance, which, with her diminutive size, made anonymity unlikely. The oddness of her dress increased after Maynard died. She constantly wore a scarf round her head, inside and outside the house, and on it might be perched some other sort of covering. Often there were many layers of clothes, with sometimes as many as three overcoats; occasionally, even in public, the layers would be demonstrated one by one, down to the underclothes. Eddie Marsh (*Ambrosia and Small Beer*, 1964) wrote to Christopher Hassall in January 1944,

> I had an amusing rencontre the other day on the King's Parade – being greeted by an odd little figure in a fur-lined hood, carrying a basket full of empty wine bottles, and realizing that it was Lydia Lopokova, now Lady Keynes.... I thought it would be fun to print a photograph of Lydia and ask if it represented 1. a *prima ballerina assoluta* 2. a female troll 3. an English peeress, or 4. the wife of a Lithuanian publican.

The following story, of which there are several versions, is an instance of Lydia's unselfconscious behaviour (which could at times be outrageous, especially if she was being egged on by Maynard). They were in the United States, to which Maynard had gone secretly and incognito, on a train from New York to Washington. As it began to cross the hideous flats of New Jersey, Maynard said, in his

clear and carrying tones, 'There, you see; this proves what I have
always said; North America is uninhabitable.' The voices of the
other passengers began to drop as the theme was expanded and then
abandoned for other topics. By the time Maynard and Lydia had
moved on to dance, everyone in the Pullman had realized who their
fellow-passengers were, and they were entranced when Lydia got
up and illustrated the point she was making by a few steps in the
corridor. When they reached Washington, everyone stood rever-
ently back for Maynard's party to leave first. Maynard and Lydia
did not notice, as, indeed, they had never noticed their fellow-
passengers.

The recipients of Lydia's letters usually found them entertaining,
and her bon-mots, often difficult to record, could come forth in a
veritable stream of funny sentences and turns of phrase. Her wit
could be astounding, and it can safely be said that her cunning misuse
of words was usually deliberate. Sometimes the words were reused,
as were her stories, and so rival accounts are possible. Maynard had
primed her before she first met my mother, the granddaughter of
Charles Darwin, by explaining about *The Origin of Species*. But
Lydia was not to be outdone: she said, 'So you are the granddaughter
of the man who wrote *Genesis!*' Sokolova tells in her *Memoirs* of
how Lydia proposed the health of the hostess at a party given by
Florrie Grenfell, whose mother had been dead for many years, and
ended the toast, 'And let us not forget dear Florrie's mother, who
compiled her!' Occasionally, the use of a 'wrong' word needs explanation: in the oft-quoted sentence, 'I don't like to be in England
in the summer, because the barristers will get into bed with me,' the
word 'barristers' should have been 'harvesters' – biting spiders, with
long legs, which Lydia encountered on her walks on the South
Downs at Tilton. Her laughter was memorable, astonishing and
marvellously infectious.

Sir Alexander Korda once asked Lydia to a grand dinner at
Claridge's, with Vivien Leigh and Laurence Olivier among the other
guests. The meal started with whitebait, a dish that Lydia did not
like, but which she knew Maynard had enjoyed. Sitting on Sir
Alexander's right, she felt she should make some complimentary
remark about the meal, and said, 'Sir Alexander, this is a good meal.
Whitebait is so wholesome.' In telling me this, she clearly appreciated the incongruity of her somewhat mischievous remark.
Sokolova recalls in her *Memoirs* how Lydia was presented to Queen

Mary during the interval of a ballet performance, and how 'the Queen looked at the little, dripping, breathless figure, whom I can so well imagine smiling up appealingly at her; but as Lydia did nothing but dab her face with a towel, Her Majesty said, "Thank you for dancing for me; it must have been trying on such a hot afternoon." Lydia bobbed and exclaimed, "Pleasure pain, Ma'am."'

Besides the way in which Lydia twisted words around, in complete knowledge of what she was doing – as Billy Chappell relates, she had a lovely way of looking round and saying, 'What have I said? Why are you laughing?' when she had deliberately done it to raise a laugh – she could also take delight in saying extraordinary things, not only to surprise but also on occasion to shock and even outrage. The following story has the perfect come-back. Constant Lambert told her that the Dutch had curiously named two of their liqueurs 'Bols' and 'Fockink', and that evening, at the end of a dinner party, she suddenly cried out, purposely mispronouncing the names, 'Have some more Bols! Have some more Fockink!' There was dead silence, and then she said, 'Huh, and now you have done that to embarrass me.' Very occasionally, it was she who was muddled. On 3 June, 1928, she wrote to Maynard, 'Why the tale of Jesus fermenting wine out of water in Cannes [Canaan] is such an important subject for wedding. Do you know?'

The story of her 'kidnap' by Vivien Leigh and Laurence Olivier is epic. Vivien Leigh had asked Lydia to dinner, so Lydia thought, one Saturday after a performance. She duly arrived at the theatre in evening dress, and Vivien Leigh asked her, to her surprise, where her luggage was – to which Lydia replied that she had none. They got into a car and drove and drove, Lydia assuming that they were driving around London to allow the Oliviers to relax before going to a restaurant. Eventually they arrived at Notley Abbey, near Thame, and had dinner. Vivien Leigh lent Lydia a nightdress, but, on being asked if she would like a toothbrush, Lydia said, 'Oh, my dear, do not worry. What is the point of cleaning your teeth? You have to lose them some time.' So she spent the rest of the weekend in her long evening dress and returned unconcerned to Gordon Square on Monday. Meanwhile she had not arrived at Lewes Station, as planned, on the Sunday, and the family and the police were alerted. Gordon Square was entered and at first there was no clue as to where Lydia was. A cheque book was found in which recent payments had been made to a mysterious Mr Hawkins, who later turned out to be a local chemist who used to cash cheques for her. There was also a chance that she was with the Oliviers, and eventually Notley Abbey was telephoned, the call being answered, most suspiciously, by a lady with a very thick German accent. But Lydia was at last found.

In any account of Lydia some mention should be made of Ruby and Auntie. Ruby Coles arrived in London as a girl from Suffolk, seeking work, and in November 1923 was told that Mme Lydia Lopokova needed a maid. She at last found 41 Gordon Square, and was taken straight away 'to the tiny figure who said in her broken English, "You are Ruby who is working for me," bowed, shook my hand and departed straight upstairs.' So began an association which lasted for over fifty-five years. When Tilton was rented in 1925, Ruby went there and met her future husband, Edgar Weller, in the local village. Edgar became the chauffeur-gardener at Tilton, and they lived in the cottage on the farm next to Tilton House, and raised a family. Ruby described the first time that Pavlova came to Gordon Square: 'The front-door bell rang, and as I answered it I bent down to pick up a letter on the floor. I remember seeing a lovely pair of legs in black stockings looking, as I later said to Madame, like the legs of a Black Minorca chicken. She laughed and said, "Yus, but lays 'noer' eggs."' Edgar Weller had an aunt, Penny Weller, who became Lydia's dresser from 1926; 'Auntie' accompanied Lydia everywhere until her retirement at the start of the war. There were three dogs at Tilton during the 1930s: a greyhound, Ross, who could chase rabbits and hares over the Downs with grace and vigour; a black and cheerful Labrador called Pushkin, and a squat, yapping brown-and-white mongrel, Patsy. Of the three, Patsy, who could not have been more ungraceful, was the most loved.

After Maynard died in 1946, Lydia continued to live at Tilton, the flat in Cambridge and Gordon Square. At Tilton she was looked after by a couple living in the back part of the house, as well as by Ruby Weller. In 1956 Lydia wrote to Richard Buckle★, 'My staff left me after ten years so I cannot invite you at the moment. "Normal service will be resumed as soon as possible."' She continued to walk on the Downs above Tilton, wrapped up against 'the curly winds' and learning and reciting the poems of Shakespeare and Eliot. She used to say,★ 'I like to be alone, yes I *do!* But I must have a man for Sunday lunch,' and she had guests very often at the weekend, though they were not allowed to stay very long, only for one or two nights.

She was contented and with the passing of time, rarely left Tilton, except when her 'staff' were on holiday or being replaced. In other letters to Buckle★ she expresses her joy in Tilton:

> I am surrounded by broad beans, green peas and weeds, my skin rattles from the sun, so rewarding and sudorous.

> ... The hay smells good and English country is beautiful, I circulate, exist like a plant with two arms.

> ... For the last days I have been sweating like a dancer. I was so hot I wished for nothing but sea shells around my neck. ...

> ... At the moment I am shelling broad beans, like a Tibetan monk with his beads, I find life a melody, away from Oxford Street.

> I am away from London to reach warm walls with my cold in the chest. I am well again, as every day I eat roast beef.

> Most of the day I am in the hills, learning poetry, bitten by invisible insects in the lower parts of my body. Still I have the taps of water to rinse me through and degrade the bites.

> I mounted the hill today [Boxing Day]. It was misty and mystical. I felt I had done 'good works' being on top.

When at the flat in Cambridge, Lydia invariably ate at the Arts Theatre Restaurant, cared for by Mr Schurch, the head waiter. She attended performances at the theatre and saw her old friends, such as Morgan Forster, George and Janet Trevelyan, Patrick Hadley, Dadie Rylands, Noel Annan, Jack Sheppard and, on two occasions, Ruth Draper, when she was performing at the theatre. In London the incomparable charlady, Mrs Turtle, worked at Gordon Square. Lydia would usually eat once a day at Antoine's Restaurant, round the corner in Charlotte Street, tended by Mme Antoine.

The upper floors of no. 46 were let off to some society for Christian aid, and when the door bell rang, Lydia would dart off to answer it and ask the astonished caller 'Are you Christian?' She had the ground floor, but the basement was scarcely used. The ground-floor front room, with its large mirror and *barre*, was her bedroom, and she entertained in a small, high back room at a table covered

★ These passages are quoted from my *Essays on John Maynard Keynes* (1975).

with oilcloth, among a pile of books and tins of food. Maynard's picture collection (in which she had a life-interest and which is now the property of King's College) was accumulated at Tilton, where the more important paintings hung in the sitting-room – Seurat's study for *La Grande Jatte*, two Picassos, two Braques, a Matisse, two Renoirs and four Cézannes. She once said, 'I also like the Cézanne apples as well as the Seurat. Cézanne painted hundreds of apples, and I have five of them.'

In London, Lydia went to the theatre, and particularly Covent Garden, for which I might be urgently summoned as an escort. She would ring up and ask, 'What do you want to eat at Gordon Square afterwards? Cold chicken, or hamburger?' but I never had a hamburger. She gave memorable meals, at which she would tear off hunks of chicken with her hands to place beside the cold salad, putting the carcass on her own plate. We would all laugh and talk endlessly, eat with our fingers and napkins, and get wittier, happier and more profound as the wine flowed. The meal might be interrupted by Lydia rising from the table to illustrate some steps in a ballet, especially if Ashton or Balanchine was there. Once, she and Balanchine jumped up in turn to dance and explain a passage from *The Firebird* to each other. On another occasion Stevie Smith recited her 'Not Waving but Drowning' poem. The other guests could be the Grigorievs, Baronova, Danilova, Arthur Waley or the Duke of San Lucar La Mayor. As a rule, Lydia used to meet her old ballet acquaintances at the Covent Garden crush bar – only Ninette de Valois and Frederick Ashton used to visit her at Tilton.

In time the University of London took over 46 Gordon Square – it is now part of Birkbeck College – and Lydia gave up the flat in St Edward's Passage in Cambridge, but her beloved Tilton continued. Here was the difficulty of 'wash-up' of the breakfast things, and one did not see her, officially, until lunch-time. She would potter around, however, earlier, doing her 'housework' (which consisted only of making her bed and washing up her coffee cup), smoking cigarettes incessantly. Her week was taken up otherwise by reading *The Times*, the *Daily Telegraph*, the *Evening Standard*, the *Listener*, the *New Statesman and Nation* and the Sunday newspapers. Lunch would entail a drive to 'The White Hart' in Lewes. As usual, the garden, except for the daffodils in spring, had no flowers (the beds had been grassed in years before), and the orchard was derelict, but there were the kitchen garden and the raspberries to nurture.

At Gordon Square Lydia had played on a grand piano, but at Tilton there was only a 'crummy' upright, bought for Benjamin Britten to use when they were planning the first production of the Auden-Isherwood play, *On the Frontier*, directed by Rupert Doone in 1938 at the Arts Theatre, Cambridge. One weekend a friend was playing a Chopin waltz on the upright, when Lydia entered in her dressing-gown, smoking her constant cigarette, and said, 'Go on.' She must have been in her sixties, but started dancing *Les Sylphides*. "Lift," she said to me in a hopeful way, and I became her last-ever partner! When it was over, she returned to the housework, but during those few minutes we could still see her wonderful, moving, lyrical quality and natural sense of music, as well as her lovely *port de bras* and inner concentration.

The last change at Tilton came when Logan Thompson, who had managed the farm there for forty years moved in, and a housekeeper-companion was engaged to look after them. The sitting-room was used less and less, and they sat in armchairs, facing one another in the hallway near the 'bogey', a grill in the floor through which, in a manner reminiscent of the subway vent in the Marilyn Munroe film, *The Seven Year Itch*, hot air formerly flowed up round the house from a boiler in the cellar. It was in this hallway that stacks of tinned food and bottles of wine had been stored, as well as in the dining-room, during and after the war years. In it, also was a long row of Lydia's footwear, with some of her many coats hanging from a rack above. At the top of the stairs was the Vanessa Bell cartoon of her and Maynard in the 'Keynes-Keynes'.

Once, at Tilton, Lydia described the process of growing old: 'Every day a little bit of me flies away, like a bird.' Unfortunately too much flew away, and she spent her last four years in a nursing-home a few miles from Tilton across the Downs. Here, she continued happy and contented, though muddled and forgetful; she still, however, had her inimitable laugh and needed demonstrable affection. She had difficulty in formulating and completing sentences, and Russian words became interposed with English. The last time I saw her I asked that she should try and avoid using Russian words, as I did not understand them, to which she replied, most logically, 'But *I* do!'

Lydia Lopokova died most peacefully on 8 June 1981, and was cremated, her ashes being scattered half-way up the Downs over-looking the back of Tilton. In July there was a fully choral memorial service, partly in Russian, in the Chapel of King's College, Cambridge, the college which Maynard Keynes had entered eighty years before.

The Lopukhov Family

Milo Keynes

In 1910, at the end of Lydia Lopokova's first season with Diaghilev in Western Europe, she went with her elder sister, Evgenia, then known as 'Lopukhova I', and her eldest brother, Fedor, to the United States. Both Evgenia and Fedor were ballet dancers, as was another brother, Andrei. Maynard Keynes was to christen the four members of the family 'The World-famous Lopukhov Troupe'.

Lydia was the third child of Vasili Lopukhov and of Constanza Karlovna Douglas, who was of Baltic-Scottish origin. Nikolai and Andrei were her two younger brothers. Vasili Lopukhov – who had strikingly long fingers and long clean nails – was an attendant, or usher, at the Imperial Alexandrinsky (now the Pushkin) Theatre, a post that Lydia said was well-paid (twenty-five roubles a month), with, in addition, very good tips from the 'boyar' families when they were shown to their boxes in the theatre. Vasili, of Buriat-Mongol extraction, loved the theatre and used to recite monologues from classical plays with gusto. His father was a lay-server at Tambov, 250 miles south-east of Moscow, and his mother a midwife. His great-great grandfather was a Tatar from Kazan, 450 miles due east of Moscow. The name 'Lopukhov' is that of a plant, the burdock.

Lydia, as we have seen, had Scottish blood in her. Her adored mother, whom she called 'Karlusha', had worn little Scotch caps when young. She was born in Reval (now Tallinn), in Estonia, in the Gulf of Finland, and spoke only German. She moved to St Petersburg to take up a post as a housekeeper; there she met and married Vasili Lopukhov, but she never learned to speak Russian well. Her great-grandfather, an engineer, had left Scotland for Sweden, where his son Gerhardt, who spoke only Swedish, worked

as a tapestry weaver. Gerhardt's son Karl, Karlusha's father, was
Clerk to the Municipality of Riga; he was also an amateur painter
and, according to Lydia, an authority on taste. Karl married Charlotte Johnson – daughter of a well-to-do merchant from Scotland –
who spoke English and wore English clothes. Karl died young.

Vasili and Constanza Lopukhov lived in an apartment twenty
minutes' walk from the Alexandrinsky Theatre and there they
brought up their family of five, with the help of servants. As well as
Lydia and her brothers and sister, there was an illegitimate half-
brother to whom Karlusha was kind, 'because she was a kind soul',
so Lydia said. Lydia always kept a photograph of her mother
in her bedroom, but her relationship with her father was not
nearly as close. At times, according to Lydia, her father would
curse her mother, and in later years there was clearly 'an alcohol
problem'.

Evgenia, Fedor, Lydia and Andrei were all educated free at the
Imperial Ballet School in Theatre Street, St Petersburg. Lydia always
spoke highly of the education there. Those pupils who, on gradua-
tion, might be chosen to become dancers at the Mariinsky Theatre
in the city received a training which was far more thorough than
basic schooling. Lydia started piano lessons and, very soon after
joining the school, began to develop a keen knowledge and deep
appreciation of music. Evgenia, Fedor and Andrei, who all went on
to become Mariinsky dancers, had nevertheless inherited their
father's interest in the spoken drama, and the two boys and Lydia
performed in plays while they were at the school. Of the five
children only Nikolai failed at the audition for entry into the Imperial Ballet School; but as he later became a successful engineer he
probably had no regrets about this.

Evgenia, Lopukhova I as she was known (Lydia was for a short
time known as Lopukhova II), graduated from the Imperial Ballet
School in 1902 and became a noted Mariinsky character dancer. She
toured Russia with Lydia Kyasht in 1904, and participated in
Diaghilev's tours in Germany, Belgium, France and England in
1909, 1910 and 1911, as well as going to America with Fedor and
Lydia in 1910. After the Revolution she was awarded the title of
'Distinguished Artist of the R.S.F.S.R.', and, for many years, her
partner was the creator of the Moor's role in *Petrushka*, A.A. Orlov.
She danced at the Mariinsky until 1924, and then became popular in
operettas. She died in Leningrad in 1943.

Fedor Lopukhov, for many years Master of the Ballet at the Mariinsky Theatre, was the most famous member of the family in Russia. He was a link between the nineteenth-century classical ballets and Soviet ballet, and became in due course Professor of Choreography at the Imperial Ballet School and a 'People's Artist of the R.S.F.S.R'. Born in 1886, he entered the Imperial Ballet School in 1896, one year after the St Petersburg presentation of the Ivanov-Petipa *Swan Lake*, and danced two years later in the 'Dance of the Arabian Boys' at the first performance of *Raymonda*, a ballet with music by Glazunov and choreography by Marius Petipa. He graduated in 1905, having danced for his examination performance the role of Acis in the première of Fokin's first ballet, a revival of Lev Ivanov's *Acis and Galatea*. Also participating were Lydia, who played the part of Cupid, and Nijinsky, for whom Fokin created a solo in the 'Scène et danse des faunes'. Despite this promising start, Fedor's dancing career was to be less notable than that of his brother or sister. At first he toured in Russia, and then in Scandinavia, in a company headed by Ann Pavlova and Adolf Bolm. In 1910 he danced with Julia Sedova and Nikolai Legat in Paris, and later that year went to the United States with Evgenia, Lydia and Lydia's partner, Alexander Volinin, appearing first at the Globe Theatre in New York on Broadway, and later touring more than thirty cities. Although he accumulated more money than he had ever dreamed of during the tour, he became distraught and home-sick, earning the nickname of the 'crazy Russian'. Pavlova, who was in San Francisco, hurried to see him; unfortunately all that Fedor could remember of their meeting, years later, was that they cried together and talked about Russia.

On returning to St Petersburg, Fedor began his career as a choreographer. One of his earliest achievements was the solo for the Lilac Fairy in *The Sleeping Beauty* – a pastiche of Petipa's style which has been accepted for all subsequent productions, except for the one mounted by Diaghilev in London in 1921, in which Lydia danced the Lilac Fairy. After the Revolution, Fedor, as Master of the Ballet of the Mariinsky Theatre, upheld the classical repertoire against official opposition, as well as staging Soviet revolutionary ballets. Written in 1916 and published in Russia in 1925, his *Paths of the Ballet Master* caused great controversy later when it appeared in the West, especially because of the author's support of symphonic ballet. At times out of favour and out of work, Fedor nonetheless directed not only the Kirov and Malii Ballet Companies in Leningrad, but also staged ballets for many others. As well as being inventive he could be lightly humorous – as, for instance, in a staging of *The Nutcracker* in which the ballerina was carried on stage upside down, doing the splits. One innovation of his (the device of a dancer carrying a ballerina high above his head) passed into general usage, first in Russia and subsequently in the West. But Fedor Lopukhov's chief concern was for the preservation of the classical tradition. He died, aged eighty-six, in 1973.

Fedor dwelt for many years in an apartment above the Imperial Ballet School in what is now called Rossi Street, and here his widow, Maya Vladimirovna, lives to this day. After finishing school in 1941, she danced in the corps de ballet of the Kirov company; eventually she became a soloist. Sometimes she was partnered by their son, Vladimir. Vladimir Lopukhov, who graduated from the Vaganova Choreographic School in 1965, is a character dancer in the Kirov Ballet, for which his début in the fandango of *Don Quixote* was a great success.

Andrei Lopukhov, Lydia's favourite brother, graduated from the Imperial Ballet School in 1916. He was an excellent character dancer with the Kirov Ballet, and in charge of teaching of character and ethnographic dances at the Mariinsky Theatre and the Choreographic School in Leningrad. He was co-author of a manual, *The Rudiments of Character Dancing*, besides being a prominent teacher. His greatest achievement was the role of Mercutio in *Romeo and Juliet*, to music by Prokofiev, which he created for the first production in Leningrad in 1940, with Galina Ulanova as Juliet and Konstantin Sergeiev as Romeo. He died in 1947.

Lydia's first recollection of ballet was of a performance at the theatre where her father had taken her for an afternoon performance, leaving her in the charge of a dancer whom she remembered as a very kind little lady, who told her of the wonderful fairy tales being portrayed on the stage.*

In their beautiful costumes and with all their grace, the ballet seemed to me at that tender age to be made up of angels. Every number thrilled me, and I finally found it impossible to keep my

---

*   The autobiographical fragments in this chapter come from the introductions Lydia gave to programmes of ballet music, on the BBC, in the 1930s.

feet from moving. When the curtain fell, I was standing on the seat, and as the music continued I began to dance and do some childish imitations of the poses and some rather bold attempts to lift my feet higher than my head, with the result that I fell from my perch and carried home a fine bump with black and blue decorations just under my curls, which had been so carefully dressed for my first attendance at the ballet. My father later told me that I had danced all the way home, keeping it up until bedtime, and that when I knelt down by my mother to say my prayers, the only petition I had to send heavenward was a heart-pulsing wish that I might be one of the beautiful angels I had seen at the theatre. The morning after the matinée, I very cautiously whispered to my brother and sister that I was going to be a beautiful angel, even if I had to run away from home, and to my astonishment they told me that they were going to do the same'.

At her audition for the Imperial School in 1901, when she was eight, she had to appear before the Faculty members as well as the Director of the Mariinsky Theatre, the Inspector and Inspectress of the school and, for some peculiar reason, the school priest. According to Mikhail Fokin (1880-1942) in his posthumous *Memoirs of a Ballet Master* (1961),

The teachers inspected the girls and boys who were standing in line. We, the teachers, would ask the children to place their knees together and then straighten them. When this was done and there remained space between the knees, or if a child could not straighten the knees without their overlapping, that candidate was considered unfit for a ballet career. The back was also checked, for possible protrusion of the shoulder blades. Most attention, however, was concentrated upon the general appearance of the child. The handsome and the well built were naturally given preference.

Lydia told me that at the audition besides lining up in front of the judges, she had also had to run for a few yards away from them, and then back again. Her right foot turned inwards, she said, but her parents had told her to be sure to turn her toes outwards at the audition as she ran. She kept on thinking, 'I must point the foot outwards', all the way up the hall. She also recalled that the judges had inspected her joints, limbs and mouth, as if they were examining a horse.

Life at the Imperial Ballet School consisted of appearing in:

> brown practice frocks, young, nervous, but very eager, holding on to the wall bars and repeating what might seem meaningless movements to the cracked notes of an old piano. First position! Third position! Circle, point, return, circle, point, return! For a year, we did nothing but simple exercises; like little nuns, we were guarded by a governess, and must not wink at the young gentlemen on the boys' side of the school. After all, we were Imperial property. We were counted before every meal, indeed we were counted several times a day. When we went to the theatre, we travelled in big black coaches with the blinds drawn. And so we went on, until the day came when we cast aside the brown dress for the pink, which was the outward reward of the little girl's progress, and then at last the white dress, which meant that we were launched into our careers, when we could exchange the tinkle of the piano for the glory of the full orchestra. When I was nine years old, I played before the Tsar the part of Clara, the little girl who is given the nut-cracker at a Christmas party, and steals down after all the guests have gone home to discover her nut-cracker in a desperate fight with the king of the rats. The nut-cracker is victorious, and then turns into a prince and carries her away to the Home of the Sweets in Fairyland. How nervous I was to remember my steps! Before me the Opera House blazed with light and the orders and jewels of the audience.

Tamara Karsavina wrote in *Theatre Street* (1930) of 'little Lopokova', who had been placed in her care at the school: 'The extreme emphasis she put into her movements was comic to watch in the tiny child with the face of an earnest cherub. Whether she danced or talked, her whole frame quivered with excitement; she bubbled over. Her personality was manifest from the first, and very lovable.'

One very cold night, as Lydia and some other children were walking in the snow after a performance of *The Nutcracker*, a grand carriage pulled up behind them. Out of it leaned Matilda Kshesinskaia, a famous and rich ballerina, formerly the mistress of Tsar Nicolas II and of the Grand Duke Sergei, and now married to the Grand Duke Andrei. She said, 'Children, let me drive you home.' Lydia later told of how she looked up and said, 'Oh, no, no, no, we mustn't go with her. She's a wicked woman.' She added, however, 'Now, I say what a fool I was to stay in the snow because she was a wicked woman.'

Lydia always emphasized that, as well as being a young dancer at the Imperial Ballet School, she was also a child actor on the Imperial Stage at the Alexandrinsky Theatre, appearing in speaking parts in operas and plays, including Shakespeare's *The Winter's Tale* and *A Midsummer Night's Dream*. She appeared with Chaliapine, Komissarzhevskaia, Savina and other great Russian actors of the old tradition. One of the majestic memories of her childhood was of Chaliapine, then at the height of his powers, as Khan Konchak in Borodin's *Prince Igor*. She first saw him on her first day at the Imperial School. Lydia was called to the blackboard by her governess:

'Tonight,' she said, 'you must be ready to come in the carriage to go on stage at the Mariinsky as one of the crowd in the opera.' I was taken in the great closed carriage in which we used to rumble over the stones of St Petersburg. I was shown into a very big dressing-room, had my cheeks rouged and a long woollen frock put over me, and taken by the hand on to the stage. It was all very dark. There, I saw a terrible monster with red legs and horns, who was doing a sort of mā-ā-ā, mā-ā-ā, mā-ā-ā in a bass voice. It was Chaliapin as Mephistopheles in *Faust*, but I thought it *really* was the devil – and fainted. This was how they used to accustom us little ones to the brilliance and spaces of the stage.

At the school, there were solo parts for the girls from the repertory of the Imperial Ballet, at a time when the prima ballerinas were Preobrazhenskaia, Kshesinskaia and Pavlova. One of the figures Lydia remembered there was Marius Petipa (1822–1910), the maître de ballet, who, even in old age, was still the great living master of the stage – and, of course, especially of classical ballet. But she considered that her schooldays occurred at a time of transition from the Petipa ballets, designed as they were for the Court of the Imperial family, to the romantic ballet of Mikhail Fokin – which gave Diaghilev his chance to bring Russian ballet out of Russia itself to Western Europe. While he was still under the influence of the older tradition Fokin staged the *Polovtsian Dances* (in which Lydia later danced the part of the Polovtsian maiden many times), and this was the start, in 1909, of the new Russian ballet.

Lydia also remembered the day at school in 1907, 'when, as we were rehearsing, the door opened and in came a tall, statuesque woman in a long white Grecian robe, with her hair in a fillet. It was Isadora Duncan, and she and her troupe opened a new world for us with their new, wavy, flowing, rhythmical movements – which clearly inspired Fokin.'

During the five years before 1909 when Lydia graduated from the Imperial Ballet School, Maestro Enrico Cecchetti (1850–1928) was back again in St Petersburg after opening a ballet school there. In a review, in 1929, in *The Nation and Athenaeum* of *Enrico Cecchetti* by C. W. Beaumont, Lydia wrote:

> In my young days in the Imperial School, I was taught by his second in command, who used to come to the lesson with a piece of cheese in his hand, as if we were mice. But once a week, Cecchetti himself would visit our class with the look of a Mother Superior, with his baton and a fierce expression. The only accompaniment he allowed was his inimitable whistle and the tap of the baton on the floor. But a great deal of the fierce expression was probably put on to produce a Mussolini effect on the little ballerinas. Afterwards, those with promise would be taken completely into his hands, and since he followed the Diaghilev Ballet from Russia, all the principal dancers of what England knows as the Russian Ballet were brought up in the Cecchetti School. To Cecchetti, men were just men, but women flowers, and in the Imperial School of St Petersburg he only taught the girls. The pupils who had talents he loved and upbraided. His abuse was terrible. All of us he would reduce to tears. But it was a bad sign not to be abused, for that would show that one had no gifts, no possibilities.

Cecchetti, who left St Petersburg to join Diaghilev in 1910 and was from then onwards concerned with his company, opened an Academy of Dancing in London in 1918. Until his retirement in Italy in 1923, Lydia was able to take lessons with him once again; the maestro was clearly a powerful and inspiring influence on her dancing career. When Cecchetti retired Nikolai Legat (1869–1937) took over as a teacher of ballet in London. Marie Rambert told me that Legat, although not comparable with Cecchetti as a teacher, was a wonderful improviser. He staged the ballet, *The Postman*, for Lydia and Stas Idzikovsky at the London Coliseum in 1925.

Lydia's public début (her examination performance) was reported in the press. The *St Petersburg Gazette* (23 March 1909) commented, 'The pupil Lopukhova has a good pirouette and much self-confidence, but still undeveloped *pointes* and not entirely correct *port de bras*. However, the majority of these young female artists suffer from this last imperfection. The pupil Lopukhova is a very nice-looking dancer but should immediately begin to divert herself from over-emphasized affectation and mannerism.' In a report on the second performance (9 April) the newspaper noted, 'The pupil Lopukhova danced much more reservedly this time and displayed a good tone and manner in the dances, from which the mannerism and artificiality of the first début were absent.'

Lydia graduated from the Imperial Ballet School, aged sixteen-and-a-half, in April 1909 and joined the corps de ballet at the Mariinsky Theatre in June; there she remained until she left Russia to join Diaghilev's second foreign season in Paris, Berlin and Brussels, in April the next year. In 1909 (when he had an opera company as well as a ballet company) and 1910 Diaghilev toured only for the summer in Western Europe, at the end of the season of the Imperial Ballet in St Petersburg and before the start of the new one. In 1911 he formed his own company, the *Ballets Russes*, which was to tour all the year round outside Russia, but by then Lydia had broken her contract with the Imperial Theatres of Opera and Ballet – she was finally dismissed from the Imperial Ballet Company at the Mariinsky Theatre on 21 December 1910 – and had left for America. She did not rejoin Diaghilev until his company arrived there in 1916.

By April 1910 Lydia had danced in twelve ballets and two operas at the Mariinsky Theatre. She danced Armide in Fokin's ballet *Le Pavillon d'Armide* on three occasions. In 1910 her salary as an employee of the Imperial Theatres rose to as high as 840 roubles a month, at a time when Nijinsky was earning 960 and Bronislava Nijinska and Vera Fokina 900 roubles. She was promoted to coryphée on 28 April 1910, just as she left Russia. Her arrival in Paris was described by Karsavina in *Theatre Street*: 'As she was stepping out of the railway carriage, emotion overcame her. She fainted right away on the piles of luggage. It had been her dream to be in Paris, she told the alarmed Bakst who had rendered her first aid; the lovely sight (of the Gare de Nord) was too much for her.'

It was Fokin who suggested to Diaghilev that they might ask Lydia to join his summer season in 1910 from the corps de ballet in

St Petersburg, possibly with a view to asking her to deputize for Karsavina if she was unable to dance in some of the performances, as seemed likely. Karsavina had earlier signed a contract with Oswald Stoll to appear at the Coliseum in London at the same time as the Diaghilev Ballet performances, a contract which she would not break, despite Diaghilev's demands. In the end a compromise was reached. She danced in Paris between appearances at the Coliseum, though she was obviously under rehearsed there. (It may have been harder to get together a good corps de ballet for the touring season that was being planned than to hire soloists.) Lydia appears to have arrived in Paris to start rehearsals as a member of the corps de ballet, but in the event appeared in this capacity only rarely. Diaghilev gave her her first big part in *Les Sylphides*, with the promise that if she did well she would, in Karsavina's absence, take her place in *Le Carnaval*.

In the event Lydia created the role of Columbine in *Carnaval* (with Nijinsky as Harlequin), although Karsavina had, indeed, appeared at a charity performance in an early version of the ballet in St Petersburg on 5 March 1910 and had danced in the premières at the Theatre des Westens in Berlin on 20 May and at the Paris Opéra on 4 June. Karsavina arrived from London to take over the part on 6 June. Lydia also danced with Nijinsky in the Blue Bird *pas de deux* (one of a series of divertissements called *Le Festin*, arranged by Fokin) on the company's first night at the Paris Opéra. On 18 June Lydia danced the flute solo in Act I of *Giselle;* Nijinsky was Albrecht and Karsavina Giselle. She achieved a personal success, although the ballet itself was not well received. Robert Brussel wrote in *Le Figaro* on 19 June, 'Mlle Lopukhova continues to deserve the particular interest which her appearance has so far aroused: her variation in the first act was encored, and in it she showed vitality and grace in equal degrees.' On 13 June he had already written that 'Lopukhova II' had danced the Prélude in *Les Sylphides* with 'adorable subtlety of expression'. Lydia danced the Polovtsian maiden in *Prince Igor*, performed in the corps de ballet in *Schéhérazade*, and appeared as a Greek maiden in *Cléopâtre*, for which *Le Figaro* gave her a special mention.

Her final and greatest success was in *The Firebird*, first presented on 25 June. At first she danced an 'enchanted princess', but when Karsavina returned to London Fokin persuaded Diaghilev to give Lydia the title role, for which, with her big jump, she was particularly suited. Her interpretation was quite different from that of

Karsavina; according to Alexander Benois, 'She was a delicate humming-bird rather than a flaming phoenix.' Robert Brussel wrote in *Le Figaro*, 'So, it is a success, a great success, for Mlle Lopukhova II to have achieved such lengthy applause in this delightful dance. This child – she is seventeen – has only just left school: but her first performances have been pretty much like those of Karsavina, who at once won herself a position of importance at the Mariinsky at the very beginning of her career.' From Paris the company went to Brussels, where it stayed until the end of the season in July. Then Lydia left for America with her sister, Lopukhova I, her brother Fedor and Alexander Volinin, never to dance in Russia again.

Lydia Vasilievna Lopukhova:
A Choreographic Portrait

F. V. Lopukhov

It is not known when Fedor Lopukhov wrote this piece, which has not been published before. The ballets in which he describes his younger sister's dancing were all performed in Paris in 1910, and in July that year he left with Lydia and their sister, Lopukhova I, for America. He returned to St Petersburg the next year, and it is probable that he never saw Lydia dancing again. Mikhail Fokin's Memoirs *(referred to* passim *by Lopukhov) were compiled over many years in the form of notes; they were not published in English until 1961, but had been available in Russian at an earlier date*

M.K.

I must first explain that I am going to write about my sister, the ballerina Lydia Lopukhova, not as a brother, but as the ballet master, Fedor Lopukhov. Lydia is almost unknown in Russia, but she had an outstanding career abroad, beginning with her work with Diaghilev. An extensive literature about her has accumulated outside Russia, which I do not propose to recount or refer to here. I shall write about Lopukhova from the same vantage point that I have adopted when writing about other ballerinas.

I saw Lydia Lopukhova on the stage of the Paris Opéra in 1910, when I had arrived in Paris to dance at the Sarah Bernhardt Theatre on a tour with the St Petersburg dancers, Julia Sedova and Nikolai Legat. Lydia, like many other young dancers, had been invited to work with Diaghilev by Fokin, with whom she had studied at the drama school in St Petersburg. Fokin had a high opinion of his pupil, had nurtured her talent while she was at school, and in due course (while I was at finishing school) had signed her on, first, for the part of Cupid in the ballet *Acis and Galatea* (in which I danced Acis) and, later, for that of the Winter Snowflake in Tchaikovsky's 'December' music. Nevertheless, when Lydia arrived in Paris it was as an ordinary member of the corps de ballet. It was at the Opéra that she made her remarkable leap from the ranks of the corps de ballet to the position of a recognized ballerina who was the talk of the ballet correspondents. I know of no other dancer who has made such a leap, which was all the more remarkable as Lydia had no 'pull', or publicity, to help her comparable with the ambiguous murmurings that surrounded Nijinsky from his days in St Petersburg onwards. Lydia Lopukhova had nothing but her talent, which no one, except presumably Fokin, had noticed; but Fokin was not going to promote anybody who might obstruct the advancement to prima ballerina status of his wife, Vera Antonova.

I do not know exactly what happened: whether it was because of illness among the ballerinas or for other reasons, but Diaghilev's ballet repertoire was in danger of collapse at this time. Diaghilev could hardly cancel the performances, since that would have posed the threat of a major financial loss, and Diaghilev's personal budget depended on box office receipts. And so, there and then, after a conference with Fokin – hurriedly, without the proper amount of rehearsal and with her roles incompletely prepared – Lydia Lopukhova was launched in the ballets *Firebird* and *Carnaval*, in both of which she appeared with Fokin.

It is possible that neither Diaghilev (who was not very interested in female roles) nor Fokin thought that Lydia, who was little more than a girl (she was not yet eighteen), would cause a stir at this early stage; they were only concerned to save the performances. But the incredible happened: I was present at those performances and can vouch for it. After Lydia's appearances in these ballets, and without the press (with which we had no contact whatever) being courted, the whole of the Paris theatre world was talking about her as a ballet phenomenon. Her success was such that Diaghilev already began to base his box office calculations on her appearances. I cannot understand why Fokin in his *Memoirs* gives Lydia hardly more than a passing mention – only sparing her a few words – when, after all, he himself had danced with her and shared her success.

Thus began the career of the hitherto unknown dancer Lydia Lopukhova, nicknamed 'Little Baby'. Paris was abuzz: a new star had arisen. My account is confirmed by articles that were written about her at the time.

Wherein lay the fascination of this young dancer who had thus taken Paris by storm? Lydia was of short stature – an elegant little doll, with eyes that shone whenever she performed. Her cheerful nature, the optimistic, youthful *joie de vivre* of her interpretations, infected audiences; any number that she danced ended with thunderous applause. Her pirouette technique was unremarkable, but her running on points was infectiously gay and light, as if she was tripping on air, without any boards beneath her feet: in general, dancing on points conveys the suggestion that the ballerina wants to leave the earth behind her. Her leg muscles were remarkable, and she could achieve an incredibly big leap, almost masculine in its power; yet, at the same time, her flight through the air – or hovering in mid-air – was delicate and typically feminine, as was her landing. It was the kind of leap of which Nijinsky was capable, but whereas his leap reminded one of the jump and flight of a grasshopper, Lydia's resembled rather the wafting and descent of dandelion down, and thus the alighting upon earth of the little angels of quattrocento painters. How accurately Fokin had sensed this quality when he gave her the part of Cupid in *Acis and Galatea*! But Fokin did not like to remember that ballet, even though it was one that laid the foundations of his own mastery. And yet, in his *Memoirs*, he ought to have recalled both the ballet itself and the Lopukhovs who took part in it – above all, Lydia Lopukhova, who was to bring success to his ballets *Firebird*, *Carnaval* and *Petrushka*.

The role of the Firebird was not in essence well suited to Lydia's gifts. It was her leap, her soaring flight, that saved her. But, as Columbine in *Carnaval*, she overshadowed even Karsavina, of whom I was a great admirer and who also danced the role with immense verve, bringing to it a unique element of sincerity. Lydia, on the other hand, created the picture of a young girl and of her first jubilant love, when everything appears in a rosy glow – everything around seems to rejoice with her and not a single black thought arises to cast a shadow over these ecstatic feelings. I can understand why Europe was swept away by her jubilation. This, after all, was 1910, a year of dark foreboding, with war clouds gathering; yet, here on stage was portrayed the very joy of existence, a great affirmation of life as being the best thing man possesses. Audiences could forget for a while the looming storm clouds and rejoice in life together with Columbine-Lopukhova. Such was the impact of the choreographer's art and of this young artist's talent.

Besides her brilliantly executed Columbine in the Schumann-Fokin *Carnaval* – such a thoroughly German Columbine, matching the equally German Harlequin of Fokin – one must mention her performance as the Ballerina in *Petrushka*. Lydia's Ballerina too was German in style, as Stravinsky himself appeared to wish when he introduced the Lanner waltz into the dance dialogue between the Ballerina and the Moor. Here Lopukhova created brilliantly the image of a simple little German ballerina. In her attitude to the Moor there was no hint of interest in his wealth (which many other interpreters of the part have emphasized). Lopukhova, by contrast, portrayed the kind of unexpected, strange attraction which sometimes possesses inexperienced young girls. She gave the impression of being sincere in her infatuation and of recognizing her mistake too late, after the tragedy of poor Petrushka, who genuinely loved the Ballerina, had occurred. Lydia was unbelievably moving, her radiant, joyful eyes filling with tears of remorse as she realized her error. Nobody else played the role like that. And had it not been for the deliberately noisy publicity created by Diaghilev for his favourite, Nijinsky, the part of the Ballerina, which is in no way less important than that of Petrushka, would have received its proper share of attention from the critics. Both Karsavina, with her romantic interpretation of this part, and Lydia, with her portrayal of apparent light-heartedness leading to tragedy, would have been properly recognized. Lydia's interpretation offered much that was true to life, and audiences were bound to acknowledge this.

Lydia Lopukhova appeared in parts created by other choreographers as well as Fokin, from whom Diaghilev eventually parted company in 1912 in order to help his favourites to become ballet masters, especially Nijinsky (who staged the notorious and choreographically illiterate *The Rite of Spring*). But I do not wish to add anything about these other productions (including my own) in which Lydia appeared. Here I end my attempt to characterize the creative essence of Lydia Lopukhova, which, in 1910, was revealed so suddenly and so memorably for all her friends and contemporaries – perhaps even for Fokin himself, and certainly for me.

Lydia Lopokova in America

Frank W. Ries

Lydia Lopokova's career in America spanned over six years, from August 1910 to July 1916, and from October 1916 to February 1917. Within that period she appeared as dancer, cabaret artist, model, vaudeville performer, and even as dramatic actress on the Broadway stage. She was to end her American stay by practically saving the *Ballets Russes* through her diplomacy with the press, her knowledge of the country and her previously established popularity in the New World. Lydia's work in America is therefore important not only in an overall perspective of her career but also for the light it sheds on American attitudes to dancers, especially Russian 'toe-dancers', in the first decades of the twentieth century.

Lydia Lopokova left France on 26 July 1910, bound for America and the fulfilment of an eight-month contract with the producer Charles Frohman at a salary of four thousand roubles a month. A special cable sent from Paris to New York aroused much speculation. The 'eighteen-year-old' dancer had apparently kept both Paris detectives and her American manager, Josef Mendelkern, busy, because she insisted on getting married and breaking her contract with Frohman. An article reported that she was engaged to a rich Polish count, 'who stated money was no object and he was willing to pay a heavy fine for the release of Lopoukhova from her American contract'. Despite this exciting possibility, Lydia, together with her brother, Fedor, sister, Evgenia, and Alexander Volinin, landed in New York from the *Oceanic*, as scheduled, on 3 August. *En route* she seems to have lost a couple of years, for the *New York Telegraph* talked of her looking 'younger than her sixteen years'.

When Lydia stepped off the boat reporters rushed to ask her questions about the mysterious Polish count. She refused to reveal his name but did tell them that he had 'a real castle in Poland', and 'with just a suggestion of a pout on her lips, that in eight months her contract with Mr Frohman would be ended and she would return to him and be married'. The Polish count never appeared during Lydia's stay and was never mentioned again after the first few interviews. The 'engagement' may have been a ruse by Frohman and his new star to establish interest in her.

Lydia appeared in Frohman's various revues and toured the United States as a 'specialty act'. The *Chicago Tribune* (26 October 1910) thought Fedor and Alexander Volinin very good, 'but we are especially pleased to have Lydia, and we thank the Tsar very much for lending her.' The reviewer commented on her 'light and graceful dancing', and, while finding her 'not as great as Pavlova', qualified this criticism by informing his readers that Lydia 'is only at the start of her career'.

> She is pretty, is little Lydia Laokowa [sic], all curves and dimples, and what is unusual in a toe dancer, she hasn't the appearance of an athletic spider with large hunks of muscles overprominently displayed. Little Lydia dances like an autumn leaf fluttering around the ground on a blue-grey October evening. She doesn't put forth any effort herself, but whisks this way and that at the caprice of the orchestra which takes the part of the October wind. She dances on the stage or twinkles in the air for a while and lands on the shoulders of Alexander Valienne [sic] of Moscow as light as thistledown.

Although this review is very crude in its description of the performance, it does give the reader some idea of what Lydia was like as a young dancer. American journalists were not used to reviewing dance, except in its vaudeville manifestations, and its technical vocabulary was quite alien to them.

Lydia's 'official' biography began to appear in various newspapers as she toured the United States. Some of it is rather obvious press-release puffery, but it is interesting to see how publicists thought a ballerina should be presented to the American public:

> Mlle Lydia Lopoukowa of the All-Star Imperial Russian Ballet is only nineteen, yet she is a prima ballerina with the greatest organization of choreographic artists the world ever saw. She is co-star with such famous dancers as Mlles Katrina Geltzer, Julia Sedova, Vera Koralli, and Carlotta Zambelli, etc. and has as partners such

leading man dancers as Alexander Volinin and the reincarnated
Greek God, Mikhail Mordkin.

'La précoce' or the precocious child, is what the Parisians fondly
called Mlle Lopoukowa when she danced at the Châtelet in the real
'Saison des Ballets Russes'. The members of the All-Star Imperial
Russian Ballet know her as 'Baby Lydia'. American critics who
have already seen her dance have hailed her as 'that adorable little
Lydia Lopoukowa'.

Coming from a St Petersburg family of Imperial Russian dancers, Mlle Lopoukowa has herself been a daughter of Terpsichore
for over half her life. She was just nine years old, when in 1901
she was entered in the Imperial Mariinsky Institute of St Petersburg. She graduated in 1908, and since then has danced not only
at the Imperial Opera House of St Petersburg, but in Paris,
London, Brussels, and Berlin.

Besides French, German and of course Russian, the little première danseuse speaks English – with a quaint polyglot accent. She
says that America is a lovely country, but that there are two things
here she does not like, hats for the hair and American shoes. In
fact Mlle Lopoukowa doesn't like any kind of shoes, even those
from Russia. Even while on the street she wears sandals.

When this biographical sketch was released, in June 1911, Lydia
had already joined Gertrude Hoffmann in the 'All-Star Imperial
Russian Ballet'. Miss Hoffmann was a revue artist who had a great
ability to mimic other performers. She had seen Diaghilev's Russian
Ballets in Paris and had the costumes and sets copied for her in
America. She simulated the choreography, played the non-dance
leads – such as Zobeïda in *Schéhérazade* – and hired dancers of questionable authenticity disguised under Russian names. Obviously
Lydia was not questionable and was one of the few genuine Russians
to appear with this astonishing polyglot company. Why Lydia
joined this imitation Russian Ballet is not known; perhaps she was
tired of the vaudeville circuit and, wishing to stay in America, felt
that Miss Hoffmann's company offered the best way of achieving
this while enabling her to continue dancing.

Lydia appeared with the Hoffmann 'Russian Ballet' from 5 June
until 17 September 1911, at the Winter Garden Theatre in New
York and then on tour in Chicago, Minneapolis, Washington and
Buffalo. She may have left the company because of professional

jealousy on Miss Hoffmann's part. All the reviews are unanimous in their praise of Lydia. After the opening night in New York, *The New York Times* noted that she was the outstanding and unquestionable star of the evening, and all the other reviews say much the same thing. This is remarkable, since Lydia did not dance the lead parts but mainly solo variations: the waltz in *Les Sylphides*, a variation in *Cleopatra*, a pas de deux in one of the *Festin* selections. Time and again she was singled out for praise above and beyond the rest of the company; one newspaper went so far as to call her 'the new Pavlova'. It was not the type of praise that would especially please the ambitious Miss Hoffmann; Lydia left the company after the cross-country tour.

Although her brother had returned to Russia Volinin had stayed with Lydia. Along with Alexandra Baldina and Fedor Koslov of the Hoffmann 'Russian Ballet', they toured the country in a programme of both national and balletic Russian dances. The reviews were again unanimous in their praise.

By November 1911 Mikhail Mordkin had joined the troupe and had become its acknowledged leader. Lydia had never liked organizing and running the company and was happy to hand over the task to Mordkin, who had just had a tiff with Pavlova and left her company. As he was extremely popular in America, the Lopokova-Mordkin partnership should have worked well. However, Mordkin was soon wounded by the acclaim Lydia continued to receive. When the company appeared in New York, the *New York Sun* thought that of 'the greatest success there could be no possible, probable shadow of a doubt – it was la Lopoukowa'. The reviewer goes on to say that Mordkin is still a great dancer, but that he had become 'affected' in performance and especially in his exaggerated curtain calls. 'For the first time in his long career he had to stand comparison, and he does not always win out, against Koslov on the male side and Lydia on the female.'

A rift was probably only to be expected. While the company was touring Lydia finally left, in Buffalo, on the night of 11 November 1911 when her manager, Josef Mendelkern, caused a disturbance because she did not appear in the ballet as scheduled for that evening. The newspapers took up the story and the matter was finally taken to court. While there is much conflicting testimony, the basic story seems to have been as follows.

At the performance the opening dance had finished and, according to the programme, Lydia was then to dance two solo numbers. Lydia told the court that she was ready to go on, waiting in the wings, when she heard that Mordkin – had given instructions to the orchestra leader to change the music. Almost instantly – according to Lydia's testimony – the curtain rose and a Miss Jane, an English pupil of Mordkin's, danced out on to the stage. Immediately after this Lydia's manager appeared in a box near the stage and told the audience that they had not seen Miss Lopokova, though they had not been informed of the programme change. Mendelkern then told the audience that Mordkin was jealous of Lopokova and wanted to foist his pupil on the public. Mendelkern was dragged from the theatre, but the audience was so stirred that they yelled and cat-called until Lydia appeared on the stage and danced for them. A newspaper noted that she 'was given an ovation that rarely befalls any artist and encore after encore was rapturously demanded'. Lydia's manager was brought before the local court and fined $25 for disorderly conduct.

Mordkin told the newspapers after the performance that he had a right to change the programme order and had always intended Lydia to dance later in the evening; he blamed the misunderstanding on a 'printer's error' in the cast lists. This excuse, however, sounded very flimsy, and Mendelkern took the suit to New York, claiming that the producers of the ballet company were responsible for his client's maltreatment and demanding arrears of salary for his star ballerina. As Lydia was still under age in the eyes of American law, Mendelkern claimed that he was also her guardian and protector and even 'the representative of the Imperial Russian government' on her behalf. The management claimed that they would love to have Lydia dance for them again, but found her manager obnoxious, nosey and domineering. Mendelkern brought the case to court, claiming $6,500 for transfer of contract and $6,200 for damages. When Lydia was forced to appear in court all the reporters noted how tired and ill she looked and that she dozed off when not on the witness stand. After months of negotiations and proceedings Lydia received her full arrears of pay, but no sum for damages. Her contract was renewed, but transferred to a different organization. Mendelkern is never mentioned again in connection with Lydia; perhaps her new management stipulated that she must not continue to employ him as her agent.

During the next year, 1912, Lydia headed a revue at the Winter

Garden Theatre in which she danced an extremely difficult *terre-à-terre* 'toe dance', called the 'Xylophone Polka', to music by Drigo. All the critics were astonished by her prowess, and the dance soon became a popular encore for her subsequent recitals. When Mordkin's company collapsed there must have been a reconciliation between the two dancers, for he partnered Lydia during her new engagement in Pavlova's old piece, 'The Bacchanale', to music by Glazunov. Once more, however, the reviews noted that he was not at his best. On the same variety programme with Lydia was Al Jolson, as well as the swimming artist, Annette Kellerman.

At about this time articles began to appear, most of them interviews with Lydia, expatiating on her desire to become an American citizen. 'Lydia Lopukova seeks naturalization papers to escape dreadful recall by Tsar of Imperial Ballet,' one headline told its readers dramatically. The Tsar, according to the article, was Alexoff Pvoffovich, ballet master of the Imperial Opera in St Petersburg. Lydia explained: 'I do not wish to go back to Russia. . . . The only fear I have is they will call me back before I am a citizen. . . . I want to live in New York always. I want to be like other American women, and most of all I want to vote.' She must have been very concerned about the suffragette movement, since there is proof that she danced for charity benefits in aid of various women's 'liberation societies' in America. 'Pvoffovich' and his threat were both inventions.

By September she was rehearsing, in New York, Victor Herbert's new operetta, *The Lady of the Slipper*. A musical fantasy in three acts based on the tale of Cinderella, it opened at the Globe Theatre on 28 October, with Lydia as the *première danseuse*. Her dancing was not part of the plot, but consisted of interpolations: one occurred during the ballroom scene; the other was a dream sequence. The reviews do not actually describe her dances, but all are unanimous in their praise of 'her delightful talents and delightful technique'. Articles continued to appear, emphasizing Lydia's desire to stay in the country, but now there was an added twist: Lydia increasingly told reporters that dancing was no longer her chief love and that light opera was more her *forte*, though she thought she had possibilities 'in other fields of the performing arts'. Despite this public reticence, it is obvious from subsequent events that she had already made up her mind about her future goals. When *The Lady of the Slipper* closed in the spring of 1913 Lydia disappeared from public view, and no one seemed to know what had become of her.

What she had decided to do was to learn English properly, so that she could become a dramatic actress. Although this was not revealed until years later, she spent the summer and winter of 1913–14 in the Catskill Mountains, studying English and taking drama lessons. It is extraordinary that one of the 'toasts of New York', with one of the highest salaries on Broadway, should have given up her glamorous career to pursue dramatic work that was not even in her native language. Throughout her life, though, Lydia was intrigued by 'impossible' challenges.

She returned to New York in January 1914, and gave a final dance recital on the New York Roof, which was sponsoring a series entitled 'Jardin de la Danse', in which both classical and popular dance forms were displayed. Lydia appeared with Edmond Makaliv as her partner and, as described by one reviewer, 'went through all the latest steps', to numerous signs of appreciation and applause. Lydia's participation in the revue series was so popular that the management presented her with a silver loving cup and offers poured in for her to go on tour with the show, at $1,500 a week. However, she refused. 'The Pet of New York', as *Variety* termed her, announced in February that she was giving up dance and becoming an actress. 'I shall continue to dance for my own pleasure,' she explained, 'but not ballet dancing. I shall do interpretative dancing – but only for myself and friends, I shall not appear publicly.'

Lydia gave a series of interviews in the next few months, explaining her decision. Many papers embroidered the facts. The *Boston Herald*, claiming that Lydia was only seventeen, also announced that she had been prima ballerina in Russia before she came to America. She simply informed the papers that she was 'tired of the dance world' for personal reasons and that dance could no longer motivate her. She had taken acting lessons during her training for the Imperial stage and had always preferred the more theatrical dance roles. She stated that this decision was 'a natural outcome' of her background and training and 'where my heart really lies'. It was at this point (1 April 1914) that Lydia legally changed the spelling of her surname (from Lopukhova to Lopokova) to avoid any further confusion, the change being officially registered in New York State.

In March 1914 Lydia revealed that the impresario, Harrison Grey Fiske, had chosen for her a play written especially with her in mind, but that she was not allowed to reveal its title or content. She did tell the press that 'it gives me great scope to prove myself as an actress, which is the thing I want to do most of everything in the world'. Lydia had first approached Fiske and his wife when she returned from her retreat in the Catskills. Mrs Minnie Fiske, a playwright in her own right, had then suggested that she prepare some of Nora's speeches from *A Doll's House*. Lydia worked alone for several weeks and in early February gave a private audition for the Fiskes in one of the theatres they owned in New York. When the audition was over a contract was immediately drawn up. Afterwards Mrs Fiske told the press, 'I have never seen parts of Nora more beautifully portrayed. The child has talent and possibly a spark of genius.' Although Lydia was never to perform Nora in America, many years later she created Ibsen's heroine on the British stage.

The play the Fiskes had chosen for Lydia was originally entitled *The Young Idea*; before it reached Broadway its title was changed to *Just Herself*. It was credited to a Mrs Grant, but a number of newspapers note that it was in fact written by Ethel Watts Mumford and her husband, Henry Watts. The story they concocted for Lydia's stage début concerns a young girl who returns to her parents' home after finishing her schooling in Europe. There, in Berlin, she had worked under a 'new-fangled' teacher who had taught her to shun any pretensions or social conventions. The home the young Miss returns to is, of course, filled with all the things she has been taught to abhor. Her father, a widower, had married his cook while his daughter was away in Europe. The cook naturally wants to raise herself up the social ladder, but finds her step-daughter's attitudes totally opposed to her new-found affluence. The young girl falls in love with the chauffeur next door - much to her parents' horror - but by the end of the play he is revealed to be the son and heir of the wealthy neighbour, so all ends as it should do.

Lydia first performed the new comedy in Pittsfield, Massachusetts, on 20 July 1914. For these try-out performances she appeared under the name of Vera Tula, without, however, fooling the press. They thought her delightful in the role of the young rebel, though she was naturally nervous in her first public speaking part. The crowded house was enthusiastic on her behalf, and so she visibly relaxed as the play progressed.

Lydia toured in the play in the traditional pre-Broadway try-out cities: Buffalo, New Haven and elsewhere. The reviews were always good as far as her performance was concerned, but rarely found any redeeming features in the play written for her. 'Miss Lopokova,' stated a Boston newspaper, the *Christian Science Monitor*, on 3 November 1914,

> needs no apologists on her first appearance in a play, for she has been schooled in the mother of the arts, the dance. She can act with ease the shallow part given her in this sketchy play; can act with charm and distinction, for her schooling in the dance involved long training in mental appreciation of emotion ... for sketchy and artless though Mrs Mumford's play is, it serves as a means of displaying Miss Lopokova's art. Even so a Corot might be contained in an apprentice frame.

Interviewed in Boston, Lydia explained that the dramatic training she had received in Russia had led her to become fascinated with verbal, rather than strictly kinetic theatrical art. 'I have so much to learn', she remarked, 'the real test is yet to come.' Though she was tired and reserved after the Boston opening, the reporter for the *Christian Science Monitor* (7 November 1914) has left a vivid word picture of the aspiring young actress:

> Shy until now, Miss Lopokova in her grateful happiness that she has pleased the playgoers here, laughed gaily, half tossed her arms as if talking with them, and at one point the fingers of her left hand did a little dance movement on their own account. Watching her mobile face [one wants] to try to store up the impressions of the evanescent moods that play in her keen blue eyes, with their eloquent lids, and about her lips that are nearly always parted in youthful eagerness; then try to pass these impressions along to a reader with their iridescence of colour and baffling nuances.
>
> But the detailed effect of her charm is elusive. You see it partly in the finely modelled head, the blond hair simply parted and softly braided into a psyche knot and banded diagonally with a ribbon of Persian silk in soft dark hues. You are conscious of the smooth contours of her rounded cheeks and slender throat, and grateful that she designed her simple blue-grey frock with its broad lace collar as a setting for her charm, not a decoration to it.

By the time the play reached Broadway in late December, a number of dramatic changes had been made in an effort to save it.

Not only was the title altered; characters were cut and other parts enlarged, to add more comic confrontations between the young girl and the upper crust. A longer dance sequence was interpolated, to allow Lydia to display her dancing, and much of the dialogue was tightened. It did not do much good, for when the play opened at the Playhouse Theater on 23 December 1914, the reviews were generally unfavourable, while giving Lydia excellent personal notices. One headline captured it succinctly: 'Lopokova appears in silly play/Little Russian danseuse goes in for acting in *Just Herself* BUT SHE ALSO DANCES/ which provided the most pleasant moments in an expert comedy by Ethel Watts Mumford.' *The New York Times* (24 December 1914), after dismissing the play as a trifle, thought it difficult to pass any judgement on Lydia because of the weak vehicle:

'How good an actress she is or may become, it would be monstrously unfair to judge by her appearance in the new piece at the Playhouse. As the small rebellious heroine of *Just Herself* she displays much piquant charm of personality and little variety.' The reviewer thought the most pleasant moments of the evening were 'when the stage was fairly well cleared, and Lopokova was left to dance her way into the good graces of the people across the footlights. Decidedly its most amusing moments come when the comedy can be observed making uneasy preparations for these displays of Lopokova's original art.' The *New York Telegram* also thought the dancing the high point of the show, and noted that Lydia was 'so youthful and pretty in some of her scenes, so captivating and spontaneous that her limitations are either forgiven or forgotten and the evident mechanical nature of some of her gestures are condoned.'

With reviews such as these the play could not last long but, if the publicity had been carefully managed, it could have had a respectable run. However it closed within a week – rather short, even for mediocre plays at that time – and its closing was a drama in itself. 'Fiske show ends/Actors Barred Out', the leader in the *The New York Times* reported on 30 December 1914. The paper went on to explain that the cast had arrived in the rain at seven that evening, only to find the doors locked on them; they could not even go in to obtain their possessions which had been left in the dressing rooms. It was all very abrupt and sudden and no one knew about the closing until the last minute, although the star, Lydia, had been told at 6 pm in her Manhattan apartment, where she remained 'secluded and upset'. It was explained some days later that Fiske had run into heavy

financial problems and could not support the play beyond its opening week. For Lydia this must have been a crushing blow, considering the year and more she had spent learning English and preparing
for her dramatic début. Now it was over before her New York
performances had barely begun, and the city papers speculated on
what her next move would be.

Lydia surprised them all by bouncing back into the theatrical
world within a few weeks, this time as a dancer again. On 15 January
1915 she appeared as the fourth attraction in the 'Moments Musicals'
given at the Waldorf Astoria Hotel. 'She showed she had not forgotten her intricate steps,' the *New York Herald* reported. Lydia
performed a Chopin prelude and a variation from Delibes' *Sylvia*.

By February she was on tour in a new revue, *Fads and Fancies*, in
which she danced 'the spirit of Pleasure'. It opened in New York on
8 March, and while many of the critics found the show tedious and
long, they also found Lydia to be the highlight of the evening:

> When she dances there is a charm to the performance, but the
> producers have failed to make use of their greatest asset in having
> this dainty person confine herself largely to ragtime and musical
> comedy dances, rather than the beautiful movement in which she
> excels. There was never a time during the performance that Miss
> Lopokova could not have danced on in filmy draperies, and, by an
> exhibition of her own art, unaided, lifted the whole performance
> to a higher plane and aroused the audience to a point of enthusiasm.

Although this criticism in the *Brooklyn Eagle* (9 March 1915) is
expressed rather crudely, the critic does point out the main problem
with Lydia's American career: she was often either underused or
misused.

Lydia tried to rectify the problem by changing over in April to a
different revue at the Palace, with only one night off between
performances. She danced a number of classical solos, as well as some
speciality numbers with a small corps de ballet. Between each of her
selections 'the Morgan dancers appeared in a repertoire of ancient
Egyptian, Greek and Roman dances.' While the authenticity of
these is highly doubtful, the contrast between the dance groups must
have been fascinating. Lydia's coaching of her corps de ballet and
observation of the Morgan girls may have prompted a comment to
the *New York Mail* (31 July 1915) soon after that opening. 'American
girls are lazy,' Lydia stated. 'Why, they don't know what work is.

At home in Russia we are brought up with the idea that to be idle is almost a crime. We know nothing but work. That's why we are such a healthy lot and that's the reason we turn out such good dancers.' Lydia concluded that not one girl in fifty in America could stand the daily grind and practice of the Imperial Ballet School, in which she had been brought up.

Although Lydia was dancing again, she had not given up her ambition to become a dramatic actress. At the end of the summer, in another one of her surprise moves, she asked for and was granted a release from her dancing contract and, turning down offers of between $1000 and $2000 per week, joined the Washington Square Players in New York at the grand salary of $100 *per month*! The Players were a group of semi-professional actors and actresses who were tired of the stock commercial plays and wanted to try out more interesting, though less profitable, drama. Many of these were one-act plays of considerable historical interest which were too limited in appeal to reach the main theatres on Broadway.

Lydia opened with the company at the Bandbox Theatre on 14 October 1915 in *The Antick*, an old play by Percy Mackaye, in which she herself played Julie Bonheur. The authoritative critic, Burns Mantle, thought her 'glorious as the little Canuck, who breaks over the well-known traces and grabs her love as she flies by him in riotous, youthful dancing. The fact that that Faery actress, Lydia Lopokova, played Julie added more to the play than Percy MacKaye anticipated when he wrote it, we dare say. She, at least, was the one who stabbed our interest in the proceedings, and help it, though she danced little.' Although her début with the players was in this rather 'fluffy' role, the next series of one-act plays allowed Lydia to sink her teeth into a more dramatic part. This was in Alfred de Musset's *Whims*, which opened for a limited run on 20 November. All the critics noted her charm in 'this hoopskirted role from the 1860's' and commented on how well she carried the difficult and poetic text which Musset had written for his heroine.

At about the time of these performances rumours began to spread about a possible announcement of an engagement between Lydia and a New York gentleman. On 11 December 1915 the *New York Review* 'leaked' the information that Lydia was to marry a journalist, though his name was still being withheld. All the newspapers expressed amazement that, during her long years in America, this was the first time that any hint of romance had attached itself to 'the fair

Russian heroine' since she stepped off the boat, pursued by the count
who never appeared. On 8 January 1916 the identity of the mysterious gentleman was revealed. He turned out to be Heywood
Broun, a drama and sports critic for the *New York Tribune*. Broun
had fallen in love with Lydia while seeing her act at the Bandbox,
although Lydia emphasized in an interview that his professional
opinion still remained unbiased! Later, when he was 'promoted' to
sports editor – it is interesting that the post of drama editor was
considered less prestigious – he proposed to her and she accepted
him.

Within the week another startling announcement was made about
Miss Lopokova. The Russian Ballet, which was planning to come
to America, would welcome her back to its fold for its engagement
by the Metropolitan Opera and for its cross-country tour. Diaghilev
was fearful about this New World venture, and Lydia, with her
Americanized English, her contacts, and her knowledge of the country, was the perfect cultural ambassador for the company. She was
inexhaustable in her interviews, her translations for other dancers in
the company interviewed by newspapers and magazines, and her
energy and enthusiasm for Diaghilev's work. Her engagement to an
American sports writer helped to make her more acceptable to the
populace, and the Metropolitan publicists continually emphasized
that Lydia 'was a normal, everyday girl' who just happened to
dance.

The Russian Ballet, or *Ballets Russes de Serge de Diaghileff*, opened
at the Century Theatre in New York, under the auspices of the
Metropolitan Opera Association, on 17 January 1916. Lydia, however, did not appear on stage until the third night, Many historians
and critics have wondered why Diaghilev did not use Lydia immediately, considering her proved personal success in America and his
weak line-up of ballerinas for the American tour. There were a
number of reasons for this. One was that Lydia had to finish her
commitment to the Washington Square Players, which included a
performance on the 17th. This would give Lydia only one day to
prepare for her performance with the Russian Ballet on its third
night in New York. Diaghilev may also have wanted to give his
other female dancers a chance, knowing that Lydia would outshine
them. This proved to be only too true when Diaghilev's 'lead'
dancer, Xenia Makletsova, became furious at Lydia's success and at
the comparison which critics were making between them, to her

disadvantage. She walked out before the cross-country tour began and later sued the company – unsuccessfully.

Lydia duly appeared on 19 January as Columbine in Fokin's *Carnaval*, and her name headed the reviews. The *New York Tribune* called Lydia's appearance 'a triumph'; it showed New York 'for the first time, dancing as the Russians have taught it to us in seasons past'. The *New York Post* noted that Lydia's recent 'lapse into acting' had done nothing to destroy her 'bewitching and piquant charm' as a dancer. Her partner in the ballet – Stanislas Idzikovsky, who danced Harlequin, was also praised by the reviewers, although it was obviously Lydia's night.

The next evening *Les Sylphides* was presented, with Lydia dancing; the *New York Sun* thought she 'demonstrated what a *première danseuse* should accomplish – she had already shown New York audiences the extent of her ability, even though her support was not comparable to that she is now receiving'. By the end of the two week engagement at the Century Theatre it was obvious who the real star had been. As one writer said in a letter to *Musical America*, 'By the aid of Mlle Lopokova and the police [a reference to the censorship of *L'Après-midi d'un faune* and *Schéhérazade*] the Russian Ballet ... ended in a blaze of glory.'

The Russian Ballet went on to Boston, then to Albany, New York, where Lydia was hailed as 'the best asset of the troupe', possessing 'personality and charm and grace in prodigal measure'. They performed in Detroit, from where they went on to Chicago. This was the one city where the company failed to draw large crowds and the local backers lost most of their investment, but even here Lydia was singled out for praise, especially for her dancing in the title role of *The Firebird*, which had now been added to her repertoire.

To avoid further disaster, preview articles were prepared for the local newspapers of the next stop, Milwaukee, Wisconsin. Lydia, acting as ambassador for the company, wrote an article in which she described the hard work the Russians put into their art and her own early days in the ballet studios and on the stages of St Petersburg. Such interviews were published frequently during the tour; Lydia was at the centre of most of them, both because of the fluency of her English and because of her American connections. In the next two cities on the tour, Minneapolis and St Paul, for instance, articles appeared on how Lydia was to wed an American sports writer, with

a banner headline in Minneapolis: ' "PLAY BALL!" CRIES LYDIA LOPO-
KOVA; WHY? SHE'S TO BE SPORT WRITER'S WIFE'. The article goes on to
explain how the charming dancer felt she had to learn all the correct
baseball terms, since 'dutiful spouses should be able to "get" Husband's Idioms.' This article, which appeared on the company's
opening night in the city, had obviously been written some weeks
before, either on tour or in New York. The irony was that, as the
newspapers reached the stands, Lydia was indeed getting married –
but to someone else.

   During the tour Lydia had become attached to Randolfo Barocchi, who was acting as Diaghilev's business manager for the tour.
She seems quietly to have broken off her engagement to Heywood
Broun, and while in Minneapolis, Lydia and Randolfo were married
in a civil ceremony – all of this would only be revealed when the
company returned to New York some months later. The papers
stated that the ceremony took place 'in either Minneapolis or St
Paul'; it has now been possible to trace the original certificate of
marriage to the city registry of Minneapolis, where Lydia was
married on 2 March 1916. The company had arrived in the city that
morning and Lydia and Randolfo were married in the afternoon,
before the evening performance. One suspects that the marriage was
kept secret from everyone except perhaps Diaghilev and a few close
friends in the company.

   Lydia continued to accumulate garlands of praise on the tour. In
Washington D.C. she danced in *Le Spectre de la rose*, with Alexander
Gavrilov, at the benefit opening for wounded Russian soldiers and
in the presence of President Wilson. Lydia seems to have been quite
bashful when presented to the President, which was unusual for her.
Some years before, when she had been presented to President Taft,
she had given him a little curtsey and, with a sweeping glance, said,
'You are as big as two men. But I think I would rather have Mr
Roosevelt as President.'

   When the company returned to New York in April for their
engagement at the Metropolitan Opera House Lydia was not ex-
cluded this time from the opening night, but appeared in *Le Spectre
de la Rose*, and later in the season in *Carnaval*, *Firebird*, *Les Papillons*
and *Les Sylphides*. At the end of the engagement *The New York
Times* concluded, 'Lydia Lopokova may well be classed as one of
the great dancers who are supposed to appear at intervals of
twenty-five years.' Such praise must be tempered, however, with

that of another reviewer who thought Lydia was a delightful performer but 'no Karsavina or Pavlova'. After the last performance, on 29 April, Lydia left America for the first time since 1910. She was to return in the autumn, after a tour of Spain with the Russian Ballet from October 1916 to February 1917. This time Vaslav Nijinsky was to head the company.

Nijinsky had already joined the company for the last few weeks of its Metropolitan engagement in April, after his release from internment in Austria. The reunion with Diaghilev, because of his marriage, was tense and uncomfortable, and the rest of the company found him more distant and aloof than in the past. Lydia danced in *Le Spectre de la rose* with Nijinsky and the reviews naturally concentrated on his performance. Most critics judged him technically outstanding, although the role itself was somewhat effeminate for American taste.

When Nijinsky returned with the company to the Manhattan Opera House in October 1916, Lydia continued to dance in *Le Spectre de la rose* as well as in the Bluebird pas de deux, which was now presented under the title *La Princesse enchantée*. As she was the strongest technican in the company, Nijinsky partnered her in the classical ballets, although he never allowed her to take a separate curtain call, which the newspapers noted and complained about. Lydia seems to have borne up well under his jealousy and probably realized that he was not fully himself since his internment – as later events were sadly to prove.

The one part which she added to her repertoire in New York was that of the Ballerina in *Petrushka*, which a number of reviewers did not think really suited her. Although she had danced the role with Massine on the previous tour, New York had not seen her in the role and found 'her acting talent surprisingly lacking for one who has had such theatrical training'. However, in such brilliant show pieces as the Bluebird pas de deux, she was praised for her 'graceful, ethereal, quick stepping display of sheer virtuosity, hardly exceeded by Nijinsky's own'. The reviews in the cities visited in the five-month tour repeated very similar opinions, and one critic noted how the applause Lopokova received 'spurred Nijinsky on to better and better dancing'. Off stage, however, relationships between Nijinsky and the other dancers deteriorated, as he switched ballets without notice, as well as the parts the dancers were to play. It was on this tour that Lydia made her only appearances as the slave, Ta Hor, in

Cleopatra. The tour finally ended in Albany, New York, on 24 February 1917, with a programme in which Lydia danced Bluebird with Nijinsky.

In the same month Lydia left with the rest of the company to return to Europe. She had spent nearly seven years in America. Very few dancers were as loved there as she was, and one cannot think of any who risked as much as she did to enter the dramatic profession, changing her career so radically in mid-stream. The fact that she was able to return to dance so triumphantly proves her inherent talent and discipline. Unlike the other Russian dancers who came to America, she accepted and welcomed its way of life; the people returned her love by applauding her talents, whether they were encased in a bad revue or in the glamour and prestige of the Russian Ballet.

Lydia Lopokova and Serge Diaghilev

Annabel Farjeon

Lydia Lopokova danced with Serge Diaghilev's Russian Ballet capriciously, spasmodically. She darted in and out of the company, a five year gap here, a two or three year gap there, between 1910 and 1927; yet the impact she made was very great, so that she is always considered as one of Diaghilev's chief ballerinas.

She had not the physique of a classical dancer, being a tiny, happy blonde, with rounded arms and the cheeky manner of a London sparrow. But, on first leaving Russia to follow Tamara Karsavina as the dramatic Firebird in Fokin's ballet, she had immediate success. This was a remarkable feat for a seventeen year old girl, one who was so emotional that she fainted with excitement as she stepped onto the platform of the Gare du Nord, fresh from the Mariinsky ballet company. Certainly she had already made her mark in St Petersburg as a soloist, for, after a performance there in company with Nijinsky, the Tsar had presented her with a diamond brooch. But Paris was different, and to succeed as the wild, poetic Firebird before more sophisticated audiences showed marvellous strength and adaptability as an artist.

It was her elevation and lightness that stood Lopokova in good stead when she danced the fabulous bird. Those darting, soaring leaps, the quick nervousness, came readily to her and, although she would not have appeared so melodramatic as the experienced Karsavina, the fearless way she plunged into the role - or into any role, for that matter - carried every audience away.

Alexander Benois, the designer, described her not as a phoenix - which is how he would have referred to Karsavina - but as a humming bird. Lydia Sokolova, the famed character dancer, remarks in her autobiography that, to everyone's astonishment, whatever Lopokova attempted came off. By 'everyone' she means her fellow dancers, whose approbation is far more worth-while than that of any outsider.

Immediately after this triumph Lopokova was lured away into the world of American variety by Charles Frohman, and was not seen again in Europe until 1916, when the Russian Ballet (to which she had now returned as *première danseuse*) was touring in Spain. Seeing the company in Madrid, King Alfonso conceived an enduring affection for it and for its leading dancers. There followed further tours, in which the Russian Ballet twice crossed the Atlantic to North and South America and travelled, in Europe, back and forth to capitals: Rome, Paris, Madrid and Lisbon. Leonide Massine, rising as Diaghilev's favourite from the ashes of Nijinsky's burnt-out career, was now the company choreographer, and he created a number of light-hearted, scintillating ballets which entirely suited Lopokova's genius for comedy. The first of these was *The Good-humoured Ladies*, based on a play by Goldoni and set in a Venetian piazza in the eighteenth century.

Of this production Serge Grigoriev, the ballet master, writes, 'Massine's choreography was considered most original and beautifully welded to Scarlatti's music. As for its execution, never had any ballet given by our company been so perfectly danced, partly perhaps because no other ballet had ever been so thoroughly rehearsed.'

Lopokova played the intriguing maidservant who holds the thread of the plot together, in which role Cyril Beaumont describes her as dancing not only with her limbs, but with her head, her eyes, her shoulders and even her lips:

> Lopokova revelled in the part of Mariuccia and was the very incarnation of the vivacious maid in Pietro Longhi's *My Lady's Toilet*. She was so full of vitality, so exhilarating, so ready to share in every prank, so spontaneous in all her actions and expressions that she radiated happiness whenever she appeared. Yet if she played the part of a soubrette, it was not a modern conception clothed in historical costume; her soubrette had a mellow quality, the glaze of a past epoch, a suggestion of period graces which gave a final touch to her performance, just as the passage of time confers a particular quality of colouring to a painting.

Beaumont's description of her seducing everyone with gay chatter, bright eyes and merry laughter could well have served for Lopokova off stage, for her spirit of joyous amusement at life and the April freshness of her performances were no masquerade. However, like all ballet dancers, she was serious and realistic about work, never in after years pretending to a success which was not there, as do many theatrical stars.

The three year period leading up to July 1919 was the longest consecutive one which Lopokova spent with the Russian Ballet; but, owing to the war, dancing in Europe had become a problem and there were months of resting. When, in the summer of 1918, Diaghilev sent a telegram to the dancers, who were waiting penniless in Spain, saying that he had signed a London contract, the question of how to transport scenery, baggage and personnel became acute, and not merely because of the shortage of trains. When the Bolsheviks retired from the war, Clemenceau was so angry that he refused permission for any Russian to set foot on French soil, and transit visas were refused to Diaghilev's company. However, one of Lopokova's admirers, King Alfonso, used his influence to make the journey possible. Even so, after three weeks of waiting for visas and another three spent waiting for transport, the dancers found the journey – which was broken in Paris because the baggage trucks had been mislaid – extremely exhausting. On arrival in England, Lopokova gave a reporter an interview: 'I did not like the terrible journey from Madrid to London. I thought we were never going to get here. We used to do our daily practice in all sorts of corners – once in the corridor of the railway carriage.'

At this time Diaghilev was in worse financial trouble than usual. He had been forced to accept an offer from Oswald Stoll to fit his ballet into a twice daily variety programme at the Coliseum, sandwiched between performing dogs, acrobats and clowns: it was the only alternative to disbanding the company. Nevertheless, this autumn season turned out to be a triumph. A critic wrote, 'By engaging the famous Russian Ballet, Mr Stoll did a masterstroke. For too long now the ordinary variety programmes have been stale.'

Up to this time Lopokova had never danced in England, but she was an immediate favourite with the London public. She was twenty-six and at the height of her technical and artistic powers. As Mariuccia in *The Good-humoured Ladies*, the Snow Maiden in *Le Soleil de Nuit*, Columbine in *Carnaval* or the Bacchante in *Cleopatra* she received rapturous notices.

Beaumont said that Lopokova's personality was a complete surprise to him, being accustomed 'to the sweet sadness of Karsavina's intensely poetic style of dancing.' Besides, she never put on ballerina airs. He writes that she

> had no exalted idea of her importance. As soon as she had taken leave of those who came to pay her homage, she would wipe off her make-up – she never put on very much – and change into a simple short skirt, woolly jumper, and tam-o'-shanter, skipping home like a schoolgirl let out of school. She had an ingenuous manner of talking, but she was very intelligent and witty, and, unlike some dancers, her conversation was not limited to herself and the Ballet.

Tidiness was certainly not one of her attributes. She was known to be the sort of dancer who has 'pig's ears' at the back of her ankles – that is, the ribbon ends on her ballet slippers stood up and were not tucked neatly away. Sokolova writes that she once helped Lopokova to get ready before appearing in *La Boutique Fantasque* and found that, disregarding the frantic exertions which she would have to make as the Can-Can dancer, she intended to rely on exactly three hairpins to fix her hair and the wreath together. (Most dancers' heads are a jammed, pine-needle mass of hairpins, inserted to keep wigs and head-dresses from toppling.) On another occasion when dancing, in *Les Sylphides*, Lopokova had to perform a *relevé* in arabesque several times. 'Her raised leg fell lower and lower; then to everyone's surprise, she stopped, tucked her hand under her costume and stepped out of a pair of tarlatan drawers. She threw them into the wings, picked up her music where she had left off and carried on as if nothing had happened.'

When, at length, things seemed to be going well for Diaghilev, Oswald Stoll suddenly gave his company two weeks' notice to quit the Coliseum. No touring dates having been booked, there was consternation. But by great good luck a revue at Stoll's other theatre, the Alhambra, failed and the Russian Ballet moved in for another season, which included Massine's new ballet, *La Boutique Fantasque*, with music by Respighi, based on themes by Rossini.

The first night, in June 1919, was a riotous triumph, the performance being held up by applause from number to number. The dancers in the final Can-Can received a thunderous ovation. Beaumont wrote:

Lopokova looked charming in her pale blue bodice and white skirt trimmed with black lace and blue bows, while her hair, dressed in her favourite ringlets, was bound with a garland of cornflowers and marguerites. Massine, dressed entirely in black velvet, save for his light waistcoat, looked, on the contrary, a decidedly raffish figure with his curly black hair and moustache and dead white make-up.

Derain, who designed both costumes and scenery, had drawn detailed pictures for each artist and laid them on their dressing-tables, to show how they should paint their faces. Beaumont continued,

Lopokova had an extraordinary resemblance to a doll, for which her rounded limbs, plump features, curved lips, and ingenuous expression were admirably suited. You could easily imagine her squeaking *Ma-ma! Pa-pa!* She whirled her leg and flirted her skirt with the utmost abandon, yet there was nothing vicious, nothing inelegant in her presentation.

Three years earlier, while in New York, Lopokova had married the business manager, Randolfo Barocchi. He was an Italian of infectious charm, who was a remarkable linguist, impersonator and raconteur, one for whom the sight of a beautiful woman passing in the street made the day memorable. Soon after the production of *La Boutique Fantasque*, Beaumont noticed an estrangement between the couple, and that in her dressing-room Lopokova would often murmur, '*Kak yah oustala!*' ('How tired I am!')

Then, on 10 July, Grigoriev received a note which ran, 'Dear Sergei Leonidovich, Since Diaghilev is away I am writing to you. For reasons of health I shall be unable, from today, to appear with the ballet – Lydia Lopokova.' Grigoriev rushed to her hotel, but she had gone, no one knew where. Barocchi also had left that morning for the Continent, yet it seemed certain that his wife was not with him. There were headlines: 'Famous Ballerina Vanishes.' The newspapers discussed the disappearance and the mysterious letter. The *Daily Herald* was suspicious that her absence was not due to indisposition caused by the strain of over-work; there was a hint of some Russian officer being involved. A few days later new headlines appeared, announcing that the ballerina had been found no farther

away than St John's Wood, in London. It was not till two years
later, on her return to the Russian Ballet, that Lopokova gave a
scrap of information about her escapade, to the *Daily Sketch*: 'One
hot night I felt so tired I could not go on. So I stayed in my hotel
and a few days later I went to France. And I never danced again for
eighteen months.' But what actually went on during these two years
remains a mystery.

On the evening of Lopokova's disappearance on 10 July, Vera
Nemchinova took over the role of the Can-Can dancer in *La Boutique Fantasque* and was hailed as the latest exciting new ballerina.
Lopokova's unprofessional behaviour caused great perturbation in
the theatre, and Diaghilev was astounded by this second desertion,
although Grigoriev remained convinced that the errant dancer
would return.

Sure enough, in the spring of 1921 Lopokova was again seen with
the Russian Ballet in Madrid and Paris. In May C. B. Cochran
presented the company at the Prince's Theatre, and the London
public seemed utterly subjugated by Lopokova's charm. 'There
were two thousand people at the opening performance,' said
Cochran, 'I could have filled the house three times.' The *Sunday
Pictorial* gave an enthusiastic welcome: 'We have not seen Lopokova
for two years and two years can play havoc with a dancer. But
Lopokova has improved. It is not merely that the exquisite plebeian
beauty of that gay, tragic soubrette is unimpaired; her joints and
muscles are in finer fettle. Long life to the joints and muscles of
Lopokova.'

Enrico Cecchetti, the teacher who trained almost all the famous
dancers in Diaghilev's company, had now settled in London, and
Lopokova went to a nine o'clock lesson every morning in his studio.
Her class was described in the *Daily Telegraph*:

> In Lopokova one sees nothing of the haughty airs and lofty graces
> of a popular favourite; of one who disdains instructions and resents
> correction because she has nothing more to learn. The relation
> between professor and pupil is that of a father and beloved child,
> but the maestro is none the less exacting. He conducts the lesson
> with the discipline and rigour of a drill sergeant ... At a correction
> she will pout her lips, become sad, then burst into laughter and
> repeat the movement until it is right. A careless movement and
> he springs upright with an angry shout of '*Doucement!*'

The work was hard: she was dancing leading roles in *Petrushka*, *Parade*, *Les Sylphides*, *Prince Igor*, *The Firebird* and *La Boutique Fantasque*. There were the usual good notices, but two are interestingly critical of her dancing in *Les Sylphides*. They give an idea of her limitations. The *Observer* said that with all her adroitness, Lopokova could not hit off the lyric quality of this ballet, while *The Times* wrote, 'Mme Lopokova has not quite the air of detachment which used to make the muzurka and valses in *Les Sylphides* the nearest possible approach of action to absolute music. She is impulsive and glowing with energy....'

For Diaghilev there remained the eternal problem of how to lure and captivate the public with some fresh production which would reveal new beauties in the art of ballet. Having noted the extraordinary success of the musical *Chu Chin Chow*, now in its third year, he decided to try for a long run with a grand classic unknown in Western Europe, but one which, over thirty years, had been tried and not found wanting in Russia. This was the five act *Sleeping Beauty*, with Tchaikovsky's score and Petipa's choreography. Negotiations were opened with Stoll, who agreed to finance the production. When the contract arrived Diaghilev made the sign of the Cross above the document and wrote his name with a sigh, saying, 'What will be, will be.'

This magnificent production, which has always been admired as one of the great theatrical experiences, was a financial disaster. Despite the ravishing decor and costumes by Leon Bakst, the pageantry, poetic music and superb dancing, with a cast led by Spesivtseva, Lopokova and Tchernicheva, the public did not like *The Sleeping Beauty* half as well as *Chu Chin Chow*. So, after 105 performances, in February 1922 the season closed. Since the ballet had been expected to run until April, there were no plans for the company, which was now bankrupt. Décor and costumes were impounded by Stoll, leaving no possibility of taking the ballet to France, and the dancers were stranded in London, penniless and out of work.

Lopokova was uncertain what to do. There is the draft of a letter in Maynard Keynes's handwriting which reads as though it had been dictated by her:

Dear Serge,
    By leaving us all here so long with no news you make a terrible

situation. The artists have no money. Everything is uncertain, and there is no one here to encourage us or tell us what are the plans. Other Directors who talk of ballet in London make us offers and we do not know what to say.

   For myself I believe the great ballet will only be with you and what others may do will be inferior. Therefore I accept no other engagement. . .

Whether this appeal was ever sent, or, if sent, whether it was answered, is unknown, but it shows Lopokova's inclination.

However Massine was still in London. He had lately been dismissed from the company on his marriage to an English dancer, for Diaghilev could not bear his lovers to leave him for the sake of women. It had happened already with Nijinsky. When Massine asked Lopokova to join him in forming a small company she did so, signing a contract via Worland S. Wheeler's Variety Agency Ltd. Sokolova and Woizikovsky (two of Lopokova's friends who, like her, had been hanging about in the hope that something would turn up) joined this company, as did Ninette de Valois and Slavinsky. Massine duly devised a show called *You'd be Surprised*, to be performed at Covent Garden as the sequel to a film.

Sokolova writes with shame, 'Massine had a chance to do something really good, but the programme he arranged was a disaster.' The company danced twice daily to half-empty houses, and at about this time the *Sphere* mentioned that 'Diaghilev's dancers fail when they leave him and court public favour on their own.' Sokolova had never expected that they would be letting themselves in for this kind of thing and, in any case, the pay was so poor that ultimately she and Woizikovsky were at a loss for a square meal. Lopokova, on the other hand, was much more inured to such larky, cheap kinds of entertainment after her American experiences. Besides, she now had the backing of a well-to-do lover, Maynard Keynes, to whom, when he was away either teaching at Cambridge or attending economic conferences, she wrote daily.

There was a troublesome ballet, *The Cockatoo's Holiday*, for which she had to make herself black. 'Oh! Maynard,' she wrote, 'I lead such a dirty life this and next week – the brown powder does not come off very well it stabilises in me, half of my body is not pure quality these days, and when I put a good deal of cold cream to have easier after Massin complaints that he cannot grasp me as I slide from

1 Constanza Lopukhova, Lydia's mother, with her two brothers, Fedor and Andrei, St Petersburg, 1900

2 Lydia as a Polovtsian Maiden, Mariinsky Theatre, 1909, aged seventeen

3 Chaliapin as Mephistopheles in Gounod's *Faust*, Alexandrinsky Theatre, 1901; he caused Lydia to faint on stage

4 Pavlova and Lydia at the San Francisco Zoo in 1910

5 Charlie Chaplin (while filming *Easy Street* in
Hollywood, 1916) with Nijinsky and Eric Campbell
('Big Bully') on his right, and Lydia and Olga
Spesivtseva in front

6 Publicity photograph of
Lydia, New York, 1910

7 'Diaghileff's Ballet-Russe' in Chicago, 1916: Massine, third from left, Lydia and Diaghilev, fourth and fifth from right

8 Karsavina as Columbine, *Le Carnaval*, 1912

9 Lydia with Nijinsky as Harlequin, *Le Carnaval*, 1916

10 Red Cross Charity Show at the London Coliseum, 1918; in front, from left: Idzikovsky, Massine, Lopokova, Cecchetti, Pavlova

11 Drawing of Lydia on the back of a menu sent to her from Paris by Picasso, December 1919

12 Picasso's drawing of Lydia and Massine in the Can-Can from *La Boutique Fantasque*, London, 1919

13 Drawing in green ink by Picasso of Diaghilev, Lydia and Massine, Rome, 1917

14 Lydia Lopokova by Picasso, London, 1919

15 Lydia Lopokova as Mariuccia in *The Good-humoured Ladies*, London, 1918

16 Lydia, posed, London 1918

17 Lydia Lopokova and Serge Lifar in *Firebird*, His Majesty's Theatre, 1926

him like a frog.' In another letter she wrote, 'I feel tired in the head, but legs are quite cheerful, like an independent body.' And from Glasgow: 'I am going to show my healthy mechanism to the healthy crowd.'

This employment in English variety was to continue, one way and another, until 1924. Meanwhile her English attachments multiplied and in some cases deepened. It was probably because of her affection for Keynes that she did not rejoin Diaghilev's company, as did Sokolova and Woizikovsky. Samuel Courtauld, an ardent admirer, and his wife became close friends. He wrote to her, 'In comedy you are of course supreme, but it is the poetic almost unearthly feeling that specially appeals to me.' Roger Fry composed some curious verses, which begin:

> Not Procne you
> Nor Ariel,
> Nor did Mozart
> Beget your ash . . .

Cyril Beaumont had long been a dear well-wisher. Now, as Lopokova's London life was settling into a solid pattern of friendships, the daily lesson with Enrico Cecchetti was essential. She wrote to Keynes of the maestro and his Italian wife with great affection, deeply regretting his imminent departure for Milan in June 1923.

In another letter (29 April) she wrote, 'I visited my dancing parents . . . Maestro as usual, was saying that Russian women were worse of all, because they did not care to be good cooks and housekeeper . . . Everywhere is the same existence of dancing peoples awful lack of work and hunger.' On 2 June she described the farewell party for Cecchetti before he left for Milan:

Saturday *Oh* emotions! when I arrived at the studio of maestro everybody's eyes were so red that my [mine] felt purple. The present was already given, as poor maestro was quite exhausted by awaiting it (not a pin, nor buttons, but a bronze statue without anything on but an Italian tamborin, dancing). I said a few words and the end was such: '*C'est ne pas possible de vous dire adieu mais seulment au-revoir.*' Then after I met Genée [Adeline Genée, the Danish ballerina], it was good taste on her side to see maestro going away. She made me think of a marionette very young she looked, correct and stiff, or perhaps she was dressed (mentally) in

late Victorians. I snatched the opportunity to be full of admiration
(as her art was admirable) in reverse I might have appeared to her
like a robot. I am convinced that you are in intimacy with
consultations, speeches, politics and progress of the World.

> Your true underworld dog Lydia.

Later in June she went to see what the Russian Ballet were doing
in Paris. On the eighteenth she wrote to Keynes,

I came back from the theatre worn out to the last degree. So
many faces so many kisses everything turned out *à la Russe*. Big
Serge gave me outwardly affectionate embrace, then Boris
[Kochno], then Picasso, then [Ida] Rubenstein, then all. Most
tragic of all Serge said: 'Nijinsky is in the box.' To verify I went
into the box and there I saw indeed Nijinsky but he did not know
me, nor anybody.

She then admitted ruefully that she could not boast to the dancers of
being overwhelmed by offers of work in England.

Early in 1924 Massine and Comte Etienne de Beaumont began
work on a season of theatrical and ballet productions called *Les Soirées
de Paris*, which was to be given in aid of French war widows and
Russian refugees. The count was a dilettante of many parts, who, in
his spare time, designed jewellery for Cartier.

Lopokova joined them, and rehearsals began in Paris, with Massine giving lessons to fifty dancers. Lopokova wrote to Keynes from
her hotel, 'I go back to slave in pink legs,' and praised a costume
designed by Derain as 'more than lovely'. Two days later: 'I feel
very small and tired and like to sit on your couch without notion.'
As for Massine's choice of programme, she thought it would have
been better to make it 'different from Big Serge, but of course they
try to imitate him, although denying it'.

The Diaghilev and Massine managements regarded each other's
activities with anxiety and jealousy, and Lopokova quoted Osbert
Sitwell's gossip 'that Big Serge in such a rage over our season that he
engage everyone with a contract *forever*'. After 'Much compliments
from the all concerned in all direction, my vanity is roused,' Lopokova noted how people's nerves gradually became frayed: 'Stas
[Stanislas Idzikovsky] is so discontent that he ever makes a sour face
at me,' and on 18 May 'I and my friends find as ever that Massin
does everything to shadow me and not make me his equal ... and

that my costume is chef d'œuvre and Big Serge can't say I am too fat.' Like so many dancers, Lopokova was a hungry creature, who would eat two pounds of cherries or nuts at one sitting. Once she admitted to Keynes that she had visited Fuller's cake shop twice in a day.

On 20 May the dreaded Diaghilev came to see *Les Soirées de Paris* and 'did not admire'. Lopokova, however, took a sympathetic view of the strain suffered by impresarios: 'of course their life is not a light burden and they are terrified of any competition.' She made time to visit the Russian Ballet: 'Last night at Big Serge's performance he gave me a very cool welcome and considered a few moments (that is how I felt) to embrace or not. Silly Serge, rather small headed this time.'

By June she confessed to Keynes that she was growing weary of the dancer's life: 'Oh I had a desire yesterday to become a rich woman again independently by my legs and my comedy powers. I saw many old dancers they are most poor or mad, life is difficult I sigh all over and lean on you.'

During 1925 Lopokova's marriage to Barocchi was annulled. The *New York World* explained that apparently Barocchi had not been legally divorced from his first wife until after he had married Lopokova. This is why she was referred to as a spinster during the ceremony at St Pancras Registry Office, where, on 4 August, she and Maynard Keynes were married, with Vera Bowen and Duncan Grant acting as witnesses. After the wedding Mrs A. V. Hill, Keynes's sister, firmly told the many reporters who were present, 'There will be no more dancing. That is all over now.' But the bride did not commit herself. Commenting on the match, the *Glasgow Bulletin* said, 'although she makes her living by the nimbleness of her toes and he by the keenness of his particularly mathematical brain, they find much in common, and the union seems likely to be extremely happy.'

Lopokova was certainly aware of the difference between her intellect and her husband's, and often referred to it, though without serious regret. In one letter she suggested that her obituary should run, 'She was fresh, radiant and simple when she made conquest on J.M. Keynes, also all her life she longed for an university degree, which was of course outside her brain-province. But on the whole it was not deficit to her character.'

Although Lopokova's third departure from his company in 1922 had been a bitter blow to Diaghilev, he again relented, and in October 1925 Grigoriev arrived with a letter from 'Big Serge', offering Lopokova her former roles in *La Boutique Fantasque, Petrushka, Carnaval, Les Matelots* (with choreography by Massine and music by Georges Auric) and *The Good-humoured Ladies*. This offer she was delighted to accept and she began to work hard, with the result that she became afflicted by 'a terrible water blister that gives toothache on the toe'. She had decided to ask for £75 a week for this autumn season in London, but in the end agreed to a fee of ten guineas for each evening.

So, in the autumn after her marriage, she was back with the Russian Ballet, and very happy. Although Diaghilev complained that she wore too many poppies on her head as Columbine, he blew her kisses from his box 'like the telegramme'. Even the dry Grigoriev wrote in his memoirs, 'She returned from nowhere and imported her usual gaiety into our lives and performances alike.'

By June 1926, however, when Lopokova was thirty-four, her spirits had begun to sag again. While she was rehearsing the new Massine-Stravinsky ballet *Pulcinella* with Woizikovsky she wrote to her husband, 'I am afraid of being second hand dancer.' She did not like Nijinska's ballet *Les Noces*, saying it was more like mathematics and that everybody on the stage had to count like mad to keep up with Stravinsky's music. She had written an article in *Vogue* which was somewhat critical of Diaghilev's latest choreographer, George Balanchine, concluding, 'If for a moment the ballet seems to have lost some of its tenderness, some of its soul, that is only to say it reflects modernity.'

Lopokova's final appearance with Diaghilev's company occurred in July 1927 at a gala performance held in honour of King Alfonso of Spain, who had always so much admired and assisted the Russian Ballet and was in London at the time. She danced the wild Polovtsian girl in *Prince Igor*. A critic had written of an earlier performance by Lopokova in this part that he never expected to see a dancer 'with a more barbaric abandon than she exhibits when she flings herself into the tornado of Prince Igor'.

By this time, Diaghilev was ill, tired and somewhat bored with ballet. Lydia Lopokova was one of the very few dancers who never feared 'Big Serge'. Indeed, she was very fond of the magnificent despot, who, she wrote, 'bluffed, scourged, and tyrannised over a list of impossible persons'. Only a month before his unexpected death in August 1929 she summed up his power in an article published in the *Nation and Athenaeum*: 'What a wonderful man is M. Diaghilev. When I see the old Buddha (or is he Catherine the Great?) sitting in his box with his face as impassive as his shirt, I know that the springs of action are there. We leave him, return to him, abuse him, court him, grow old or pretend to be young, but he goes on forever.'

Bloomsbury and Lydia

A letter from Quentin Bell

Dear Milo,

You asked me to write about Lydia and Bloomsbury. I refused and said that I would try to write you a letter, since it seemed easier. But I find the task even harder than I had expected and the result, I dare say, will hardly be worth publishing.

The fact is that I don't want to write about Lydia. She will not read this, I know, but the circumstances are such that I shall have to say some things that would have given her pain at one time; and this makes it an awkward, unwelcome, ungrateful job.

Why then do I attempt it? The answer is that I am irritated; not a very good reason but one which it is hard to resist. What irritated me was the article by Richard Buckle in the collection of essays concerning Maynard which you published a few years ago, entitled *On Loving Lydia*. Mr Buckle thought that Bloomsbury 'missed the point' of Lydia, and this indeed argues gross hebetude; but there is worse to come: their insensibility was, as he sees it, not even honest; it arose, not from a genuine though mistaken feeling, but from a craven submission to orders; 'they' complied with the dictates of an 'autocrat' who 'ruled the roost' and in some manner enforced her wishes upon the rest of the gang. And this odious tyrant was my mother, Vanessa Bell!

Yes, as I said, I am irritated, and I am afraid that my irritation may show itself in what follows. Nevertheless I will try to confine myself to a brief account of the facts as far as I know them.

I first saw Lydia in 1918, when I was eight years old; she was I think on the stage of the Coliseum and perhaps I didn't even see her there; it doesn't matter. But a few years later I began to know her, and indeed to love her. I think that it must have been before my eleventh birthday – but again I am vague – that I was allowed to join the grown-ups at lunch at 46 Gordon Square. Lydia was there; also I believe Massine and Karsavina, my father, Clive, and Maynard. At that time there was a widespread notion that in the presence of Russian dancers one talked French. At any rate, everyone on this occasion did talk French. I don't know if you remember my father; if so, you may also recollect that when there was an excuse for talking in French he took it, and sometimes indeed he took it when there was no excuse. On this occasion he had a double motive; not only did he enjoy the chance to exhibit his command of the language, he also enjoyed the opportunity to flirt with Lydia while Maynard, whose spoken French was awkward and hesitant, could hardly get a word in. I had even less French than Maynard and for me that party was an affair of incomprehensible exclamations and laughter in which it certainly appeared that Clive 'saw the point' of Lydia, and saw it with very great enthusiasm. Maynard, not unnaturally, was vexed and at the end of the meal he exclaimed to me, his fellow-sufferer: 'Why do they jabber away in French like that? I don't believe that they really understand what they are saying themselves.'

If, as I suppose, this party took place during the summer of 1921, then in the same year I was given a first chance to improve my knowledge of French when, in the autumn of that year, the family moved to the South of France. It was here, in December 1921, that my mother and Duncan Grant learnt that Lydia had learnt English, with notable results.

Maynard, in a letter to Vanessa dated 20 December that year, wrote, '... my other chief news is the progress of my affair with Loppy. I told you, I think, that she came to lunch here last Sunday week. Last Friday I took her to the Savoy after the ballet where we chatted until 1 a.m. and now she has asked me to tea. What is to be done about it? I am getting terrified.' On 6 January 1922 Maynard wrote to Vanessa again: '... I'm in great need of much good advice from you. You needn't be afraid of marriage, but the affair is very serious, and I don't in the least know what to do about it. I begin to think it's a good thing I'm going to India. However she's very adorable.' And again on 9 January: '... I'm in a terribly bad plight almost beyond rescue. Clive simply grins with delight at seeing me so humbled. However I long to have a good gossip with you.'

One must no doubt allow for an element in these letters of half comic exaggeration. Nevertheless it can hardly be doubted that at this time Maynard's feelings were strangely mixed. She was indeed 'very adorable'. In another letter he speaks of her 'knowing and judicious use of English words', a playful coquetry with the language which Maynard was not alone in noticing and finding extremely attractive. Her nature was both sweet and happy; she seemed to find the world a source of perpetual and delightful astonishment; herself surprised, she was herself surprising. Gifted with tender delicacy of sentiment, which led one ballet critic in an unlucky hour to call her a 'dainty rogue in porcelain', there was all the same something sensible, honest and unpretentious, earthy even, about her. You, who knew her, will not be surprised that Maynard fell in love with her, and will agree that, certainly, there was much to adore.

Why then the terror, the appeal for rescue? Why then was the idea of marriage so swiftly (if unconvincingly) dismissed?

I don't think that one needs any very profound psychology to answer such a question. Marriage is a momentous and serious business. It has its dangers, particularly when your wife is a foreigner, never mind how delightful a foreigner: some one with entirely different interests and from an entirely different background. A few months earlier Maynard's companion had been that charming and erudite person, the late Professor Sprott, at that time a very elegant and seductive youth. Vanessa sometimes referred to him as 'Maynard's wife'. Sebastian, as he was then called, was never a member of the Bloomsbury Group, but his union with Maynard never caused the slightest difficulty with Maynard's other friends: he had been at Cambridge; he was an Apostle; he could meet those friends on their own ground and be accepted by them without difficulty. More than this, he caused not the slightest disruption to the easy, agreeable bachelor existence which Maynard had built up for himself ever since, in 1912, he had become one of the communal group which settled in Brunswick Square. That existence seemed to suit Maynard and his friends perfectly; it allowed him to be entirely independent and yet to be very sociable; it enabled him to live his own very strenuous public life, and at the same time to see a great deal of and frequently to travel abroad with his friends, and in particular with Duncan Grant and Vanessa Bell. He might persuade himself at times and attempt to persuade them that this pleasant, friendly intimacy would survive his marriage to Lydia. But in fact he must have known that it would not. Marriage would inevitably change the picture; it would no doubt bring its delights but it would demand sacrifices, sacrifices that he found it hard to contemplate. That phrase in the marriage service which enjoins the couple to 'forsake all others' would, for him, have a special and poignant meaning. He longed to see his friends and to have the benefit of their 'advice', but what could they advise but that he find some way of avoiding marriage? They were as anxious as he to continue a state of affairs which had been so pleasant for so long. Where Maynard, a man very much in love, could see the matter with such desolating clarity, his friends may perhaps be forgiven for being equally clairvoyant.

Just what happened when Duncan and Vanessa returned from France I do not know. Vanessa used to say that Maynard had implored her to extricate him, and this seems to me likely enough, although how the feat was to be performed it is hard to say. I do however remember what may have been one little attempt at extrication and, since it is first-hand evidence, it seems worth offering, even though inconclusive.

The time would be 1922 or 1923, the place Vanessa's sitting room at No 50 Gordon Square, the actors Lydia, Vanessa and myself (a walking-on part):

Lydia (suddenly and gaily): 'Maynar' says I write to Barocchi and say to him: does he still consider himself married to me?'
Vanessa (gravely and with meaning): 'My dear Lydia, matrimony is a very serious business. I should be very careful about saying or doing anything.'

I was shocked. I hadn't thought of Lydia as being married, and she had never said anything about it to me, I who saw her every day.

At about this time, say three years before they finally were married, Maynard was, I think, attempting a sort of compromise policy. He was trying to educate Lydia in the kind of things that his wife would need to know; also I think that he was trying to transplant her, as it were, to get her to flourish in the soil of Gordon Square. In order to put these measures into effect Lydia was installed at No. 50 Gordon Square; down below were the Adrian Stephens, up above there were the Bells, or at least a sample of Bells. Lydia wandered upstairs and downstairs; she spent a great deal of her time in our kitchen. But at weekends Maynard would descend upon us in order to further my education. Of course, it had to be *my* education, I was the child and indeed sufficiently in need of education; but, of course, Lydia came with us and could hardly dodge the splendid shower of information. Maynard was always kind to me, ever since at the age of five I threw his straw hat into the waters of Chichester Harbour, and I have no doubt that he took a benevolent pleasure in my obvious delight: but if Lydia had not been there I very much doubt whether those educational excursions would ever have taken place. We drove off in a hired Daimler (that in itself was enough to make my day), and we visited Westminster Abbey, Hampton Court, the Tower of London, etc., and Maynard talked brilliantly about English History, the Constitution, the Church, and heaven knows what else. It was wholly delightful, and I'm sure I learnt a great deal and was very sorry when I had to go to a boarding school and stop learning. How much Lydia gained by it I do not know, but from my point of view the thing was an enormous success.

From my point of view it might also be said that Lydia's transplantation was also a success. I have said that she was much in the kitchen, and it is there that I chiefly remember her talking incessantly with me and with the extremely nice young woman who was later to become the family 'treasure' – cook-housekeeper, and much more – our dear Grace. Sometimes Grace and I would go to the Coliseum with tickets given us by Lydia to see her transformed, etherealized, almost unrecognizably lovely upon the stage. We enjoyed this tremendously, although I cannot say that we didn't enjoy George Robey and Little Titch with equal passion. And one notable evening Maynard burst into my room and hauled me off to the first night of a revue. We had a box, and Lydia came to see us there, either before or after her act. She was there when the curtain rose upon a scene set by a lake around which were posed a score of lovelies sketchily dressed as Red Indians. The girls remained still as waxworks, there was no music, no sound in all the great house save for Lydia's reverberating whisper: 'Oaah, it makes you to *vomit*.' I think that some faces must have turned to the box from whence that appalling comment had issued. The spectators would have seen Maynard, Lydia, Vanessa, Duncan and a fat, a monstrously fat, boy with red hair cut in a fringe, his bulk tightly but untidily covered by a black and white striped football jersey and – but they would hardly have been visible – badly frayed shorts and stockings that crept in wrinkles down to dirty boots. A disturbing sight, no doubt.

I digress: let me come back to the second part of Maynard's campaign, the introduction of Lydia to Bloomsbury. As I have said, Lydia made her way into the kitchen, and here she was an unqualified success. She told us about Russia, about the Nevski Prospekt and droshkis and zakuskis and wolves and samovars. It was lovely.

But when Lydia went up another flight of stairs and, with the same artless good humour, set herself to entertain Vanessa, the results were less happy.

Vanessa, as you may know, was not a very sociable person; she devoted her time mainly to her art; to this, certain hours of the day were sacred and not to be interrupted without good reason. She could also find time for her family which in this context means her children. For Duncan, Virginia and indeed Maynard, and three or four other old friends, she could just find time, usually fairly late in the day when work was done and the younger children were in bed. A casual visitor, a dropper-in, dropping in during the daylight hours was anything but welcome. It is one of the difficulties of the art of painting that it takes a very long time and can be very seriously disturbed by any intrusion.

Maynard must surely have known this, and would, one would have thought, have told Lydia that she could not always be welcome. Either he neglected to do this, or he was in some way misunderstood by Lydia. She made herself perfectly at home; she might look in at any time of the night or day, as she was separated by no door; she was always well received in the kitchen, why not also in the sitting-room or the studio? And indeed there was always a smile for Lydia, as it would have been too cruel to deny her a friendly salute. But the constant visiting, the endless chatter, the entirely innocent annexation of every spare moment, and of moments that in truth could not be spared, became for Vanessa a misery. It seemed that it was, after all, she who had married Lydia and, while Maynard enjoyed all the comforts of matrimony, she, Vanessa, was expected to accept all the tedium. In the end Vanessa took what seemed to her the only possible step. She went to Maynard and told him that Lydia's visits must be rationed. Personally, having known what it is like to try and produce a work of art under conditions far less difficult than those which Vanessa had to endure, I do not blame her.

All the same it was very hard on Lydia. She ceased to be a constant visitor; she moved to another house in Gordon Square, so that Vanessa was protected by a front door. One must suppose that whatever it was that Maynard said met the case and was, therefore, distressing. If Mr Buckle got the impression that Mrs Bell was a hard-hearted woman and an autocrat, perhaps that was only to be expected.

It is a tame and a boring conclusion, but in the end it does seem to me difficult to blame either party. Lydia certainly must have known that Vanessa's door had been shut in her face, and she may well have known or divined that Vanessa was active in trying to prevent her marriage. If from time to time she said; 'Oh Wanessa, you frighten me to death,' and she did say this, one can at least understand her feelings. The tragedy is that I do not think that she could possibly have understood why it was that she exasperated Vanessa.

Leonard Woolf, in his autobiography, describes how Wittgenstein, a man with a reputation for saintly behaviour and high moral sense, once turned upon Lydia with such savagery that she burst into tears. Leonard considered that there was a nasty, sadistic streak in Wittgenstein, and since I didn't know the great philosopher and wasn't there when the tears were shed, I must allow that he knew best. But it seems to me possible that Lydia had unwittingly said things which had brought Wittgenstein himself to the verge of tears. I know that she did this to me on one occasion.

It was at Charleston in the spring of 1940. Maynard and Lydia had come over after dinner, and naturally there was talk about the war. The Germans had just invaded Norway, we had won a naval action and had landed troops at Trondheim; the circumstances were sufficiently cheerful to encourage Maynard into one of his great bursts of optimism. The Germans, he declared, were about to be crushed; they would suffer a crippling defeat from which Hitler's prestige would never recover. He was done for.

Clive, who was always irritated by what he called Maynard's hubris, took the other view; he said, and truly, that it was much too early to claim a victory and that it would be very wrong to underestimate the strength of the forces that Hitler could throw into the struggle. I dare say that Clive was rather provoking in the way in which he said this, and that he didn't choose his words as carefully as he should have, but he certainly did not deserve the reply that he got, not from Maynard, but from Lydia.

'Oaah!' (but I cannot transliterate Lydia's extraordinary vowel sounds made even more extraordinary by violent emotion) 'Clive, you shall not say that you want the Germans to win. They shall not win and you MUST NOT say it.'

Clive, astonished by this outburst, objected that he had said nothing of the kind; he had merely pointed out the dangers of being too optimistic.

But he was not allowed to finish his sentence. Every time he opened his mouth he was met by a passionate denunciation, and when he did manage to say something Lydia refused to listen; and so it went on, despite some efforts to change the conversation, or to direct it upon more rational lines. As may be imagined, the evening ended badly.

To say that I was almost reduced to tears is perhaps too much, but I, like everyone else, was profoundly exasperated. Why should our conversation be reduced to this silly shouting match?

O Diamond! Diamond! thou little knowest the mischief done! Of course, one was cross with Lydia, but one did not seriously blame her. It never occurred to her that, at a moment of intense and agonizing interest in public affairs, we were being deprived of the voice of one of the people who knew most, and could talk best, and could, despite his over-optimism, tell us things that we badly wanted to know. Indeed, it was Maynard who amazed and still amazes me. He made not the slightest attempt to stop Lydia from making a fool of herself, or Clive from losing his temper. And yet with a joke, a paradox, some very slight exercise of that incredibly brilliant mind of his, he could have set everything straight. Instead of which he sat there, almost smiling, with the bland, indulgent air of a fond parent whose spoilt child is smashing someone else's teacups.

I suppose that this ability to withdraw from the discussion, this readiness to allow Lydia to have her way with the conversation, was an element of the art of being married to her and may be justified by the fact that it was a very happy marriage. But, speaking as an outsider, I must say that there were moments when I wished that Maynard could have paraphrased that poet, whose name I forget, but who said to his mistress 'Sois charmante et tais toi.' I must add that, when she ventured upon what were for her dangerous topics – politics, philosophy or science – Lydia could often be absurd, but

I do not think that I ever saw her so violent in the expression of her absurdity.

Do you see what I am getting at? Properly to say what I am trying to say would be a considerable feat of letters. One would have somehow to convey the fact that Lydia could be a bother, an enemy to good sense and even, as on this occason, to good humour. But at the same time one would have to make it clear – no, rather to *insist* – that she could be, not merely good fun, but really impressive, that her natural sincerity, her gaiety, her complete lack of side, could make an evening with her not merely delightful but instructive. It was when she knew more about the subject under discussion than one did oneself that she was at her best, but let me repeat that, even at her most absurd, Lydia was thoroughly sincere, and even when tilting at windmills she rode uncommonly straight. Perhaps one of your contributors will reproduce Lydia in the old days with Diaghilev, or the still older days in St Petersburg. And perhaps someone who saw more of her in the last years of Maynard's life will be able to paint a very different picture, for by then it was not windmills that she was charging. For my part I got no more than a glimpse of that later heroism, when she was spending all her magnificent energy and vitality in caring for Maynard and keeping that troublesome patient in some kind of order. At that time, undoubtedly Lydia was heroic and, whatever his previous doubts may have been, Maynard may have realized that he had a wife of whom he could most justly be proud.

There were, as you will see, two different aspects of Lydia, and if one were to try to describe the relationship between her and Maynard's older friends it would be necessary to give each its proper value. For this you need a skilful and a highly judicious author. As I said, my own chief motive for writing was irritation; it is not a qualification for the kind of contributor you need, for how am I to escape the charge of partiality? In this matter I am not a judge, but a witness, and as such I claim merely that I have tried to tell the truth; I am in fact yours most sincerely,

                                                                Quentin

Lydia Lopokova

Anton Dolin

There have been many great dancers I have known, and many whom it was my good fortune to have danced with during my long career – Adeline Genée, Tamara Karsavina, Olga Spesivtseva, Yvette Chauviré, Irina Baronova, Phyllis Bedells and, of course, Alicia Markova. None of them, except perhaps Irina Baronova, possessed the exuberance, vitality, and sheer *joie-de-vivre* of Lydia Lopokova, one of the most beloved dancers of this century. She had the utmost sex appeal, and I fell madly in love with her when, as a youth of fifteen, I first saw her dancing with the Diaghilev Company at the Prince's (now the Shaftesbury) Theatre during the First World War. I met and spoke to her for the first time in 1921. It was at the Savoy Hotel, where I had gone with my mother to sign my contract for the production of *The Sleeping Princess*, and it was Serge Diaghilev who introduced me.

My monthly salary and rehearsal pay were very small, but I think I would have danced for nothing, knowing I would be seeing her almost every day for many months to come. How adorable she was – and, I am sure, continued to be up to her death – though it was a long time ago that I last saw her, listened to her delicious English and enjoyed her bubbling effervescence! Few, if any, knew, and certainly not the music or dance critics, that as the Lilac Fairy in Diaghilev's marvellous Tchaikovsky-Bakst production she did not dance the traditional solo of this role but the much more important one of the Sugar Plum Fairy from *The Nutcracker*. For since she was the British public's favourite dancer, Diaghilev felt, and rightly so, that he must cater to her many admirers by allotting her this major solo. Of course, she also danced the part of the Enchanted Princess, with Stanislas Idzikovsky as the Blue Bird, in the famous pas-de-

deux from the last act. Never once during the three months that *The Sleeping Princess* lasted in production – it should have been at least six – did I ever miss the chance of watching with adoring, admiring eyes from the wings of the Alhambra Theatre (now the Odeon Cinema, Leicester Square) those twinkling feet and sparkling eyes, that pretty, pouting little mouth and well filled out cheeks. She exuded charm, and a radiance that captured every member of the audience, as she danced and moved, not merely executing brilliant steps. It was 'the little boy with beautiful brown eyes', as Leon Bakst called me, who worshipped her.

Though Diaghilev had christened me 'Patrikeef', and it was under this name that I first appeared as a very unimportant member of his famous company, my real name was Patrick Kay, which I soon changed to Anton Dolin. As the latter, I was again to have a most helpful encounter with the adorable Lopokova. I was rehearsing and learning my first leading role, that of Daphnis in Ravel's ballet *Daphnis and Chloe*, in Monte Carlo in December 1923. At that time, speaking no Russian and understanding very little French, I was having great difficulty in understanding what the role was about as well as the story of the ballet. Although Lydia was there on holiday she watched the rehearsals with her usual enthusiasm, and she explained in the most detailed way the story and, in particular, the dream sequence that had been puzzling me so much. I was to see her again on many future occasions.

In 1929, Lydia, Balanchine and I met in London to take part in the filming of a ballet scene in the film *Dark Red Roses*. How amusing she was that day at her house in Gordon Square! A meeting had been arranged to decide on the music that was to be used, and everyone who had anything to do with the making of the film was there. Lydia seemed to have bought every record of Russian music that ever existed, and also tried in her amusing English to explain to the film producers the deep significance of what they were hearing. The rehearsals for the ballet took place at my studio, but I felt that Lydia thought I was going to ruin the enterprise when she kept on saying, 'Oh, Pat, you must be serious. It is most tragic, you know.' Finally the ballet was ready to be filmed. We drove down to the studio at Isleworth after lunch and were told to be ready at about four o'clock, when work would start. Twice we made up, dressed and waited, before being told that nothing could be done that evening.

We duly reappeared on another evening. While we were waiting to be filmed, I bought an evening newspaper, and as I opened it saw a small photograph of Diaghilev on the front page. Without reading, I knew what this meant, and with a cry, 'Serge Pavlovitch est mort!' I dashed over to where Lydia and Balanchine were sitting. How sad we were! Lydia kept saying, 'Big Serge, poor, poor Big Serge! He was so tired, so very tired. But he died in Venice, Pat, think of that. Oh God, how good of him to Big Serge!' For Diaghilev had often expressed the desire that he should die in Venice. Three very sad figures sat on the stage into the early hours, well wrapped up in rugs, waiting endlessly for the filming of the ballet to begin. At about two-thirty a.m. they started. How we managed to dance I do not know. 'Big Serge' seemed to be looking on, but no longer were we to hear him say, 'Pas mal, pas mal,' as we had heard him so often say after a performance. As Hannen Swaffer wrote, 'the puppets had lost their master.'

After Diaghilev's death the Camargo Society was formed. Lydia, now very happily married to Maynard Keynes, was to play a great part in it. Indeed, they both played important parts in forming it: he with his brilliant brain, and she with her dancing genius. One of the ballets which the Camargo Society mounted was *Job: A Masque for Dancing*, devised by Lydia's brother-in-law, Geoffrey Keynes, and first produced by Ninette de Valois in 1931. The music was by Vaughan Williams. I created the role of Satan. After one performance Lydia said to me, 'Dear Pat! Perfect typecasting! Most beautiful Satan, emoting gorgeous wickedness and lovely sinew and sin!' Both she and Maynard visited me backstage at the Metropolitan Opera House in New York after my performance in the ballet *Bluebeard* – with choreography by Fokin and music from Offenbach – one of my most exhibitionist roles. 'Pat dear,' said Lydia, 'You are still a most ripe cantaloup'; this was not the first time she had mixed her words up and knew well she was doing so. The first time she had called me a cantaloup had been after the Camargo Society production of *Pomona*, one of Ashton's very early ballets, with music by Constant Lambert. Of course, I hope she meant 'antelope'!

The first occasion on which Lydia and I danced together was the month's season of the Camargo Society at the Savoy Theatre in June 1932. We appeared in *The Origin of Design*, with choreography by Ninette de Valois and music by Handel. How enjoyable it was!

A more recent memory of Lydia is of a meeting in October 1956, after the first performance of the Bolshoi Ballet at the Royal Opera House, Covent Garden. No, she did not enjoy the performance. 'It is all so acrobats, my dear Pat. Of course, Galina Ulanova is wonderful, but it hurts me, perhaps her too, to see her being hoisted into air propped up with two hands on her stomach. Most unbecoming for "Juliet", I feel sure, and also for her.'

I should like to end by quoting an earlier instance of Lydia's wickedly eccentric handling of the English language. She and I were among the guests at a luncheon partly given by Lady St Just [Florrie Grenfell] at her home in Cavendish Square during the 1930s. Lady Oxford [Margot Asquith], who used to dominate all conversation, was there also. During a lull Lydia took full advantage: 'Margot dear, I had the most wonderful weekend recently at a country house where there were the most exotic birds, as well as the most beautiful *ovaries* I have ever seen.' Darling Lydia was fun personified, as well as one of this century's truly great dancers.

Les Soirees de Paris

Lynn Garafola

It was in January 1924 that Lopokova first heard of plans for a month-long season of ballets to be produced that May in Paris. Massine was to be the choreographer, Georges Braque one of the designers, and the season would take place in a legitimate theatre – not a music-hall. With alacrity Lopokova accepted Massine's offer.

The season that promised to unite 'all that [was] best in painting and music' became *Les Soirées de Paris*. Organized by Comte Étienne de Beaumont, and with dancers from all over Europe participating, *Les Soirées de Paris* was one of the decade's many attempts to duplicate the success of the Russian Ballet by aping Diaghilev's post-war modernist 'recipe'. Beaumont himself was a long-standing friend of Cocteau, and was close to 'Les Six', the group of young French composers, and a member of the Franco-American Painting and Sculpture Exhibition Association. Like Rolf de Maré's Swedish Ballet a few years earlier, *Les Soirées de Paris* aspired to replace the Russian Ballet at the vanguard of the Paris artistic world.

By contrast with its more distinguished predecessors, *Les Soirées de Paris* has remained no more than a footnote to the dance history of the twenties. Few memoirs have recorded the drama of its creation, and its brief existence has had to be pieced together from press notices and reviews. Hence the incalculable value of Lopokova's letters to Keynes, now at King's College, Cambridge. Penned nightly in the full flush of rehearsals and performances, Lopokova's letters provide an eyewitness account – from a *dancer's* point of view – of *Les Soirées de Paris*, from its gestation to its less than glorious demise.

Lopokova had responded with enthusiasm to Massine's offer of a place in his new company. Artistic considerations, however, quickly gave way to financial ones in the first of the dancer's wrangles with Beaumont about money. Although, at first, the Count had asked her to name her 'price' (20 January 1924), Lopokova was forced to take a heavy cut in her usual salary – 5,000 francs less than her 'lowest possible fee'. A draft (the original is in French) of her letter to Beaumont on 8 February explains her position:

> Monsieur Massin must have told you that my regular salary in London is 100 pounds a week. Before I saw you this afternoon, my idea was that, given conditions in Paris, my lowest possible fee was 20,000 francs a month (which comes to a little more than half the amount I receive in London). When you offered half of my half, I didn't know what to say. But the project and artistic ideas associated with it are very appealing, and I want to avoid difficulties about money; still, thinking of the future, it is difficult for me to lower my regular salary so much. Nevertheless, I will accept 20,000 francs for the engagement of a month-and-a-half.

As preparations for the season went forward, rumours flew fast and furious between Diaghilev's headquarters in Monte Carlo and London. Despite Massine's concern for secrecy, reported Lopokova, Osbert Sitwell's 'latest gossip' on 25 February was that 'Big Serge' was in 'such a rage' over Beaumont's project, which would coincide with the Russian Ballet's regular Paris season, that he was engaging 'everyone possible with a contract *forever*:'

> Stas [Stanislas Idzikovsky] arrived soft as a peach with me, the Count engaged him also for Paris with Massin, he said (the Count) that Diaghileff ... was pleading for a favour and should not engage Stas for Paris season, the Count promised, in the meantime Big Serge tried behind his back to destroy Count's season, so that now Count is furious and engages Stas for spite.

> 10 March

On 24 April Lopokova was in Paris. From the outset, things seemed to go wrong:

> Boulevard Raspail is hell after Gordon Square especially for sleeping ... The Count and Countess received me with enthusiasm, asked me for lunch with Stas ... The house is beautiful and two big rooms are given for rehearsing and all the furniture is taken away; I have a complex about my exercises, my room is

too small, as for the Count's room Massin gives a lesson in the morning to thirty dancers, and to study with them is of no use. Massin looks ill and seems pleasant to everybody.

26 April

Absolutely without any strength, my legs twitch incessantly. . . . Stas begins to make difficulties . . . and asked me [for] a 100 francs.

28 April

As Lopokova was doctoring a brief illness with French cheeses and cream ('I do not dare to weigh myself'), rehearsals went ahead for the season's eclectic repertoire, which included not only dance, but two theatre pieces: Tristan Tzara's Dadaist 'tragedy in fifteen acts', *Mouchoir de Nuages*, and Cocteau's 'adaptation' of Shakespeare, *Romeo et Juliette*. Loie Fuller, by then a fixture of *le tout Paris*, was in charge of lighting. Eight ballets were presented. *Salade*, a Commedia dell'Arte 'counterpoint', with music by Darius Milhaud and designs by Braque, Lopokova judged 'too futuristic'. *Mercure*, a series of 'plastic poses', had a score by Erik Satie and designs by Picasso. *Les Roses*, a plotless 'divertissement' by Henri Sauguet, featured designs by Marie Laurencin (mysteriously credited on the programme as 'N . . .'). For *Gigue*, a suite of courtly dances to themes of Bach and Handel, André Derain confected the 'costume of a princess' for Lopokova in shades of grey, green, and blue. *Vogue*, 'three danced pages' 'illustrated' by Valentine Hugo, was dressed by the couturière Lanvin. With the rage for Spanish dancing at its height, José-Maria Sert's *Ballet Espagnol* (performed by Diaghilev's original Cleopatra, Ida Rubinstein) provided the requisite touch of Iberian colour, while a medley of 'contemporary dances' by the revue star Harry Wills nodded to the jazz craze. The most popular item of the repertoire, however, was *Le Beau Danube*, a frothy evocation of the Second Empire by Constantin Guys, set to the music of Johann Strauss. Here, Lopokova added the role of the Street Dancer – later made famous by Alexandra Danilova with the *Ballet Russe de Monte Carlo* – to her delightful galaxy of soubrettes.

The programme for the season at the Théâtre Cigale was both 'advanced' and 'chic', being calculated to appeal to the sophisticated taste-makers of *les années folles*. Although Lopokova was not, strictly speaking, a 'classical' dancer – her strength lay in demi-caractère and *soubrette* roles – she became increasingly perturbed by choreography which she felt did not show her to best advantage. Her critical attitude was bound to end in emotional fireworks.

A new choreograph the Count himself! The ballet called 'Vogue' [a 'poem' by the fashionable novelist Paul Morand] our tableau about three minutes with a young man a young girl who is like a boy, and I the woman of the smart set. We lie on the beach in Lido and the man and the boy are 'getting on' so that I must produce a vexed face and stand in the middle, showing a costume made up of miroirs (dernier cri naturally). I do all I am asked except that I cannot look jealous, not in my nature. . . . Massin does not interfere, it is not worthwhile either. A good reclame for Vogue, but perhaps I sound too sarcastic.

                                                                    5 May

Massin this morning asked me an advice to give three ballets or two and a one act play. I thought with the play is better, because his 'Salade' and 'Mercury' are all the same in movement, and also better to make it different from Big Serge, but of course they try to imitate him, although denying it. They should also aim at the 'grand public' and not for the little groups. Big Serge always knew that. I wonder if they realize it. Older I am more critical I become.

                                                                    6 May

Oh I have been through fire and water . . . as last night I came to a decision that I could not do 'Vogue' ballet, and with V. and G. [Vera Bowen and her husband Garia, or Harold, Bowen] a letter was composed and dispatched. This afternoon when I saw him [the Count] 'Did you receive my letter forgive me.' The Count 'je vous déteste'. So I received his answer with a smile and now I am a free woman again.

                                                                    12 May

With the opening night a few days off, nerves became frayed, and it was the dancers who bore the brunt of the shortened tempers and squabbling among the organizers.

We spent from 2 till 7 in the theatre . . . I plead [with] Massin to have clear lights in the scene where the phsyxcological moment develops, but he is difficult. My costume is good, but my rehearsal skirts are much better as a costume with the decor. The ballet

'Salade' how I like it is with singing, music is stirring and the decor of Braque very attractive, and the ballet is of a structure that develops like a building. The order of the programme first a play, then 'Salade' then 'Blue Danube'. Big Serge asked for three seats.

11 May

In our company are 'too many cooks' the dancers waited in the theatre to-day from 2–6 while Loie Fuller tries the light and hides all the movements of the dancers.

12 May

By now I am like theatrical rat, always in the theatre, and without end we wait, there is not one controlling voice in the situation, except the Comte's polite but weak falsetto. I think V. and G. would achieve more results for the lights than Loie Fuller, what a big fat thoad, perhaps she is very clever.

13 May

Scenes and scenes, the direction now decided for me to have a wig, but it is made of black straw, and I looked ugly, so I made an unsympathetic face, they gave me another, but it is out of style with the others, too modern.

16 May

Opening night 17 May found Lopokova with her 'fibres ... in a state of perpetuum mobile' – a quaint phrase for first-night jitters. The performance, however, came off with great success, although, as she noted to Keynes, no more than a hundred people turned up at the following day's matinée. Not unexpectedly, Lopokova's letters of the next few days were concerned with the impression she had made both on friends and critics.

and my friends find as ever that Massin does everything to shadow me and not make me his equal, but also V. and G. think I have never looked better or danced better, and that my costume is chef d'œuvre and big Serge can't say I am too fat. However we can't change nature of Massin, it is always twisted in the wrong direction.

18 May

Today, in the 'Comoedia' is a criticism not at all stupid, but I receive hard knocks. 'Lopokova conserve la candeur touchante et *l'incertitude technique d'une débutante de 17 ans. Tant mieux pour la femme, tant pis pour la danseuse.'* You see how badly I am established in Paris.

20 May

Meanwhile, reports from the 'enemy' camp began filtering back:

Last night big Serge came to the theatre, but reports are that he did not express any admiration, he sat with Nijinska and 'favorite' and when Nijinska applauded he seemed dissatisfied. To-day in the restaurant Grigorieff-Chernicheva at the other table thought I had an unsuitable part and also irritated by the idea that Massin might have engagements in other countries, of course their life is not a light burden, and they are terrified of any competition.

21 May

He [the Count] and Massin speak of nothing else but 'enemies' and although to-night there is a première of big Serge a certain *princess* will arrive to Cigale instead and that satisfies our set.

26 May

Although *Gigue* was given its first performance on 29 May, the better part of the company's energy that week was devoted to rehearsals for one of Beaumont's famous fancy-dress balls to be held on the thirty-first. Once again, Lopokova was angered by the Count's attempts to allow Massine to upstage her:

I went to a rehearsal for that damnation ball to-morrow. Stas came into the dressing room with a newspaper ... and it said how this charity ball includes all the amateurs society and L. Massin. As it is a thing of *charity* I absolutely want my professional name, and as Count is very busy, I left the dirty theatre. ... Besides my costume is the same as corps de ballet and they do not take least trouble to make it better. ... The Count must not overlook these matters, and if he does, there is penalty for him; the announcement certainly comes out of his organisation. To-night I shall tell him so.

30 May

Last night I had my 'conversation' with the Count, he of course pleaded not guilty that he never edited this advertising e.c. and he asks a *favour* to do it for him, so you see Lydochka agreeing ...

but very independent telling him that director should be a director and not overlook mishaps.

31 May

Yesterday's ball seemed very prosperous, the Count's perfect 'metier'. Stas and I were prosperous also in success, although we danced with a net in front of us, and Massin in another scene without it. I register facts that do not encourage me with devotion to M.

1 June

A few days later, she spent sixty francs on a ticket to see 'big Serge's ballet'. Diaghilev himself was very 'cool' towards her, as he 'considered' whether to 'embrace or not'. The house, she noted, was 'beautifully' dressed, and Picasso's curtain of two giantesses bounding along the seashore, she found 'moving and alive'. About the performance, which included Nijinska's *Les Fâcheux*, however, she had reservations. It was 'smooth and professional', 'but nothing or no one stirred' her. Sounding the theme of such contemporary critics as André Levinson and Valerian Svetlov, she found herself longing 'for very old fashioned ballets without abstract ideas. I want simplicity and *Poetry*; Massin or Nijinska choreography clever as it is have too much intellect' (5 June).

On 10 June, Beaumont's dancers found themselves once again at the beck and call of society – appearing this time before a minor royal personage for whose convenience a private performance had been arranged:

> Last night we had to dance after our representation once more to an empty theatre 'Gigue' and 'Divertissement' because in the middle sat the Queen of Roumania coming after the Opera, so when the dance was over Massin, Stas ... and I shook the hand of the Queen ... Then Loie Fuller [long an intimate friend of the Queen] began her repertory with lights, that looked like insides of the stomach, or oysters or kinds of Easter eggs or simply eggs, and we poor worn out dancers had to wait and admire it.

10 June

Lopokova's gastronomic fantasies are to be pardoned, for the dancers must have been as hungry as they were tired. The post-performance recital capped a long day, for the company had been rehearsing a complete new programme: *Les Roses*, *Mercure*, and a 'sketch about a girl who dreams of dolls' (11 June), Lopokova being one of the dolls. Her letters of the next few days talk of little except physical exhaustion and maltreatment. They evince none of the enthusiasm that Massine's initial proposal had excited. In fact, they are pervaded by a tone of disillusionment – not only with the enterprise itself, but also with its overall aesthetic and its pandering to fashion:

> I still work like an elephant . . . I told Massin that he must give us one free night before Saturday to come into a normal condition, and also I have not washed myself for a week, because a hot bath wears me completely out, so I wait for the night of liberty.
>
>   12 June

> In the theatre from 2 till [8.30] for ever waiting, trying on costumes, and [have] not been able to dance with the orchestra except for 7–8 minutes. I told Massin that except [for] himself, he considered the other dancers as mud (in the Roses he does not dance) but the ballet with him he rehearsed for hours so that musicians when tired were logic[al] to stand up and depart . . . To-night is the night of liberty. I shall put my worn out legs into the embrace of hot water and recite.
>
>   13 June

> Last night the 'furore' of the evening was Stas. He had to repeat his variation, in it he does the same turns in the air as in the 'Lac de signes'. I looked very well, but there is no chance for me to develop any dance, as all the pieces are too short. 'Mercure' to me seems a decadence. Picasso perhaps wanted to pull the noses of the public, the colours are very good but the way they [are] brought on or executed or what they represent is beyond any measure of comprehension. It is no ballet, no parody, but somehow a stupid farce. Smart audience and success, as always on the first night.
>
>   15 June

The première of *Mercure* was marked by fireworks behind the curtain and in the hall. Lopokova nearly 'came to blows' with the Count when she refused to don the 'cheap', tasteless flowers of her costume. Beaumont stamped his foot. 'Mum [L. L], his stubborn adversary won the day.' (15 June). Venturing into the theatre later that evening, Lopokova found herself in the eye of another artistic storm:

> *Oh* what a demonstration last night. 'Mercury' being the last on the programme I went into the 'promenoir' to look steadily at the ballet and have a firm opinion about it. First tableau began with cries 'vive Picasso' the other party replies 'vive Erik Satie.' ... 'En bas E. Satie et vive Picasso.' After the [second] tableau pro-Picasso-sists became enormous and shouted 'Vive Picasso seul, En bas E. de Beaumont les garçons, et toute soirées de Paris.' I was only a few steps away from the young man who proclaimed this. Then the policeman rushed to him and arrested [him], the anti-Picasso group ran to his box and shouted 'En bas Picasso.'
>
> 16 June

The remaining days of the Beaumont season were uneventful by comparison. The dancers continued to rehearse 'to perfect ourselves or to give something to do to the Count or M.' (18 June). Cherries came into season. Lydia spent forty francs on a picture of Fanny Cerrito. On 20 June the letters break off.

For Beaumont and Massine, the season was not a success. Reviews were mixed, perhaps the worst notice appearing in the *Dancing Times*. ('The *corps de ballet* was, without exception, the worst I have ever seen', wrote Gilson MacCormack.) Houses were rarely full. The eagerly awaited engagement by the London producer Charles B. Cochran failed to materialize. Most tragically for Massine, his attempt to form a successful repertory group, at the level of Diaghilev's Russian Ballet or Rolf de Maré's Swedish Ballet, came to nought.

Lydia Lopokova
and English ballet

Ninette de Valois

'Never mind, my dear, you have nice legs. . . .' As my final flounderings round the classroom came to an end I heard these words, and I saw the laughing figure leaning on the *barre*. Gratitude overwhelmed me – for I was very near to tears, due to Maestro Cecchetti's sarcastic shouts of 'aeroplane' singing in my ears.

Was it the start of a friendship? I think that it may have been, for it was soon after this incident that Lydia Lopokova – star of the Diaghilev Russian Ballet – took an interest in me and helped me in many ways. She even arranged that I should join her private lessons with Cecchetti. I only paid the weekly class fee, but had the advantage of studying alone with her in her special private lesson with the maestro. Today we do not meet such individual performers as Lydia in the ballet. Personalities have become discreetly submerged, and are dedicated to the relationship of the part to the whole. What use would the modern choreographer have for her freely expressed exuberance, that had to be employed with a judicious sense of compromise? What would he do if confronted with the task of harnessing an energy that he felt his methods would not be equal to exploiting? Yet, this artist never lacked a fundamental sense of discipline, nor the necessary sense of submission to the demands eventually made on her. She was, by nature of her inheritance, a proud product of the great Imperial Ballet traditions – and she was ever aware of the significance of this fact.

It was Diaghilev who, with his usual foresight, discerned in this remarkable artist the muse that was necessary to inspire Massine to create certain roles for her in his early masterpieces. Who could ever forget her in *The Good-humoured Ladies*? Who has ever approached her perfection in this role, ever 'eaten' in the famous supper scene with a richer abandon, or has ever made more demands on the efforts of a knife and fork to accompany her all the way? Again, there is *La Boutique Fantasque*. The wild abandon of Lydia's 'Can-Can', and later the piquant charm of the variation in which she wears the expression of a disillusioned cherub – who has ever surpassed, or even equalled, her reading of this role? How aptly did Karsavina, in her autobiography *Theatre Street*, describe her face as 'the face of an earnest cherub'.

She jumped like a gazelle. One might say, with more dignity, that 'Madame Lopokova had a remarkable elevation'. But this would not be the whole truth, for it would not take into account her gazelle-like spring, that made you feel every movement was in its essence a jump, and the ground a springboard that never permitted her to stay on it for more than a split second. She had three instruments of highly developed expressiveness: her face, her beautifully arched feet and her delicate, shell-like hands; together, they acquired something of the deft assurance of a pawnbroker's sign, bent on conveying a certain symbolic force. She was the darling of the twenties' balletomane public. When Diaghilev produced *The Sleeping Princess* in 1921, with the decorous performances of the lined-up Mariinsky ballerinas, it was Lopokova, as the Lilac Fairy, that the house demanded time and again, and there was the added joy of her appearance in the Blue Bird pas de deux with Stanislas Idzikovsky. By popular demand she later appeared in the role of the Sleeping Princess herself. On the last sad night of the ballet season, with the house knowing that bankruptcy faced Diaghilev and that his artists must expect a long period with no work, the final curtain call was taken by Lopokova. Summoning her quick wit to her aid, she made the following announcement: 'We will come back – very Good Humoured Ladies,' and the house roared its wishful thinking.

Lopokova did come back, and back. She danced time and again in the late twenties and early thirties, and after she left the Russian ballet she danced with the embryo English companies. She was the inspiration behind Frederick Ashton's Milkmaid in the 'Jodelling Song' and in the 'Tango Pasodoble' in *Façade*. She was the first Swanilda in the Vic Wells production of *Coppélia*. Her occasional guest appearances were a valuable box office draw and greatly helped the struggling companies.

To me, she was a true friend and a most lively and witty companion. I can recall the joy for me of her guest performances when I was a member of the Russian Ballet; she was already married to Keynes and no longer a permanent member of the company. I remember once going to her hotel in Paris, knowing she was with us for one of her fleeting guest visits. Lydia was surrounded by innumerable ballet shoes and a hastily emptied suitcase – actually its contents had been hurled on to both the floor and the chair as well as the bed, for she never 'unpacked' in the orthodox sense of the word. 'My dear, he is giving me [I forget the sum Diaghilev was paying her] for this visit. Don't tell.' I swore myself to secrecy over a sum of money modest by today's standards, but nevertheless one that left me speechless with excitement at the time, just as such a revelation would have left some of my Russian ballet companions speechless with rage.

Over the years I visited Lydia on her Sussex farm, set among the South Downs near Lewes. As forthright and wise as ever, she lived there a life of quiet seclusion in retirement. Always a wonderfully self-contained person, she never knew the meaning of loneliness, which has become today such an obsession with so many of her generation. She would say to you, 'And now goodbye, my dear …', and you folded up your conversation as you would a packet of left-over sandwiches and took your leave of her. The leave taking was always so simple, so direct, so honest. Lydia Lopokova was too intelligent ever to seek flattery or to bestow it. You accepted anything that she said, however unflattering it might happen to be! She was uninhibited in both heart and mind, with effects that were always refreshing and sometimes most illuminating. 'Better to be a 'undred years behind the times than twenty-five' was her cryptic comment on the revival of a ballet that was brought back too soon to the scene of its former triumphs.

Of all the things that my 'nice legs' may have done for me, this friendship ranks high in importance. Who knows? Perhaps if I had not floundered round the classroom so disgracefully, and thus drawn Lydia's quick powers of observation towards a pair of wildly kicking legs, the owner of them might have had further to travel, and might never have known a relationship that widened those powers of perception that are so necessary to a young artist. This may appear to be a simple tale of friendship, but the secret of its importance lies in the part that Lydia Lopokova played in the encouragement of

English ballet in the early 1930s. Her marriage was an extremely happy one, her dedication to the ballet being shared by Maynard Keynes, who, through his own interest and his wife's determination to help, did much for us, both financially and in other ways. Lydia was a wonderful wife, and, despite her very different background and upbringing, was acutely aware of her brilliant husband's career and of its importance to his country. During his last years before he died in 1946, her devotion and her protection of him were as touching as they were effective. She stood by – a bodyguard to be reckoned with. Gone were her former interests, and now only Maynard, his health and his work mattered. I remember her saying to me, after his untimely death, that whenever they returned to their Sussex farmhouse, Tilton, 'we were like two children setting out on a long, long holiday'.

Lydia got to know and love the Sussex Downs. In her early years there she would stride out, taking long, ambitious walks. 'When I am on the Downs in the morning I feel that I am having a cocktail with God.' Personally, I always found lunch and an argument with her an invigorating cocktail, leading, at her command, as it did, to 'the ballet gossips, please, my dear'. What a bundle of honesty, what a friend, and what a generous spirit to have encountered! But now I shall dwell on another aspect of her life, one to which I have already referred: the interest and help which she bestowed on the English ballet. In particular, she took an active part in the founding of the Camargo Society, which was formed just over fifty years ago.

What was the role of the Camargo Society – named in honour of Marie-Anne de Cupis, La Camargo (1710–70), prima ballerina at the Paris Opera and courtesan? I would say that it played the role of an important fairy godmother for English ballet, and it played this role for two or so years at the beginning of the thirties. In fact, it was a role identical to that of the Stage Society. The Camargo Society (with Maynard Keynes as Treasurer) found time and money to organize the production of new ballets with which to enrich the English repertoire. The ballets were presented on a Sunday night and a Monday afternoon in a West End Theatre, three or four times a year. The nucleus of the dancers was drawn from the already existing Mercury Theatre Ballet Club in Notting Hill Gate (today, the Ballet Rambert) and the Vic-Wells Ballet (today, the Royal Ballet), recently installed, with a ballet school, at Sadler's Wells Theatre as an opera-ballet. Many famous dancers appeared as guests in the Camargo performances, including some who were appearing in West End theatre productions, as well as ex-dancers from the Pavlova and Diaghilev companies. These dancers were all willing to give their time and services, as the venture was far removed from the ordinary theatre, nor could a Sunday evening and a Monday afternoon performance interfere in any way with their professional commitments. I think one can say that honours were equally divided between the Camargo Society, the two young companies and the guest performers. The companies could not have afforded to stage certain of the ballets presented, yet these ballets could not have 'lived' if, in the final analysis, the Vic-Wells Ballet and the Mercury Theatre Ballet Club had not been able to take over, between them, the more successful ballets mounted by the Camargo Society and preserve them in their repertoires.

In this way, we had magnificent backing from the Camargo Society; small wonder that both managements and their artists saw what there was to be gained by this ingenious method of helping the English dance. After two years (including a four-week season of ballet at the Savoy Theatre in June–July 1932) the Camargo closed, mainly because of the increasingly successful activities at Sadler's Wells. The Society divided its productions between the two companies, with Sadler's Wells Theatre taking over the larger ones that required an orchestra (of which Constant Lambert 1905–51, was the musical director). From all this, we can see what an important weekend venture the Camargo Society proved to be. Even before it closed, ballets it had mounted were 'lifted' into the rapidly expanding Vic-Wells Ballet. One of these, for example, was *Job: a Masque for Dancing*, founded by Lydia's brother-in-law, Geoffrey Keynes, on William Blake's 'Illustrations of the Book of Job', with music by Ralph Vaughan Williams and choreography by myself. This was presented at the Wells by the Vic-Wells Company within a short period of its first presentation by the Camargo Society on a Sunday evening. At the beginning we mounted such productions 'by arrangement' with the Camargo Society, but when the Society closed, it generously presented us with ballets that were considered successful and which had been originally staged mainly with our dancers. It should be noted that Camargo performances were supported by both the Vic-Wells and the Mercury Theatre ballet companies from their existing repertoires.

The whole organization of the Camargo Society, part initiated

18 Lydia Lopokova and Leonid Massine dancing the Can-Can in
La Boutique Fantasque, Alhambra Theatre, 1919

Laura Knight

While listening to the Prelude by

19 *Opposite, left:* Lydia Lopokova by
Augustus John, 1921

20 *Opposite, right:* Lydia Lopokova by Glyn
Philpot, 1920

21 *Opposite, below:* Lydia Lopokova
listening to music, by Laura Knight, 1919

22 *Right:* Lydia Lopokova by Duncan
Grant, signed and dated 1923

23 *Right:* A lost portrait of Lydia Lopokova
by Vanessa Bell, 1923

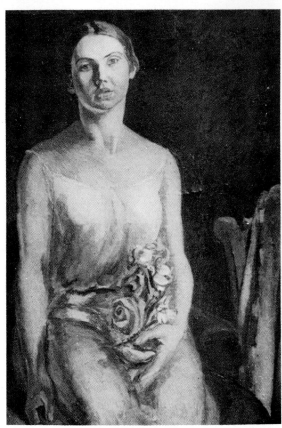

26 Lydia as the Lilac Fairy in *The Sleeping Princess*, Alhambra Theatre, 1921

27 Lydia as Princess Aurora in *The Sleeping Princess*, Alhambra Theatre, 1921

24 *Opposite, above:* Diaghilev, Vladimir Polunin and Picasso in Polunin's studio in Covent Garden, 1919

25 *Opposite, below:* Outside the Alhambra Theatre in 1921; from left to right: Vera Nemchinova, Florrie Grenfell (Lady St Just), Lydia Lopokova, Igor Stravinsky and Bronislava Nijinska. The woman behind Lydia is unknown.

28 Lydia dancing with Duncan Grant, Studland, 1923

29 Virginia Woolf with Lydia, Studland, 1923

30 At Studland, in Dorset, 1923; standing: 'Dadie' Rylands and Raymond Mortimer; seated: Leonard and Virginia Woolf, with Lydia in front

31 Maynard and Lydia Keynes at Tilton, 1925

32 Maynard and Lydia Keynes after the Registry Office wedding in 1925

33 Lydia Lopokova as The Dancer and Nikolai
Zverev at The Moor in *Petrushka*, London Coliseum,
1925

34 Lydia Lopokova as The Dancer, *Petrushka*, New
York, 1917

by Keynes and his wife, was inspiring, with Constant Lambert as musical director and Philip Richardson (editor and founder of the *Dancing Times*), Arnold Haskell and Edwin Evans (Chairman) among the other directors, as well as a larger committee for those interested in helping the ballet. Without the Society, the progress of the Vic-Wells company, hampered as it was by its theatre's lack of finance, would have been far slower. It was Lydia who arranged that season of ballet at the Savoy Theatre in 1930, for which Nikolai Sergeiev (who joined the Vic-Wells company within eighteen months of its foundation) came over from Paris and mounted *Giselle*, with Olga Spesivtseva and Anton Dolin in the title roles – a performance to be remembered to this day.

The Camargo Society was a well timed venture, bestowing urgently needed aid and encouragement on English ballet. At Sadler's Wells we had to try and stabilize ballet in this country as a proper wage-earning part of the theatre world in a theatre built for the purpose. The ballets presented to us by the Camargo Society were a great help at that time to forward the venture that grew into the Royal Ballet. When the Royal Ballet (then still the Sadler's Wells Ballet) opened in the Royal Opera House, Covent Garden, after the war in 1946, there was a further link, for Lord Keynes was the first chairman of the Royal Opera House Board of Governors. The ballet chosen was *The Sleeping Beauty*, in which Lydia Lopokova had danced for Diaghilev those many years before.

The position of Lydia as a member of the Camargo Society's committee – her actual title was that of 'choreographic adviser' – made her the prime mover in the engagement of guest artists between their other appearances; in fact, it made her an impresario. The picture is, needless to say, a lively one. It was only with great reluctance that she joined the committee, and it was her first such task. Initially, she felt she had better be a spectator rather than an active participant, as, after all, it was a serious step, 'like parting with one's virginity'. Her approach to being on a committee, though, left no doubt about her attitude towards the responsibilities involved. There was a true dedication and an honest desire to help the English scene, accompanied by what she called, with a degree of impatient suspicion, 'my committee mindedness'. Arnold Haskell, in his *Balletomania* (1934), quotes the following exchange:

Lydia Lopokova (always very correct, now that she had taken the great decision to join the committee): I propose, Mr Chairman, that we put on *Casse Noisette* on a grand scale, as it was done in Russia.

Constant Lambert: Yes, and with a really fine orchestra. ...

Arnold Haskell: We must get Benois or Dobujinsky to do the costumes.

The Treasurer (J. M. Keynes): I can allow you exactly £57 3s. 4d. Will that be enough?

The system of occasional performances was wasteful: each one cost about £500 (with the expenses being the same as for a long run), even though the dancers gave their services without fee. Various schemes which seemed to offer tempting possibilities, were discussed, but the committee had to be practical about what could be achieved. When the Society wound up magnificently with two gala performances at Covent Garden in June 1933 – mounted for the edification of the members of the World Economic Conference, of which Keynes was an organizer – the immediate economic problems were solved by turning a large deficit into a small balance, later given to a fund for the Vic-Wells Ballet. The first two acts of *Coppélia* were given (with Lydia, Stanley Judson and Hedley Briggs as the three principals, and with Ninette de Valois, Ursula Moreton and Frederick Ashton leading the character dances), and the second act of *Swan Lake*, with Alicia Markova and Anton Dolin.

A thorough survey of the productions financed by the Camargo Society, especially those that survived over the years in the Sadler's Wells repertoire, should make interesting reading, and give us a conspectus of the adventurous path followed by English ballet in the early thirties. The list includes *Danse Sacrée et Danse Profane* (Debussy, de Valois), *Cephalus and Procris* (discussed below), *Job* (mentioned above), *Rout* (Bliss, de Valois), *The Lord of Burleigh* (Mendelssohn, Ashton), *The Origin of Design* (again, discussed below), *Pomona* (Lambert, Ashton), *La Création du Monde* (Milhaud, de Valois); *Rio Grande* and *Façade* (both discussed below). Diaghilev was dead; Pavlova was dead: as a result, the two renowned professional companies that had toured the world in the twenties were finished. Perhaps this loss gave us Dutch courage, and it was the Camargo Society that ensured that we could progress on our own resources.

Lydia danced in six ballets for the Camargo Society. The first, in January 1931, was *Cephalus and Procris*, with music by Grétry, choreography by myself, and designs by Chappell; it was later performed both at Sadler's Wells and at the Old Vic, in May and November. In April 1931, she appeared in *Follow your Saint - The Passionate Pavan*, with music by John Dowland, arranged by Constant Lambert, choreography by Frederick Ashton and costumes by William Chappell; the other principal dancers were Ashton and Harold Turner. This was repeated as a masque, *Beauty, Truth and Rarity*, at the Arts Theatre, London in December 1930. In this masque there were also performances of *Dances on a Scotch Theme*, with music by William Boyce arranged by Constant Lambert, and with the same cast as for the Dowland ballet. This was taken over by the Ballet Club a year later and renamed *The Tartans*, after it had had a charity performance at the Cambridge Theatre in March 1931; it was not done, however, for the Camargo Society.

The third of the ballets mounted by the Camargo Society in which Lydia danced, also produced in April 1931, was the most successful: *Façade*, with music by William Walton, choreography by Frederick Ashton and designs by John Armstrong. Lydia created the role of the milkmaid in 'Jodelling Song' and danced in the 'Tango Pasadoble' with Ashton. *Façade* was transferred to the Mercury Theatre Ballet Club in May 1931; it did not reach Sadler's Wells until 1935. In November 1931 Lydia danced in *A Day in a Southern Port*, with music by Constant Lambert, choreography by Ashton and sets by Edward Burra; the ballet was duly performed at Sadler's Wells in 1935 under the title of Lambert's original score, *Rio Grande*. In 1932 Lydia appeared in *The Origin of Design*, with music by Handel, arranged by Sir Thomas Beecham, choreography by myself and designs by William Chappell; Sadler's Wells took over the production later in the year. The Vic-Wells production of *Coppélia* (with choreography by Nikolai Sergeiev, based on that by L.I. Ivanov) in March 1933 at Sadler's Wells, in which Lydia danced, was also given twice at Covent Garden, by the Camargo Society, in June; these were the last performances which Lydia gave in public as a dancer.

Lydia was a great believer in the future of the Vic-Wells Ballet, and later helped me to convince Nikolai Sergeiev forcibly that he should leave Paris and give up any thoughts of forming a company of his own there - an obviously impracticable project. Between us we got him to come to Sadler's Wells on a full-time contract, beginning in 1933, about a year after the Camargo Society had given up its pioneering work for good. Sergeiev, who had been *régisseur* at the Imperial Theatres in St Petersburg from 1904 until 1917, had left Russia in 1918 and had come to London to reconstruct *The Sleeping Princess* for Diaghilev's 1921 production at the Alhambra Theatre in which Lydia had delighted the London public. He spoke little French and less English, but Lydia translated letters, and acted as interpreter (both of language and of ballet parts) at rehearsals. Sergeiev had worked at the famous Stepanov notation, devised to record the choreography and production detail of the great ballets in the repertoire of the Imperial Russian Ballet, and since this system of notation could only be used for ballets composed according to strict classical principles, and was uselesss for recording the modern productions with which the Vic-Wells Ballet was concerned, Lydia'a assistance as interpreter of the roles was crucial. When Lydia was asked for her youthful recollections of the Stepanov notation, she said in her emphatic English, 'It was once a week; it was a bore, I did not listen, we were not fit subjects for black magic. . . .' What does this conjure up but a picture of small, fidgeting Russians who would respond trustingly by the hour to the demand for hard physical exercise, but regarded with suspicion and defiance poor Sergeiev's messages on the blackboard – expressing in theoretical terms the movements that their obliging anatomies performed for them every day in practice?

Maynard Keynes built the Arts Theatre, Cambridge partly for Lydia, and handed it over to the University and City of Cambridge after its building in 1936. The Vic-Wells Ballet opened the theatre on 3 February that year as promised by Lilian Baylis, who controlled the destinies of both the Old Vic and Sadler's Wells theatres. Miss Baylis knew that she could obtain more lucrative engagements for the companies in larger theatres, but explained that her main concern was for future audiences, and it was to the universities that she looked for these. The programme danced was *Les Rendezvous* (with music by Auber, arranged by Lambert, choreography by Ashton and costumes and decor by Chappell), *The Rake's Progress* (with music by Gavin Gordon, choreography by myself and designs by Rex Whistler, after Hogarth) and *Façade*. The dancers included June Brae, Frederick Ashton, Robert Helpmann, Michael Somes, Harold Turner and William Chappell, and the orchestra was conducted by Constant Lambert.

In the following year Molière's *Le Misanthrope* was produced in

English at the Arts Theatre, Cambridge and then afterwards in London. Lydia acted the part of Célimène and the sets were by Derain. The play was preceded by a short ballet, *Harlequin in the Street* (with music by Couperin, arranged by Lambert, choreography by Ashton and costumes and decor by Derain), which was taken into the repertoire of the Vic-Wells Ballet in 1938. In 1957 the Sadler's Wells Theatre Ballet celebrated the twenty-first anniversary of the opening of the Arts Theatre with a week's programme of ballets given there. In those twenty-one years a total of seventy weeks of ballet had been presented at the theatre, the Sadler's Wells (twenty weeks), Ballet Rambert (fifteen weeks) and Ballets Jooss (ten weeks) companies being the most frequent visitors. Indeed, English ballet has been well served in Cambridge, as Maynard and Lydia Keynes would have wished.

Finally, I should like to mention Lydia in connection with Keynes's chairmanship of the war-time Council for the Encouragement of Music and Arts (CEMA), a body which, under his guidance, developed into the Arts Council. The effect which CEMA and its successor have had on subsidized theatre, particularly opera and ballet, in Britain has been far-reaching and incalculable. Beside Keynes, during those years of planning, was this small, much loved artist of the Diaghilev days, concentrating now, at the end of her career, on her deep concern for progress in the field of English ballet.

It has been with a great sense of gratitude and affection that I have written on Lydia Lopokova - my friend of Maestro Cecchetti's studio who stayed with me through the years.

Lydia, the Enchantress

Frederick Ashton

The first time I met Lydia was when she was going to do *The Postman* at the Coliseum. This was a ballet by Nikolai Legat, to an orchestration of a Beethoven piano sonata, which was performed for three weeks in 1925. A friend of hers, T.H. Marshall, who had seen her prance down a street to post a letter in a red pillar box, had got the theme of the ballet from this, seeing her as a maid, hurrying to drop a fatal letter to her lover into the box, then, quickly regretting it, waiting for the postman to empty the box so that she can grab the letter back. Having achieved this, she scampers off on the postman's bicycle (something that gave her much trouble when the ballet was performed) with the letter in her mouth. The postman was danced by Idzikovsky. She came to Legat's studio where I was a student, to rehearse her part; I asked her, 'Can I stay and watch?' and we shook hands. This charming ballet was never repeated.

On one occasion in performance, I remember, she lost her shoe – Lydia was often untidy, always losing things or popping out of her dress – but she went on dancing. When she took her curtain call, she came out holding the shoe apologetically, and of course, the audience adored it. I think she sometimes did such things on purpose, for she knew how to get at her public. She was not really a great ballerina, nor was she among the most technically expert of dancers, but she had incredible charm and was always a strong and most interesting dancer to watch. When she appeared on the stage in *La Boutique Fantasque* the effect was like champagne corks popping. There was such intensity and vitality and childlike eagerness; this was especially well shown, too, when she danced the Polovtsian girl in *Prince Igor*. She was so pretty at that time, with pretty arms, as in Frank Dobson's bust of her, and very delicate hands. Her feet were beautifully expressive. I liked her nose; strangely enough, when she was on stage it looked as though it was upturned, though really it was not. William Chappell said she had a nose like a turtle dove, and could peck like one. She could certainly be quite difficult and put people in their place very quickly and severely; occasionally, if she did not like someone, she could either be fiendishly rude or stand-offish. If she was fond of someone and something went wrong, she loved it, and she could be terribly nice at first, but then extremely outspoken and frank.

Lydia did not dance for the Ballet Club when I was there. The Mercury Theatre Ballet Club (now the Ballet Rambert) was started by Marie Rambert, and at first Billy Chappell and I were the only boys in the company, later to be joined amongst others by Harold Turner, Anthony Tudor and Walter Gore in quite a strong group. At that time the Ballet Club was really the only ballet company going in this country as Diaghilev and Pavlova had died. When the Camargo Society, in which Lydia took such a strong interest, started we all became very much involved. The first time I appeared with her was in a programme of poetry and dance which Maynard Keynes presented at the London Arts Theatre Club in December 1930, under the title *Beauty, Truth and Rarity*. With Harold Turner, we danced a pavane by Dowland, also a piece called *Dances on a Scotch Theme*, with music by William Boyce, arranged by Constant Lambert, our conductor. Lydia and other speakers recited some Shakespeare and Milton. George Rylands directed; Harold Turner and William Chappell designed the costumes. It was very pretty, and the programme was illustrated with photographs taken by Cecil Beaton. But *Beauty, Truth and Rarity* was somewhat esoteric for some tastes. Later the Scottish piece was taken up by the Ballet Club, who produced it as a ballet called *The Tartans*.

My fellow-dancers and I were all very much involved with the Camargo Society. I first danced for the Society in a mixed bill which included *Pomona* (with music by Constant Lambert). Lydia did not take part in this, but she appeared in the Society's production of *A Day in a Southern Port* (later called *Rio Grande*), dancing the Queen of the Whores divinely, though it was not really the right part for her. Lambert always underrated his marvellous score, used for this ballet. Lydia did *Coppélia*, dancing Swanhilda, at Sadler's Wells in 1933 which was later included in two performances at Covent Garden for the Camargo Society the same year. In 1934, *Casse*

Noisette - The Nutcracker - was also done at Sadler's Wells, and Lydia rehearsed the young dancer taking the part of Clara - a part which she had danced before the Tsar during her school days at the Imperial Ballet School in St Petersburg at the age of nine. She had never danced in, nor seen, the ballet again until the Sadler's Wells revival, but could still remember the steps. And then, there was *Façade*, with Lydia very charming as the milkmaid; we danced the 'Tango Paso-doble' together. In this she showed the ecstatic intensity with which she did everything in the theatre, even the smallest ballet piece. Her comedy also had a great intensity, but it was not what one would call 'throwaway comedy'. In the 'Jodelling Song' in *Façade*, for which I had composed the choreography, I told her she must milk the cows properly. She said 'Yes, I will milk them, I will milk them.' And she milked with such a sense of commitment that one almost felt that the milk really was beginning to squirt out between her fingers.

What was she like to direct? I was slightly in awe of her at first because I was only a beginner. She was very good, and not alarming. She was forgetful, and one had to keep going back over points, but she did everything with such intensity that this helped. She was not temperamental and if she liked something she would exclaim, 'No, it is glorious!' (She loved the word 'glorious'.) I did not give her her head more than I did most dancers and although I allowed her latitude in the interpretation of a part, I always decided what the actual steps should be: she never developed a part herself choreo-graphically. I found her very receptive, very eager to do something different when dancing with a new partner. She might ask to change a step: 'Can I do it on this side rather than on that?' She knew how to project her personality as no other dancer knew, and was a joy to work with because she was so game and lively and funny.

As I have already implied, Lydia was not a classical ballerina, but she was a marvellous *demi-caractere* dancer. This stood her in good stead in *The Sleeping Princess*, as she was a greater draw than the galaxy of ballerinas from Russia - Spesivtseva, Tchernicheva, Tre-filova, Nemchinova and Egorova - whom Diaghilev had also at-tracted to dance in the famous production at the Alhambra in 1921. The impresario, Sir Oswald Stoll, made her dance at every perform-ance because of her popularity with the public, and she was lovely in the Blue Bird pas de deux. Apart from *Coppélia* and *Les Sylphides*, she never appeared in the great classical roles - never in *La Sylphide* or

Swan Lake. Le Spectre de la Rose, in which she danced with Nijinsky, is not technically very difficult; it has not the awesome strictness of the classical roles. On the other hand, in the character parts of *La Boutique Fantasque* (in which she danced with Massine) and *The Good-humoured Ladies* she was wonderful. Perhaps what made her different from anybody else in the eyes of of the public was that she got carried away in performance and reacted tremendously to the audience. Her performance in, say, *La Boutique* was quite different from that of anyone else, such as Danilova. It was marvellous of course. When she lifted up her dress at the start of the Can-Can, she lifted it up with such a wild ecstasy of delight at the mere thought that she was going to do this dance: she started enjoying it before she had taken a step.

Musically Lydia was not very strict; but perhaps this was because the exuberance of her dancing hindered her from listening carefully enough. Like most Russian dancers even to this day, she probably expected the conductor to follow her to some extent. Perhaps this is a Russian tradition, and perhaps musicians make too many concessions to Russian dancers. Makarova slows up the music so as to make no mistakes. But, although she could on occasion go off the beat, Lydia was not unmusical – as Spesivtseva, for example, was. Far from it: she loved music, and danced to it extremely well.

I have some recollections of Lydia's associations with Karsavina. In June 1926 I saw Lydia dancing at the first performance of *Les Noces* (the Nijinska-Stravinsky ballet) in London; Karsavina and Trefilova took part in the same programme. When, in November that year, Lydia danced in *The Firebird*, she was given a different costume from the one which Karsavina had worn in the same role. Diaghilev explained that this was because Lydia was so fat; the costume designed for her (by Goncharova) was a kind of pair of gauze Turkish trousers. (As is well known, Lydia left Diaghilev's company several times; once, when she offered to return, he said to her, 'I don't want old bones,' at which Lydia roared with laughter.) When Karsavina was in sore straits after her retirement Lydia wanted to help her. So up she went to her Hampstead house, and at the gate she took a hat out of her bag and put it on. 'What was all that juggling with your hat at the gate?' Karsavina asked. 'I put it on out of respect,' replied Lydia. What a charming tribute to a great baller-ina! Karsavina would not take a penny. 'Oh, you cannot help

Tamara,' said Lydia. 'It is hopeless. She has Russian pride and English pride and false pride.' Later, however, Lydia did start a fund for her.

Lydia's laughter was marvellously infectious – as natural as a child's. I remember once, when we were coming back in a taxi to her home, I said something that made her roar with laughter, and she continued to roar until we reached Gordon Square. I said to the taxi-driver, 'How much is that?' 'Nothing,' he said, and I replied, 'What do you mean: nothing?' 'To hear that lady laugh has done me more good than anything,' he answered, and he still refused his fare. One of her ways of amusing you was to make you laugh by saying exactly what she thought, even if it might be embarrassing or hurtful. Or it might be contrived, like some of her actions. For instance, when she and Maynard went to the White House to see President Roosevelt, she took her straw bag with the words, 'Sennet, Fishmonger, Cambridge' stamped on it. Her indecent remarks might be extraordinary, and if she was bored at a ballet or a play she began talking loudly. I remember once going with her and Maynard to a ballet performance. The curtain went up and all was quiet until Lydia's voice rang out: 'Oh, Maynard, look at her mouth. It is indecent. It looks as though it belongs somewhere else.' After I met Fedor, Lydia's brother, I mentioned it to her and she said, 'Oh my God! I hope they don't bring my brother. I hope they don't bring my brother. I send him watches, I send him food, but I hope they don't bring my brother.' When asked about Fedor as a choreo-grapher, she said, 'Och! he's awful.' She was completely frank about herself. 'I am a hoarder: I collect tins and toilet paper'. Tilton for a long time after the end of the war was crammed with tins.

I first visited Tilton, the Keynes's Sussex home, in 1930 and Constant Lambert was with me, and we wanted to discuss with Maynard and Lydia the programme we were doing at the Arts Theatre, London. We arrived on the Friday, and Constant who loved his drink, found nothing but water. Then Saturday came and Maynard arrived, and with him was a full symphony of wonderful wines from Cambridge. He told us about the pedigree of each, and the ensuing evening was one of great gaiety and laughter. On Sunday it was back to water, and Constant went off to the pub, which was a long way away, saying he must go for a walk. I remember lunching with Lydia to discuss *Harlequin in the Street*, and meeting Derain and his wife. Constant was there also, as he had arranged the music by Couperin which Derain had suggested. I was to do the choreography. Madame Derain never said a word, and when I told Lydia afterwards that she seemed rather dull Lydia said, 'Och! No. She's a good housekeeper. What more does a great man want than someone to look after him?' *Job* was a ballet she admired. 'Wonderful ritual: wonderful score. Good dancing parts. It should come back as a landmark, since it is so much a sort of conception of ballet of that time.' She preferred the original Gwen Raverat costumes and scenery to those of John Piper.

Maynard was chairman of the board of the Royal Opera House, Covent Garden. On the evening when the house was reopened after the war in 1946 Lydia had to greet the King and Queen and show them to their box, as Maynard was at first unwell. He soon recovered and was able to watch the ballet, *The Sleeping Beauty*, while Lydia and I smoked cigarettes on the floor of the box undisturbed, until the house fireman arrived and told us to stop. The tobacco smoke had been seen wafting into the auditorium.

After Maynard died Lydia rather fell out of love with ballet. I used to see her socially and once stayed at Tilton. She went to Brighton to see my new ballets and would say, 'Och! Too much ballet. The dancers are not highly enough developed; they do not get their legs up high enough.' At Tilton I teased her about the Cézannes, which were all skied. 'Why do you hang them so high?' I asked, 'I can't see them.' She replied, 'Och! I do not really care about them. I cannot sell them. They don't belong to me; they are all going to King's College.' And of Maynard at that time she would say, 'I used to think about him every day, but now I don't think about him at all.' Her frankness and realism were wonderful. At first after he had died, she used to wear his pyjamas and his vests. She was a wonderful wife. Someone told me that on an aeroplane journey it was incredible how she looked after him, getting icepacks to put on his head. She cosseted him and covered him with wool. If people came to see him she would suddenly throw them out when she thought they had stayed long enough, as the doctor had told her to do. '*Now you must go!*'

Lopokova as an Actress

Dennis Arundell

Most critical people in a theatre audience, professional or amateur, are swayed by their personal enthusiasms or convictions: but performances by a rightly popular artist do not necessarily show first-rate ability. The magical warmth of Ellen Terry, which could, it has been said, make others acting with her 'vanish', persuaded most of her audiences that she was a great actress – except for her niece, John Gielgud's mother, who, writing of her other aunt, Marion Terry, said she 'looked upon her ... as a more *accomplished* actress than the more famous Ellen', or Bernard Shaw, whose love for Ellen kept him pestering her to prove she could do far better.

With Lydia it was much the same. Her piquant charm when she danced was also there when she acted, and so most who saw her in a play accepted as part of that charm – or as unimportant compared with that charm – her clear but strange pronunciation of English, though that, of course, improved considerably over the years. Professional critics of her acting were often, as will be seen, either tactfully prejudiced in her favour because of the traditional respect for Caesar's wife, or against her on the equally illogical grounds that her frequent contact with amateurs limited her efficiency.

When Lydia first spoke on the English stage – that of the Cambridge Amateur Dramatic Club – in November 1928 her accent was certainly not what an English audience expected, especially as this was the first staging of Shakespeare's poem *A Lover's Complaint*, which was probably unknown to most of those present. Although at that time I was involved only with amateur theatre, I had directed and been directed by professional actors and singers; but I had never worked with anyone as internationally famous as Lydia.

Before our first meeting six months earlier I felt I could respect and accept her interpretation as easily as I trusted Maynard Keynes's senior knowledge. But when she began reading Shakespeare's lines, sitting on the floor of Maynard's King's College rooms, I was surprised not only by her accent but also by the ultra-regular rhythm of her speech. Her first lines were spoken mechanically, like this:

Fa*ther*, though *in* me *you* be*hold*
The *injury* of *many* a *blasting hour* . . .

Tentatively suggesting a more humanly emotional approach, I was even more surprised when Maynard authoritatively approved her accentuation as being according to the mechanical scansion. To me, this seemed as unvaried as the ticking of a clock, without the sparkles of characterization I had seen when she danced for Diaghilev.

I did not then know that, apart from having appeared in plays in Russia as a child (including the small speaking parts of Mamillius in *The Winter's Tale* and Pease-Blossom in *A Midsummer Night's Dream*), she had not only studied English speaking and acting in America in 1913-14, encouraged by the famous American actress, Mrs Minnie Fiske (1865-1932), well-known for her naturalistic style of acting, but had even acted both on tour and in New York in a play called *The Young Idea*. Had I known this my surprise would have been greater still – not because of her accent, but because, to my ear, meaning and emotion were lacking.

Yet when she first read to me the lines Shakespeare had given to 'The Afflicted Maid' her enthusiasm was so unpretentious that she was like a child eager to please, and, when rehearsals started they were most happy, with Michael Redgrave, then an undergraduate, as the lover, and a young professional from the Festival Theatre in Cambridge just beginning to make his mark as actor, mime-dancer and designer, Hedley Briggs, in the non-speaking part of the blustering 'reverend' man. Maynard had originally suggested the brilliant drama-loving classical don, J.T. Sheppard, for this part; his white hairs, Lydia thought, 'might save us the cost of the wig' – an example of amateur enthusiasm. I acted the poet and also composed the music. The set and costumes were designed by Duncan Grant.

The papers thought *A Lover's Complaint* 'rather dull', and 'better left in the book'. In the *Nation* (which was owned by Maynard) Francis Birrell reported,

The Shakespeare poem seemed to be neither acted nor read aloud but presented from another angle in another medium. Mr Grant exquisitely emphasized the visual side of the poem with his decorations, and suggested how curiously the sister arts might illustrate each other if they chose. Here Madame Lopokova showed genuine dramatic talent, and her accent was no more foreign than that of the Elizabethans would have been. Indeed, it would be delightful if she would employ her sympathy, imagination, and wit in thus translating for us other famous poems.

In a triple bill at the ADC, *A Lover's Complaint* was preceded by the first public performance in England of Stravinsky's *The Soldier's Tale*, called at that time *The Tale of the Soldier*. It was followed by three dances, in two of which Lydia took part. The main attraction was, of course, the Stravinsky, which was 'read, played and danced' as printed in the published score, with Michael Redgrave as the soldier, Hedley Briggs as the devil and myself as the reader. Lydia played the non-speaking part of the dancing princess – a part said to have been created for her by Stravinsky. She had, in fact, danced the part the year before, in July 1927, at the Arts Theatre Club in London, when the piece was 'broadcasted'. The critics were puzzled; the *Observer* found it 'curious but rather tedious', and *The Times* recorded that Lydia, 'when she dances the Princess into health with exquisite, childlike pretence of clumsiness like the clumsiness of a flower buffeted by the wind, is the pattern's centre'. When the play was performed in Cambridge the *Daily Telegraph* found the two actors 'so good that when Mme Lopokova danced ... there was no feeling that here was a great dancer graciously consenting to appear with others far below her form – only that we had seen a remarkable performance'. The *Nation*, however, reported, 'The acting, save that of Madame Lopokova, was amateur, but on the whole that lent a sincerity to the performance.'

A year later, in November 1929, Lydia again acted on the stage of the ADC Theatre in Cambridge: this time in *Life's a Dream*, by the seventeenth-century Spanish dramatist Calderón, translated by J.B. Trend and Frank Birch, who also directed the play. The performances were given by a mixed cast of Cambridge amateurs, headed by the later well known V.C. Clinton-Baddeley, and professionals, including Hedley Briggs, who not only played two parts but also,

as the programme says, 'directed' the costumes and scenery with
Arthur B. Woods.

Lydia appeared in the leading part of Rosaura, a lady of Muscovy
and a disguised princess in a 'world of rhetoric and great gestures'.
Her long speeches would have been difficult even for an experienced
poetic actress – as *The Times* suggested, the play 'may easily fall into
the fustian of melodrama', though the ingenious production with
artificial gestures that 'often seem part of the scenery ... transports
us to an unreal world'. The *Cambridge Daily News* reported that
Lydia's performance 'will remain an exquisite memory for those
who have seen it. The precision and point of her gestures, the lithe
grace with which every syllable of a delicate voice was subtly
accentuated by her whole attitude, are things that deserve to be
rescued from devouring Time.'

On 1 August 1930 Lydia wrote to Marie Rambert:

Dear Mim,
    I have had the boldness to take the Arts for a week at the end
of the year, with a small programme in which I use my tongue
more than my legs. But my legs are to appear once in a short
ballet. I am asking Fred Ashton to help me with this. Fred owes
so much to you.

yrs. L.K.

The 'Arts' was the Arts Theatre Club in London, and the programme was entitled *Beauty, Truth and Rarity: A Masque of Poetry,
Music and Dancing*. In an interview with the *Observer*'s theatre critic
on 7 December, Lydia explained that poetry was intended to be the
unifying element of the entertainment: 'Not only the poetry of
language will be represented, but also the poetry of music and of
motion. In some items we shall combine the three.'

After a prologue entitled 'The Young Man and the Preacher',
taken by George Rylands (who was to produce the dramatic items)
from The Song of Solomon and Ecclesiastes, a new staging of *A
Lover's Complaint* was to follow. As Lydia said, 'It is such a lovely
poem, and I find that scarcely anybody has read it, or even heard of
it. For the first time in London I am taking a speaking part and
appearing as one of the two lovers in Mr George Rylands' delightful
arrangement of the verse.' Then she would dance in a ballet based
on Thomas Campion's poem, 'Follow your Saint', to music by John
Dowland, act as the Lady in a version of Milton's *Comus* (ending

with a dance to music by Purcell), and, after an all-male 'Debate of the Infernal Peers' from *Paradise Lost*, she would appear in *Dances on a Scotch Theme*, to music by William Boyce. The ballets had all been 'composed' by Frederick Ashton. As she said in the *Observer* interview, 'You must admit it will be an unusual evening, but it will be an interesting one I think.'

The Arts Theatre was, exceptionally, open to the general public for the nine performances of the masque between 10 and 16 December. Apart from Rylands and Ashton, the young participants included Constant Lambert (who arranged and conducted the music), William Chappell (who shared the designing with Glyn Philpot) and a Cambridge contingent of actors: Donald Beves, Winyard Browne, Robert Eddison, Peter Hannen, Michael Redgrave and Geoffrey Toone; there was also Cecil Beaton, who took the photographs that illustrated the programme.

In these performances George Rylands acted the poet, Lydia 'the afflicted fancy', Donald Beves 'the reverend man' and Michael Redgrave 'the false jewel'.

This production of *A Lover's Complaint* (presented 'in a series of three tableaux'), and Lydia's acting, divided the critics as much as the Cambridge production two years earlier had done. They were however united about her dancing and miming. As *The Times* wrote,

> Certainly one could never forget that she was a dancer, and it is impossible not to give to all her movements as much attention as to her speech. A turn of the wrist, a walk, a nod of the head, even when it is the obvious and necessary accompaniment to the words, seems also to be in time to some music which we cannot hear. But she has also to speak ... in competition with such accomplished and melodious speakers as Mr Rylands and Mr Michael Redgrave. She does more than hold her own, and though she acts and moves more elaborately than the others, this is not to supplement any deficiency in her recitation. She speaks with a faint foreign accent, but the verse comes through with its full clearness and force, perhaps even with an added pungency.

The *Observer*'s critic thought much the same: 'her present happy alliance, as an actress, with Shakespeare and Milton charmed rather than surprised me ... when she began to put her pretty perplexities to the test of speech and gesture, her tact with our (to her) recalcitrant language, and the clear emotion with which she suffused it, were most endearing.' Others, like the *Evening Standard*, were blunter: 'For those who like their Shakespeare with a very broken accent, this was a charming experience. The rest can only regard it as a laudable attempt, though preferable to the sibilant lispings with which some of those undergraduates adorned their mother tongue.'

Francis Birrell's long article in the *Nation*, on the other hand, might seem even more prejudiced than his criticism of two years before. Calling the programme delightful, he thought the Shakespeare 'almost the last word in aristocratic beauty ... Mr Rylands and Mr Redgrave ... struggled through to triumph over the extraordinary difficulties of the remote and inspissated diction, while Madame Lopokova's still slightly foreign accent positively helped to carry the unearthly Masque into a still more remote and faery region.' But it is a personal comment in the *Evening Standard* which seems to have summed up most accurately the magic that was Lydia's:

> Her miming is exquisite. And in her voice mingle the clipped consonants of Bloomsbury and the liquid labials of her native tongue.
>
> I sat last night trying to plumb the secret of Lopokova's fascination. I decided that the dominant element is dignity – the compelling dignity of a child. And against this stand out the vivid colours of her humour, her vivacity, and her complete mastery of technique.

On 26 March 1933 HG (Hubert Griffith) of the *Observer* described an interview he had had with Lydia, who had injured a knee while dancing at Sadler's Wells. Although she was actually forty-one, he began,

> Being still very young, and an actress in the most charming sense of a misused word, she can temporarily turn this injury to the fullest account; can review her 'past dancing career' from her tea-table in Bloomsbury with as detached an attitude as though she were nine hundred. ... 'Yes', says Mlle Lopokova, 'I am like a middle-aged footballer. All of us, middle-aged dancers and middle-aged footballers, have knee trouble if we do too much in too short a time.'

She then added, 'when I have finally said farewell to dancing ... I should like to act. I should like to be a comedy actress. I wish I could find a manager to give me the small part of a soubrette!' Lydia then, in the words of HG, queried, 'Could I do tragedy? How could one do tragedy with a nose like this! But I think I could do dramatic parts. I should like to do a dramatic ingenue, if such a part exists. Ibsen particularly. What about that girl in *The Master Builder*? I should like to do her.'

Six months later Lydia was acting at the Old Vic, with an all-professional cast for the first time. This was the famous season that changed the style of that theatre's performances, with actors of established and promising reputation, headed by Charles Laughton and Flora Robson and directed by Tyrone Guthrie. Among them were Athene Seyler, Ursula Jeans, Roger Livesey, Leon Quartermaine, Basil Gill, Richard Goolden, the young James Mason and Marius Goring, Elsa Lanchester and myself.

As Laughton could not leave Hollywood in time for the first play, *Twelfth Night*, the best known name at the first performance on 18 September was Lydia's. She played the part of Olivia, and was presumably engaged only for that one play. During rehearsals, Athene Seyler, who was playing Maria, said of Lydia in an *Observer* interview, 'She is charming and intelligent and quick-witted, a lovely intrinsic personality, a "pearl among women". I do not know what exact lines her Olivia is to take yet; but all acting is a magnifying glass of the true personality – dispute this or not; I have always found it to be so – and this will come out in her acting.'

What did come out was the inevitable difference of opinion among the critics. The *Daily Express* carried the headline: 'Great Dancer Turns Actress. Lopokova's Superb Olivia. Audience of 2,500 spellbound.' The report said that 'when she floated down the steps' to take her call, the audience rose to their feet and cheered 'not Lydia Lopokova, the dancer, but the actress'. It added,

> Not since her feet built her reputation had she such a tense, critical audience to win over. All preconceived ideas of Olivia the haughty beauty, she brushed aside at the outset by the magic expressiveness of her hands. They acted for her. The audience was fascinated.
>
> The immortal words twisted her tongue, but Mme Lopokova only regarded them as guide-posts for her sensitive, full-blooded acting.

The Times, on the other hand, while on the whole complimenting the rest of the cast, remarked, 'What to say of Olivia one hardly knows, Madame Lopokova speaking Shakespearean English with so strong an Illyrian accent that much of its sense and all its music vanish.'

Unfortunately, although I was in that production, I remember nothing of her performance because I only met her at the rehearsals of the last act, in which I appeared in one of two small parts, and, of course, I never saw the play as a member of the audience. Flora Robson, however, who was not to appear in the season till *The Cherry Orchard*, was in the audience. She made the following comment in a letter written to Milo Keynes in 1979:

> This was quite a new interpretation from Tyrone Guthrie at his best. Hitherto, Shakespeare was mostly played by Repertory companies, so 'Ophelia' become 'Viola', and 'Lady Macbeth' 'Olivia'.
>
> When you examine *Twelfth Night*, the strong and faithful one is Viola; everyone else changes his or her mind about the loved one, except Viola. Olivia is first in love with her dead brother and will have nothing to do with Orsino. She then falls in love with Viola [disguised as Cesario] and is in the end quite content with her brother Sebastian. Orsino is mad about Olivia, but cheerfully accepts Viola.
>
> Therefore, Olivia should be played by a sentimental, darling nit-wit. So for the first time, audiences saw NOT Lady Macbeth (many thought it quite wrong!) but the real Olivia.

Dame Flora then added the following comments, which give perhaps a true picture of Lydia both on and off the stage:

> The other piece of acting I remember (also from the audience), and I don't know what play [? *A Doll's House*], was Lydia running to the door, to stop someone from leaving. She cupped her hands outside the handle in two curves, as much as to say 'NOT THROUGH HERE'. The man could have put his hand between hers and opened the door. It was a Ballet gesture – not realistic. We were amused as it showed up the difference in our training.
>
> She also made us laugh a lot with mistakes in her English, which we relished. (I believe she thought these out!) 'Oh, I feel like Mary, Queen of SPOTS!' Also, when her Russian (?) divorce came through successfully, she said – 'Thank God, I am a virgin again.'

Robert Eddison wrote, 'I was entranced by her Olivia, though her marked accent must have seemed rather peculiar to strangers; I can still hear her saying "Malwolio".'

Virginia Woolf wrote a long, highly polished article on the Old Vic *Twelfth Night* in the *New Statesman and Nation* which is reprinted here as an appendix. The suggestion in her review, which is borne out to some extent by Dame Flora, is that Lydia was beautifully out of key with the other actors and the production: but the more professional, frank and expert judgement was by Sir John Gielgud when in 1979 he wrote about Lydia's performance: 'The language quite defeated her efforts, though otherwise she was her usual beguiling self. . . . I don't think she could really be any good in straight theatre with such a strong accent and peculiar English.'

Despite her doubtful success in *Twelfth Night*, Lydia was bravely determined to be recognized as an actress: so in March 1934 she played the part of Nora in Ibsen's *A Doll's House* at the Arts Theatre Club, London, produced by Mrs Grein under her pseudonym Michael Orme. It was in some of Nora's speeches that she had been coached twenty years before by Mrs Fiske, but now Lydia was playing the part with experienced actors – Walter Hudd, Austin Trevor and Wilfrid Grantham.

As before, the critics varied in their reactions to Lydia's acting. The *Morning Post*'s dramatic critic said she 'gave an extremely beautiful performance', but added,

> Though they interfered much less with Ibsen than with her recent performance as Olivia in *Twelfth Night*, Mme Lopokova's accent and deliberation in speaking English are still a trouble. In the early scenes, too, she was not quite Helmer's supposed doll-wife. But the final scene of Nora's quiet challenge, with which 'modern drama was born', could not have been done with a finer sincerity.

The Times was both more detailed and more enthusiastic:

> The special merit of her Nora lies in her careful guardianship of her reserves. The first act is cautiously preparatory, and no strength is wasted in over-decoration of Nora's frivolous moods. Thereafter the part is led steadily towards its climax, which Mme. Lopokova recognises in the rehearsal of Norá's dance while Krogstad's letter lies in the letter-box, and in this scene the emotional emphasis is brilliantly timed, every movement and

frightened intonation contributing to an impression of a woman whose world is crumbling beneath her feet.

The final speech to Torvald is less successful, perhaps because this declaration of feminine independence relies for an effect of passionate sincerity on a grave precision of phrase that Mme Lopokova cannot certainly control. For the same reason her slower movements are generally less persuasive than those taken at high speed, but her performance as a whole is, in the highest interpretative sense, a genuine criticism of the play.

Lydia was to meet her greatest challenge as a straight actress early in 1936; as the *Star* announced on 2 March,

> Lydia Lopokova, the ballet dancer (now Mrs John Maynard Keynes) is returning to the stage in a new role. She is to appear with Jean Forbes-Robertson in four Ibsen plays at the New Arts Theatre, which is to be opened at Cambridge on Monday.
>
> Mrs Keynes will be active in helping to run the new theatre and after the Cambridge performances she will appear in Ibsen in London.

Maynard, according to the *Observer* of 23 February, wanted 'to see how Ibsen wears' and, being 'largely responsible for the venture', chose to present *A Doll's House*, *The Master Builder*, *Hedda Gabler* and *Rosmersholm* because he had 'very much in mind that the four plays are a continuous commentary on the emergence of the modern woman.'

Perhaps for this reason he not only engaged 'Michael Orme' to direct *A Doll's House*, as she had done two years before, and the brilliantly common sense producer Irene Hentschel to direct the other plays, but also engaged the expert women designers who collaborated under the increasingly famous name of Motley to be in charge of both scenery and costumes.

Lydia (who did not appear on the stage with Jean Forbes-Robertson, as the *Star* had implied) again took the leading woman's part in *A Doll's House*, and also in *The Master Builder*, while the mysteriously submerged passion of Jean Forbes-Robertson dominated the other two plays. This inevitably challenging comparison with a well known actress was obviously more alarming because it had already been arranged that the four plays should move to London. They were to be presented by Leon M. Lion, in association with the Cambridge Arts Theatre, as 'A Cycle of Ibsen (1879-1892)' at the Criterion Theatre. This would be the first non-club London theatre in which Lydia appeared as an actress.

The leading actors in *A Doll's House* were Wilfrid Grantham as Krogstad, as he had been two years before when Lydia first played Nora at the Arts Theatre Club, D.A. Clarke-Smith as 'a very solid but moving' Dr Rank, and as Torvald, the husband, the twenty-five-year-old Geoffrey Edwards who had been especially urged by Maynard to take the part, although at that time Lydia, as the young wife, was forty-four. Lydia had the same actors with her in *The Master Builder*, when at last she appeared as Hilda Wangel, the 'dramatic ingenue' she had told the *Observer* three years before she would 'like to do'.

Both the *Manchester Guardian* and the *Morning Post* carried glowing reviews of Lydia's performance in *A Doll's House*, and when Leon M. Lion transferred the four plays to London the *Observer* wrote, 'Miss Lydia Lopokova cannot sweep through Nora's part on personality and experience; she has worked everything out, and the detail of her performance is of the utmost intelligence. As was said, Nora's rebellion was once more an exciting thing.' Horace Horsnell, in the same paper, thought her Hilda Wangel 'enchanting. Her purity of gesture, stillness, and imaginative naivety were particularly helpful when they were most needed. Sheer strength may have been lacking at the end to support the swoop of calamity; but her mimetic sleight – her poses are lovely – and her emotional intelligence were always fancy free.'

But just as her Olivia in *Twelfth Night* three years before had been criticized in a mixed fashion by both professional actors and members of the audience, so were Lydia's Nora and Hilda in 'A Cycle of Ibsen'.

John Laurie, who played opposite Jean Forbes-Robertson in the other two plays, wrote in 1979 [in a letter to M.K.] about his memories of Lydia as an actress:

Across forty-three long years my impressions have dimmed sadly. Also, I shared only one of the four plays with Mrs Keynes – *The Master Builder* – and then in the tiny role of Solness' old clerk. I don't remember meeting Hilda, even in rehearsals! I saw her rehearsing, of course, and recall a slight, shy lady with the grace (and face) of a dancer, tackling roles which test the most talented of actresses. Alas! the critics, I recall, were unkind to her. Were we? I pray not; but we were a tough lot and I have my doubts, and sincerest regrets that maybe we 'pros' failed to extend our most generous and helpful encouragement to a very great little lady, paramount in her own art and venturing into the shoals of another.

At the time, the dramatic critics scrupulously praised Lydia's good points, which were outstanding, in spite of what seemed lacking in her performances. Two members of the audience who were not professionals were not so enthusiastic. Professor Tom Marshall, of Cambridge, wrote,

> Of course I remember Lydia went in for acting Ibsen, and there was talk about it – at least as regards *A Doll's House*. I have no recollection of *The Master Builder*. I am not even certain that I saw *A Doll's House*, but my vague memory of this affair is that comment was not very favourable and her venture on the legitimate stage was not taken very seriously by her friends and was not a great success. But then some of her 'friends' had sharp tongues.

Frances Partridge, Marshall's sister, recalled [also in a letter to M.K.] that with her husband she 'did go to *A Doll's House*, and didn't think Lydia was a success. Great admirers of her dancing and mime as we were, we felt 1. that her charming Russian accent somehow interfered with Ibsen's text, 2. that his peculiar brand of ironic tragicomedy was not in her power to capture. So, alas, we didn't go to *The Master Builder*.'

Virginia Woolf, however, recorded in her diary on 29 February 1936, 'Lydia is a great success at Cambridge' and, on 4 March, 'The Doll's House last night. Lydia very good.'

Lydia's next acting part was Célimène in Molière's *The Misanthrope*, in a new verse translation by Elsie Elizabeth Duncan-Jones, which opened on 7 February 1937 at the Arts Theatre, Cambridge. It was directed by the actor-producer Robert Atkins, who was well known for his work at the Old Vic and more recently at the Regent's Park open-air theatre, while the costumes and scenery were by André Derain.

W.A. Darlington, the theatre critic of the *Daily Telegraph*, although he criticized the play, recorded with his usual honesty and tact that 'Lydia Lopokova as the heartless Célimène gave the best performance I have seen from her since she turned articulate on the stage. Her English intonations have improved most markedly since I last heard them.' *The Times* was more specific:

> Madame Lopokova would not permit the naughty wit of Célimène or her butterfly fondness for social sunshine to be distorted into vice. She drew her as a woman fairly representative of the society of her day, indulging in malicious character sketches not so much because she is heartless as because she had the capacity for enjoyment that can be found within the conventions which are fashionable.

Lydia's last appearances as an actress were unfortunate. A year before the Second World War, she appeared in a pacifist play by Auden and Isherwood, *On the Frontier: A Melodrama in Three Acts.* This was presented by the Group Theatre at the Arts Theatre, Cambridge, between 14 and 19 November 1938; one performance was given later at the Globe Theatre, London, on 12 February 1939.

The play was directed by the Group's usual producer, Rupert Doone, with scenery and costumes by Robert Medley and music by the twenty-five year-old Benjamin Britten, who was also the pianist. Once again Lydia was acting with experienced professionals, this time with Eric Berry, Wyndham Goldie, Ernest Milton and Tristan Rawson, and some sixteen others, including John Moody (later well known as the director at the Bristol Old Vic) and Peter Pears, then twenty-eight, each of whom took five different parts.

The theme of the play, according to the correspondent of *The Times*, was 'modern war with its psychological aspect', with 'grim and revolutionary scenes between the non-aggressive dictator of "Westland" and the aggressive neighbouring state of "Ostnia"'; there was also 'a love theme between younger members of the opposing factions' (Eric Berry and Lydia Lopokova). The report made only a brief comment on one performance – Ernest Milton's – but the *Manchester Guardian*'s 'University Correspondent' gave a stronger idea of the play:

> As a whole the play is too propagandist, but its passionate seriousness carries it to success.... The least successful episodes are the most ambitious, two meetings, out of time and space, between the son of one hostile family and the daughter of the other. The

second of these meetings is the epilogue of the play, and even the brilliant acting of Eric Berry and Lydia Lopokova cannot make either scene convincing.

Apparently no other national newspapers reported on the play, whether because of political prejudice or not, and it is interesting that the two which did publish comments relied on local correspondents.

When the play was presented at the Globe Theatre in February, the London critics were no more enthusiastic, though *The Times* thought that 'the play ... has a considerable spark of theatrical life and can be watched with continuous interest, even by those who did not come to the theatre in the same spirit in which they attend a political meeting.' Lydia was not mentioned in that review, but by the *Daily Telegraph*, which, alluding to Auden and Isherwood, found the play 'less interesting than most of their work' and added: 'Only in the poetical passages where a Westland boy and an Ostnian girl meet in their dreams, does this play cease to be any modern war play by any author. These speeches – better spoken by Eric Berry than by Lydia Lopokova – express the undying human hope of a time when war shall be no more. ... They are worth the rest of the play.'

Nine months after the production of this anti-war play the Second World War began and all theatres were closed for a time; when they reopened there was a need for plays whose lightheartedness or romance helped audiences to remember the past, forget the present and look forward to the future. There was unlikely to be much need for the 'dramatic soubrette' that Lydia quite rightly felt was her sort of part. It was unfortunate that the last play in which Lydia acted had not been first-class: similarly, the first time she acted in England was in a work never intended for the stage.

When she acted in plays by Shakespeare, Calderón, Molière and Ibsen, however, and especially when she was with experienced actors, she showed her determination to succeed. But each time there were many differing opinions from professional critics and actors, members of the audiences, friends who could be over-enthusiastic, and others whose views might be either so enhanced or so dampened by their attitude towards her husband, politically or socially, that they could not forget that she was Mrs Maynard Keynes. It is, indeed, difficult to appraise Lydia's acting ability because one cannot easily forget that it was Maynard's influence that encouraged her appearance on the British stage as an actress in the first place.

Two facts, however, remain. In Russia, her theatrical training had enabled her to develop her exceptional skill in characterization as a dancer, and her training in ballet had endowed her with her mastery of expressive miming. It is easy to say that as a dancer she acted well and that as an actress her movements were lovely, but the truth of both these statements made her exceptionally attractive as a stage performer in many varied fields, though, as an actress in England, she was naturally hampered by her Russian accent.

She had, I suggest, as Virginia Woolf said, 'the genius of personality', an inborn gift that cannot be learned or taught, and which Lydia possessed, whether dancing or acting or in private life. But her chief quality was that she was always as straightforward as a child, and her eager enthusiasm for trying something new or challenging - no matter how different or difficult - was the enthusiasm of a child. This quality fascinated all audiences, whether she moved or spoke - even those who were troubled by the accent that she worked so hard to lose: in fact, it is remarkable how often her childlike - not childish - quality was referred to by critics or by those who worked with her. Even in 1930, when she was nearly forty years old, the *Evening Standard*, 'trying to plumb the secret of Lopokova's fascination', decided that 'the dominant element is dignity - the compelling dignity of a child'.

There is no question but that whenever she appeared on the stage, in whatever capacity, she lit it up with the charm of what Gielgud called 'her usual beguiling self', even for those who were honestly critical of her technical ability; and that charm came from the joy of living that one senses in an unspoilt child. Everything she did on and off the stage she turned, as Laertes said of his sister Ophelia, 'to favour and to prettiness'.

Plays in which Lydia Lopokova acted

Before 1910	*The Winter's Tale*, by William Shakespeare (Mamillius)	Alexandrinsky Theatre, St Petersburg
	A Midsummer Night's Dream, by William Shakespeare (Peaseblossom)	Alexandrinsky Theatre, St Petersburg
1914	*The Young Idea* (title changed to *Just Herself*), by Ethel Watts Mumford (Euphemia Kenda)	United States: on tour, then at the Playhouse Theatre, New York
1915	*The Antick*, by Percy Mackaye (Julie Bonheur)	Bandbox Theatre, New York
	Whims, by Alfred de Musset (La Comtesse de Chavigny)	Bandbox Theatre, New York
1928	*A Lover's Complaint*, by William Shakespeare (the Afflicted Maid)	Amateur Dramatic Club, Cambridge
1929	*Life's a Dream*, by Pedro Calderón de la Barca (Rosaura)	Amateur Dramatic Club, Cambridge
	The Prisoners of War, by J.R. Ackerley (Marie)	Amateur Dramatic Club, Cambridge
1930	*A Lover's Complaint*, by William Shakespeare (the Afflicted Maid), and *Comus*, by John Milton (the Lady)	Arts Theatre Club, London

1933	*Twelfth Night*, by William Shakespeare (Olivia)	Old Vic Theatre, London
1934	*A Doll's House*, by Henrik Ibsen (Nora)	Arts Theatre Club, London
1936	*A Doll's House* (Nora) and *The Master Builder* (Hilda Wangel), by Henrik Ibsen	Arts Theatre, Cambridge, then the Criterion Theatre, London
1937	*The Misanthrope*, by Molière (Célimène)	Arts Theatre, Cambridge
1938–9	*On the Frontier*, by W.H. Auden and Christopher Isherwood (Anna Vrodny)	Arts Theatre, Cambridge, then one performance at the Globe Theatre, London

No. 6 Harvey Road, Tilton and No. 46 Gordon Square

Polly Hill

As the eldest of the eight nieces and nephews of Lydia Lopokova and John Maynard Keynes, I have vivid memories of life in my grandparents' house, 6 Harvey Road, Cambridge, during the years 1933–6, when I was an undergraduate. Both Maynard and I (together with my brother, David Keynes Hill, from 1934) usually attended the excellent Sunday lunches provided there during Full Term. Very rarely Lydia also was present. If the occasion happened to be over-weighted by the presence of some of the sombre, heavily built siblings of Maynard's mother, Florence Ada Keynes (who was herself strangely thin), the atmosphere became uniquely aerated, my great uncles and aunts instantly losing stones of weight. (Maynard himself felt rather oppressed by some of these kinsfolk, two of whom were teetotallers unable to enjoy the fruit of John Neville Keynes's excellent wine cellar, which, later on, he unhesitatingly depleted when supplies became scarce.)

Contrary to the widely held contemporary belief that Maynard was the creature of a grand, bourgeois background, 6 Harvey Road was no stately home; it was not even terraced, but a mere 'semi'. Built in the awful early eighties, and still ugly to our eyes today, it was part of a building estate then inhabited almost entirely by academics, the younger of whom, like my grandparents, were far better off than their counterparts today. It was comfortable, yes, and my grandmother never had occasion to boil an egg; but, unlike some of their friends, who had had their own conveyances and horses, my grandparents had never had a carriage there, and after the introduction of pneumatic tyres in about 1895 the residents were essentially cyclists, though Maynard had suffered a cycling accident as early as 1892. My grandmother's background had been far from opulent. As the eldest of the six children of Dr John Brown, the penurious and learned pastor of the Bunyan Meeting in Bedford, she had lived in fairly straitened bourgeois circumstances, especially in her early years, before her mother had established a school for girls.

John Neville Keynes (whose father had been a successful horti-culturist and mayor of Salisbury), was a man of taste and elegance, with no particular interest in furniture or architecture, who had inevitably clothed the walls of 6 Harvey Road in fashionable Morris wallpaper. In her little book *Gathering up the Threads: A Study in Family Biography* (1950) my grandmother mentions the furniture in the dining-room which had been made in Salisbury by an excellent cabinet-maker 'from whom my husband's mother ordered for us a complete set of dining-room requirements' (p. 49). The original table having collapsed with a crash when the cabinet-maker jumped on it to demonstrate its stability, 'another table had to be constructed on still more solid lines, with legs shaped out of old oak beams from a church tower, and this table has borne without flinching the weight of provisions for many family celebrations.' This table, with its many leaves, was remarkably expandable. There was room in the dining room for the pianola owned by this notably unmusical family. Somewhat surprisingly, there was a food-lifting device, which ascended from the servants' basement, raising a portion of the dining-room floor beneath Duncan Grant's lyrical portrait (now at King's College) of Maynard, as a young man at work. On the immense, ornate and hideous sideboard there was always a green dessert plate of ginger biscuits, put out to soften by my grandfather, who had very bad teeth. The room was very cold, heated only by a semi-cylindrical gas fire which was lit shortly before meals. Much alarm was occasioned by wine-spilling, which necessitated raising the stain on the formerly immaculate white tablecloth with a wine glass.

My grandfather always sat at the south end of the table, carving the immense joints with consummate skill and patience, always calm and kind; my grandmother, to the north, apportioned the 'pudding', which was not a 'dessert', for that was a later course of fruit, accompanied by finger bowls. Maids served; I do not remember any of them, and I doubt if I made much impression on them either.

The size of the company at Sunday lunch was as variable as the table; the smaller the better was the view of both Maynard and myself for this gave him full scope to relate, schoolboy-like, the exciting events of the past week, and for me, as a student of both economics and human nature, who doted on her uncle, to listen enthralled. Maynard loved his parents and was at pains to entertain them. But as my grandmother was an active public figure, who had been Mayor of Cambridge in 1932-3, when she was over seventy years old, local dignitaries, as well as heavy kinsfolk, were apt to expand the table. In his letters to Lydia, in London, Maynard often mentioned the lunches and the over-crowding:

> At Harvey Rd today a great family party – large numbers of large bodies ... Low's portrait [a caricature of himself] is not at all a success at Harvey Rd – especially with Fil [Lydia's nickname for her father-in-law] who desires to throw it into the wastepaper basket. It isn't much of a success in the Combination Room [at King's College] either.   29 October 1933

> A fine turkey for lunch at Harvey Rd today, beautifully carved by Phil [sic] – but so many guests, as there always are nowadays.   25 November 1934

> I am just back from Harvey Rd where I stayed on to tea after the luncheon crowd ... had gone away. Polly thought it extraordinary that you should get 20 guineas for your BBC contract.
>   2 December 1934

On more intimate occasions calf's head was one of our delicacies: 'Calf's head for lunch today at Harvey Rd, so Polly and I had 3 helpings each' (15 November 1936).

Besides my parents, other relations and local dignitaries, occasional Sunday lunchers included old friends of the family (such as Professor H.S. Foxwell, Mrs Alfred Marshall or Dr Harry Bond), Maynard's particular economist friends (notably Richard (now Lord) Kahn and Piero Sraffa) and a few undergraduates. In a letter to Lydia (1 December 1935) Maynard wrote,

> An enormous party at Harvey Rd today including Piero [Sraffa] ... Old Dr Bond, who was there, reminisced how he used to go with Archer to the Café in Rome where Ibsen took his coffee and Archer would go across and speak with the terrifying old gentleman, but Harry Bond never dared.

But in general I have found Maynard's letters to Lydia of little help

in evoking the atmosphere of Sunday lunch; he was in too much of
a hurry when writing and too discreet. Besides, his letters were
largely taken up with tedious details of college business, and of the
little walks which he used to take in Cambridge, during time
snatched from his duties, to buy books, second-hand furniture for
Tilton, or even shirts.

After the meal my grandfather withdrew to the study for his
afternoon nap, which he had taken daily since time immemorial,
while the others repaired to the drawing-room, situated to the
south, overlooking the garden. Since my grandparents always sat
together in the study when they were alone, or entertaining grand-
children, the drawing-room felt uninhabited, dead – it was even
more hideously furnished than the dining-room, though its appearance was much relieved by the many 'Nonesuch' volumes, edited
by Maynard's brother, Geoffrey, which were on the shelves. But
overlooking the garden was a lovely addition to the house, a
strongly-built open wooden verandah, with wicker chairs, sweet
briars and steps down to the demure and charming garden. Originally a small strip behind the house, the garden had been enlarged by
discreet purchases and had become T-shaped, the asparagus bed,
trained apple-trees and gooseberry bushes, which were my grandfather's delight, being invisible from the verandah.

The study was the life and soul of the house. Originally part of
the next-door house, after its annexation it had been separated from
the dining-room by two doors, one covered with green baize, so
that my grandfather should not be disturbed when dozing. My
grandmother sat to the north, at her desk facing the road, answering
all letters by return; my grandfather's roll-top desk was to the east,
facing the wall. They nearly always sat at their desks, unless they
were taking tea or entertaining visitors, though my grandfather
sometimes decided to sit by the fire reading the novels of Rafael
Sabatini who, born in 1875, was his junior by twenty-three years.
According to my memories of the mid-1930s, my grandfather's
constant occupation at his desk was philately, his valuable collection
being attached to neat sheets, ruled by himself. In earlier years he
had collected butterflies with Geoffrey, and elegant, expensive,
wooden butterfly cabinets were ranged in the study which was
otherwise almost entirely book-lined, the heavy wooden shelves
containing runs of many learned journals and university records,
putting our modern white airiness to shame. A reproduction of

35 Lydia at Garsington Manor, Oxfordshire, home of Lady Ottoline Morrell, 1925

36 & 37 Lydia Lopokova in a
divertissement, *Scotch Reel*, at the Royal
Opera House, Covent Garden, in 1922; and
Duncan Grant's drawing, *L'Ecossaise*, of her
in this part

[Duncan Grant]

38 & 39 Lydia Lopokova in *The Postman*,
London Coliseum, 1925; and Nikolai
Legat's cartoon of her in this part

40 Lopokova as The Lady in *Follow Your Saint: The Passionate Pavane* at the London Arts
Theatre, 1930

41 & 42 *Above:* Lydia Lopokova and Frederick Ashton in The Tango Pasadoble from *Façade*, Camargo Society, Cambridge Theatre, 1931

Right: Lydia Lopokova and Leonid Massine in *Ragtime*, Royal Opera House, Covent Garden, 1922

44 *Above:* Mrs Maynard Keynes with
her husband at the Liberal Summer
School in Cambridge, 1927

45 *Above, right:* Lydia and Maynard
Keynes at Tilton, 1927

46 *Below:* Double portrait of Lydia and
Maynard Keynes by William Roberts,
1932

47 *Right:* Lady Keynes at the Bretton
Woods Monetary Conference, USA,
1944

48 *Above:* Lydia Lopokova with Anton Dolin and George
Balanchine in the ballet *Jealousy* from the early British sound
film *Dark Red Roses*, 1929
49 *Below: The Tale of a Soldier* (later, *A Soldier's Tale*) at the
ADC Theatre, Cambridge, 1928: Boris Ord, conductor; Lydia
Lopokova, The Princess; Hedley Briggs, The Devil; Michael
Redgrave, The Soldier; and Dennis Arundell, The Reader
50 *Right:* Lydia Lopokova as Nora Helmer in *A Doll's House*,
Cambridge Arts Theatre, 1936

51 *Above:* Lydia at
Gordon Square, 1951

52 *Left:* Lydia in old
age, 1980

Leonardo's *Last Supper* was over the mantelpiece and there was space elsewhere for a few photographs (of surprising excellence) of the three Keynes children. The room, though cold, was warmer than the rest of the house; it was heated by a coal fire, which usually consisted of a single, mildly-glowing lump which I was too apt to encourage with the poker. Neither of the desk-lovers ever gave the faintest hint of being disturbed at their labours by an abruptly entering grandchild (of course, in those days the front door was never locked by day), the invariable warmth of welcome contrasting with the physical temperature.

My grandfather was very, very old and I believe (though there are some who differ) that he much enjoyed this state, except when incapacitated by various illnesses. He had a special dignity, kindness and courtesy. He wore hand-made shoes, which needed a button-hook. Handsome, gay and dapper in his youth, he had long been immensely bald.

Timorously, Lydia may have first entered this house some ten years before these memories begin. Anyway, by February 1924, over a year before her marriage to Maynard and before she was confident of being granted a divorce from her former husband, she was on intimate terms with her future mother-in-law, as she says in a letter to Maynard. 'We, your mother and I, unloaded our feelings for you and for each other in relation of your being our entire idol.' In March 1927 she reports meeting her in-laws at my parents' house in Highgate, London:

> From 1 o'clock till after tea I have been with M.i.l. and F.i.l. in Highgate, she has read her *own* speech, it was very touching, we held each other's hand and ended with a mutual kiss ... I used buses extravagantly as I wanted to suck the spring air.

But despite her intimacy with my grandmother, and her effervescent effect on Harvey Road, I am sure that the large gatherings oppressed her, so that she was obliged to put on her very best performance on entering. Of course, in any company, other than the small and domestic, her aesthetic and conscientious purpose had always necessitated a *performance*; and her very great sense of discretion might not have allowed her to mention, even to Maynard, the special problems at Harvey Road, though her visits there must have tired her.

I can recall the uproarious delight caused by Lydia's normally belated arrival in the dining-room at 6 Harvey Road, in one of her tiny, cheeky hats. The great aunts and uncles, unhinged by such unfamiliar sensations, forgot their need to disapprove and were shaken by giggles. Fil patiently resumed his carving. There were many unaccustomed embraces. Unfortunately, no letters record Lydia's own feelings, for Maynard was always there as well.

Some very discreet people make a point of appearing to be exceptionally indiscreet: both Maynard and Lydia were like this. At the Sunday lunches Maynard appeared to tell *all* to his parents, while actually saying nothing about many topics which would not only have shocked them but would really have been unimaginable: their sexual *mores* had nothing in common, even less than their furniture. Lydia was enchanting, partly because she appeared to be saying things which the relatives would have expected to have found profoundly shocking; the reason they were not shocked is that she was 'unshocking' – i.e. deeply discreet.

With the exception of Vanessa Bell, whose very fecundity made her the mother of Bloomsbury (she had two children by Clive Bell and one by Duncan Grant), the core members of old Bloomsbury were nearly all childless. It was no accident that Virginia and Leonard Woolf, Lytton Strachey, Saxon Sydney-Turner, E.M. Forster, Arthur Waley, Gerald Shove ... all, like Maynard Keynes, lacked children. It is not sufficient to regard the homosexual propensities of some of these people as an instinctive protest against Victorian philoprogenitiveness as such, for the apprehension that children, with their high animal spirits, might impair their artistic and intellectual creativity seemed positively frightening. Though there is some slight evidence that Maynard and Lydia regretted their childlessness, I think that Maynard was in too much of a hurry, and too much a child of 6 Harvey Road, to have been likely to have achieved fatherhood; and surely he would have been inadequate as a father, never having outgrown his own precosity?

Maynard predeceased both of his parents, (one of whom died at the age of ninety-six and the other at ninety-seven) and was quite unlike most members of old Bloomsbury (notably the Stephen siblings, who founded Bloomsbury owing to being orphaned as early as 1903) in the extraordinary continuity provided by 6 Harvey Road, which, as a house and home, was nearly sixty-four years old at the time of his death in 1946. Having myself been spiritually more a child of Harvey Road than of my parental home in Highgate,

which had been bought in 1923, I have some inkling of the dangers
of never growing away from such a long-standing habitation,
because there was so much old-fashioned and familiar love around.

Concern about ill health in the family also made leaving home
difficult. Victorian and Edwardian middle-class parents were ob-
sessed by the probability that death would follow illness, however
slight, and transmitted their fears to their children. Admittedly, in
Maynard's case his parents' apprehensions had some justification,
for, as a young man, he had twice narrowly escaped death. When he
was at King's College and Lydia was at Gordon Square he used to
call for his mother when ill, as he recounts in a letter to Lydia:

> The last two days I have been having a pain in the side of my
> stomach – not much but enough to wake my curiosity. So today
> I telephoned to Mil to come to touch it. She thought it might be
> my gall-bladder a little wrong, and so sent me to Uncle W. [Sir
> Walter Langdon-Brown, then Regius Professor of Physic at
> Cambridge.] But he says that it is not in the right position for that
> ... but is probably an adhesion from my old long-ago appendi-
> citis. So my curiosity is satisfied, and I have nothing to worry
> about.   13 February 1933

Again: 'I am playing the invalid for a couple of days ... Mil came
around with a splendid new contraption for spraying the throat' (22
October 1933). In January 1937, at the onset of his very serious
illness, it was his father who took command: 'My breathing muscles
were so wonky today that I only just managed to walk to Harvey
Rd. So Fil in a loud voice, strong will power and a most tyrannical
manner insisted on sending for his favourite doctor to see me' (24
January 1937).

It was not long after this that Lydia assumed full charge of his
health for the rest of his life.

Extreme remedies were sometimes resorted to. My grandmother,
who believed that her constitution resented all fresh fruit and veget-
ables, had all her teeth extracted in her seventies, not because of
decay but in the false belief that she would feel better as a result. My
grandfather's deep pessimism was associated with severe migraines.
But bad health could also be a laughing matter. After suffering very
bad health throughout the winter of 1931–2, John Neville Keynes
recovered in time to fulfil his duties as 'Mayoress' of Cambridge in
1932–3. 'Fil in the highest spirits,' wrote Maynard to Lydia, 'saying

that he has a bad knee, a bad head, a bad arm and bad something else, but he has forgotten what it is' (30 October 1932). Mentally and physically infirm again in 1934, Fil yet declared that he would go up to London to see Lydia perform in Ibsen's *A Doll's House*:

A quiet lunch at Harvey Rd. Fil looks well but declares that he is very infirm. He can only walk the length of the garden on his legs, and feels that he will never play golf again. He still declares that he will come to the Doll's House if he gets any stronger than he is now. I hope he will.

Maynard to Lydia, 11 February 1934

At lunchtime during the thirties it would have been easy to suppose that Maynard's more fundamental attachment was to his eager and talkative mother, whom we all adored; but this was because his father (who was nine years older than his mother) derived so much pleasure from the golden silence of very great age, which had enhanced his life-long shyness and reserve and, incidentally, had reduced his deep pessimism. Maynard was usually very reticent about his love for his father. But deep though this was, he seldom, if ever, acknowledged his intellectual debt to him or gave any hint that his revolt against the neo-classical economists, which reached its final expression in his *General Theory of Employment, Interest and Money* of 1936, intimately involved his father, who was, after all, the author of (among other works) an excellent book on economics, *The Scope and Method of Political Economy* (1890), a work which is being currently reissued. Even in his splendid tribute to his father at a luncheon held in King's College in August 1942, to celebrate his ninetieth birthday and diamond wedding, he wholly ignored his father's intellectual, as distinct from administrative, achievements.

After saying that his father had always seemed to him at all times in the last sixty years to have been the *same* age, he continued,

I should like to imagine him as he was *before* I knew him.... Elegant, mid-Victorian high-brow, reading Swinburne, Mere-dith, Ibsen, buying William Morris wall-paper, whiskered, modest and industrious, but rather rich, rather pleasure-loving, rather extravagant within carefully set limits, most generous, very sociable; loved entertaining, wine, games, novels, theatre, travel....

He became a perfect, loveable, dependable parent, generous, reserved and shy, leaving you always to your own will and judgement but not concealing his own counsel. . . .

. . . I was able to see him for a long period as he was in the University. For thirty-three years he was one of the best administrators there ever was, and during those years this University was a better place in my judgement than it has ever been before or since. . . .

Maynard never entirely freed himself from the influence of the Harvey Road furniture, though with the help of Duncan Grant, Vanessa Bell and a few others, he made slight efforts to do so. I have alluded to his Cambridge walks, when he used to buy second-hand furniture for Tilton. As emerges from his letters to Lydia, he was very casual in his approach to these purchases; in one of them he mentions his unfortunate love of auctions:

I have taken quite a pleasant holiday today sitting between Mil and Fil at Uncle Albert's [Albert Lloyd, the late husband of Florence Keynes's sister Jessie] sale – you know how I love an auction. Since the prices were very poor, I felt I had to assist the bidding to get them up a bit. . . . The result was I had to buy rather an awful lot, including some entirely by mistake, but also a few 'genuine bargains'. But don't be afraid. Everything will be kept in the house until you arrive here; you shall choose what you want; and everything else will be given away and shall not inhabit either London or Tilton.

I swear that is the bargain between you and me.

20 November 1936

While rejecting Victorian sideboards, he was as uninterested in good antiques as in good modern design; above all, he wanted to be comfortable and to stretch his legs in a deep easy chair, while holding a green baize writing board. At Tilton, he also had a fine, comfortable, Victorian bed, on huge cast-iron casters, with wicker ends, where most of his original, solitary thoughts may have occurred.

It was at Tilton that Maynard, with Lydia's encouragement, indulged his love of literature. He was not only a poet *manqué*, who sometimes over-embellished his prose as a result, but (unlike his brother and sister) lacked the power to express himself artistically in any other medium and had no real outlet for his aesthetic feelings.

The advent of Lydia changed all this. Certainly, she was already a perfectly formed and trained artistic personality when he first met her; certainly, she was not in any sense his toy; yet, somehow, she became *his* discovery, *his* creation, the evocation of his own frustrated artistic humanity. Besides, when at Tilton, they could read so much poetry together, his soft, rounded sensuous Victorian tones contrasting so delightfully with Lydia's idiosyncratic, versatile, pertly poetic mispronunciations.

George ('Dadie') Rylands says that it was at The Knoll, Studland, a Dorset house which Maynard had rented in September 1923 for entertaining his friends (including the Woolfs and Raymond Mortimer, as well as Rylands), that Maynard introduced Lydia to Shakespeare in English – which she often read later for her private pleasure. Lydia always regretted that she had had so few opportunities to perform, or read, Shakespeare in public. Why was this? Certainly it was hard to comprehend the hostile criticism of her accent in performances of Ibsen. Although she was absurdly ill cast as Olivia in *Twelfth Night*, Rylands believes that a number of Shakespearean roles, such as Miranda or Ariel (though not Puck) would have fitted her, and he thinks that her performance as the lady in Milton's *Comus* (in the masque *Beauty, Truth and Rarity*, performed at the Arts Theatre, London, in December 1930) was 'the most enchanting thing she ever did'. In a letter to Rylands dated 25 December that year Lydia wrote,

> Here I am a quiet woman in the Sussex Downs contemplating over our season and what a happy affair it has been.... I look forward when we shall conspire another programme but *oh* it is so difficult....

She lacked persistent, long-term ambition, as many events in her tumultuous early professional life showed; as a result she was less well known in verse-speaking roles than she would have wished.

After dinner at Tilton was the time for the reading aloud of Shakespeare, Ibsen, Chekhov and other writers – I remember *Uncle Vanya* as a special favourite. During the years 1930–37 the economist Richard Kahn (Lord Kahn) was a much more regular visitor to Tilton than anyone else, especially after he had become second bursar at King's College when he was there for part of most university vacations. I am most grateful to him for his reminiscences of the rhythm of life at Tilton during those years. All Maynard's serious writing, he reports, was done in the morning – no more than three hours daily. Lydia enjoyed solitary walks and pottering and as her main interest lay in helping Maynard to get on with his important work, she was happy that he and Kahn should walk together in the afternoon discussing economics and college business. Then all three would usually reassemble in the drawing-room for tea, conversation and reading, though they occasionally visited nearby Brighton where they might speculate about the characters of the people they saw on the pier. No alcohol would have been served at lunch and they might have contented themselves with a post-prandial brandy in the evening.

Kahn praises Lydia as a marvellous conversationalist. He knows of no marriage which was so happy and he cannot remember a single angry word passing between the couple at Tilton. Maynard's life had been transformed by Lydia as was shown by his diminished restlessness and increased devotion to creative work. 'How', asks Kahn 'could two such entirely different people get on so well? To see Maynard's countenance when Lydia visited him in Cambridge was remarkable – his face lit up.'

During Maynard's most creative years he must have spent about half the year at Tilton. He seldom visited Cambridge out of Full Term. As H.G. Durnford wrote in the collection of memoirs published by King's College in 1949, *John Maynard Keynes, 1883–1946*, 'it seemed as if he needed the pulse and movement of the College working in all its arteries to keep him happy'. Also, at that time he seldom went abroad.

Despite her mixed Siberian and Scottish blood, Lydia always regarded herself as fundamentally a Russian peasant – one who had accidentally followed her elder brother into a career in dancing. She was, of course, wrong about this, since until she was forced by war time shortages to open tins of Frankfurters she had had few manual pursuits. In one's unreliable memory the sun shone so constantly that she was usually sitting bare-breasted beneath it, in the garden with her back to the house. Unlike Maynard she was not given to weeding.

Once each vacation they would visit Virginia and Leonard Woolf at Rodmell, which was nearby. On one particular Saturday, Kahn, as an Orthodox Jew, insisted on walking there over the downs, while Maynard and Lydia took a car for part of the way. Unfortunately they got lost on the Ouse marshes; Lydia became hysterical

and Maynard had difficulty with some playful horses they encountered. Much anxiety resulted from their lateness.

As is well known, two of Maynard's most extraordinary characteristics were his ability to turn his attention from one matter to
another (from pig-rearing to theorems, for example) at a moment's
notice, and his genuine power of relaxation amid deep preoccupation. Whereas in Cambridge he was involved in a strict, rigid
routine, at Tilton there was a more harmonious diurnal rhythm.

Although Lydia could seldom be persuaded to visit Cambridge
– Kahn attributes this partly to her fear of trains – we can better
appreciate the charms of Maynard's life at Tilton with her, if his
Cambridge routine is briefly outlined, again with the help of
Richard Kahn. Arriving by train on Friday afternoon, he would be
ready to supervise a number of students at 6.30 p.m., having read
their essays in advance. On Saturday morning there was often a
meeting of the College Council or Governing Body; in the afternoon he often visited second-hand bookshops with Piero Sraffa.
Sunday morning was devoted to writing his current book. (Reclining in an armchair, he wrote rapidly in pencil, despatching the
manuscript straight to the printer, who sent him sets of galley proofs
which he distributed to his professional colleagues for criticism.)
Then there was usually lunch at Harvey Road. Monday was largely
devoted to bursarial work, but was also the day on which he gave
his university lectures – only eight in the year for he had long since
ceased to hold a university lecturing post. His famous political
economy club also met fortnightly on Monday, in his rooms after
dinner. He worked in bed in the mornings, after reading newspapers
and letters, getting up at about 9.45 a.m. He spent most of his
evenings in King's, often in the senior combination room, where he
was very approachable, though generally pursuing his own occupa-
tions, such as reading or playing patience. He usually returned to
London, and Lydia, on Tuesday – certainly in April 1934 he reported
spending his first Wednesday in Cambridge for nearly twenty years.
The routine ended after his serious illness, which began in May 1937,
and nothing was ever the same again.

Many people think that it was only because of Lydia's care and
devoted nursing that Maynard survived for nearly nine years after
his first serious heart attack. Strict though she was, especially in
denying access by his friends, she never tired or irritated him by her

attentions – partly because, as Rylands suggests, 'he enjoyed a nur-sery atmosphere'. Besides, Maynard had always preferred a reclining position and it was no hardship when Lydia suddenly rushed for some ice packs which she applied to his horizontal chest. Who first recommended these packs I do not know, but they certainly dis-turbed the harmony of lunch at Harvey Road.

According to Roy Harrod's biography (*The Life of John Maynard Keynes*, 1951, p. 495), it was on 7 June 1940 that Maynard had a good report from Dr Plesch, his revered physician, who pronounced him 'fit for any moderate activity' – perhaps he had become invi-gorated by the news from the German front. It was in that month that he was asked to join the Consultative Council of Churchill's new Chancellor of the Exchequer, Sir Kingsley Wood, a room in the Treasury being provided for him in July. Now he lived mostly in Gordon Square, working as a full-time 'unpaid civil servant'. Lydia's medical regime was much relaxed.

Unlike Maynard, I was so frightened of bombs that my memory of the six months or so in which I took refuge at 46 Gordon Square between September 1940 and May 1941 (when Maynard, accom-panied by Lydia as his 'nurse', left by air for Lisbon on the way to the United States) are very hazy – much hazier than those of pre-war Harvey Road. As Maynard reported to Lydia (then at Tilton) in a letter of 16 September announcing my arrival, he was to sleep in the basement kitchen, I in the wine cellar (where I had the companionship of Cézanne's early painting, *L'Oncle Dominique*), and various other people in the pantry and passages. On the 17th he wrote to Lydia again, telling her that his devoted secretary, Mrs Stephens, had also joined us in the basement – her neighbourhood had been so knocked about that she lacked gas, water and electricity. He added,

> I went home quietly to lunch, rested on my couch both before and after lunch and opened a glass of tongue! ... The bombs we heard whistling past us last night landed in Fitzroy Square and Fitzroy St. Tell Vanessa and Duncan that their studios are still intact, although those higher up the street have disappeared.... We were consoled to find that even if these bombs had fallen on 46, we should have been all right in the basement.

On 18 September Maynard told Lydia that our neighbourhood had been quieter and that we had 'all slept in our bunks rather like life on board ship'. According to Harrod, we were all obliged to evacuate No. 46 for as long as three weeks owing to an unexploded bomb that fell nearby on that day while we were dining in the kitchen. According to my recollection, however, we very soon returned to the house, which had, indeed, been slightly damaged by a landmine which had fallen nearby. However this may have been, Maynard soon abandoned the basement for the comfort of his bedroom on the ground floor. Though there was a shelter under the Gordon Square garden he never entered it. I once retreated there briefly, only to suffer agonies of 'mourning' for the inhabitants of No. 46, which I was certain had been destroyed, though it turned out that it was undamaged. Subsequently, I always slept in the basement cupboard under the stone stairs.

By this time Lydia had abandoned all interest in her appearance – an interest which was never to be regained. Very different was Maynard's old friend, Margot, Lady Oxford, who braved the blitz one evening to enjoy dinner in our kitchen, attired in a white satin full-length gown. As always at dinner, whatever the company, Maynard was genial, talkative and relaxed, alcohol being no longer lacking. After dinner we repaired to the first-floor library, where his valuable books were continuing to defy the bombs.

After some date in 1940, which I cannot now recollect, Maynard seldom slept at Gordon Square, and usually commuted to the Treasury from Tilton. Others of us, including Mrs Stephens, continued to endure the basement siege. After returning from the United States in the summer of 1941, however, Maynard sometimes stayed at Gordon Square. In 1979 Henry Moore told me in casual conversation that he had once talked to Maynard for some forty-five minutes while he was lying in bed at Gordon Square, as Maynard was resolved to buy some of his Underground war shelter drawings.

No. 46 Gordon Square still stands intact today, having been embellished, comparatively recently, by one of the Greater London Council's commemorative blue plaques, recording Maynard's 'occupation' for over thirty years, from 1916 to 1946.

Lydia Lopokova

David Garnett

At the first sight of Lydia, I fell in love – the love of the moth for the star. She was dancing in *The Good-humoured Ladies* with Massine. It was a love full of respect and of tenderness. For though her body was obviously as strong and as elastic as whalebone, she was, I knew, vulnerable: her spirit sensitive and responsive.

That I should ever meet her, speak to her, or even gaze in adoration, except from the gallery, seemed impossible. But actually the miracle came about at once, when Lady Ottoline Morrell pushed ahead of me, and I followed, to Massine's dressing-room, and then Lydia appeared, vigorous, laughing, talking and wiping greasepaint off her forehead.

I saw her again at parties given by Clive and Vanessa. Duncan Grant and she appreciated each other from the first.

I only got to know her after she had married Maynard – it seemed to me that they were ideally suited. He amused and protective, Lydia turning constantly to him for the sympathy and approbation which were always forthcoming.

One day Maynard asked me if I would collaborate in – or ghost – an article which Lydia was to write for the *Evening News*. It was delightful. We talked it over. I think I gave Lydia confidence – but I hardly wrote anything myself – the whole point seemed to me not Lydia's ideas about cookery but her enchanting use of the English language. I haven't seen the article for forty years or so, but I remember that she began her recipe for sorrel soup with the words: 'You can find a bland grass growing in the fields ...' 'Bland' is the last adjective I should use to describe the sharp acidity of sorrel, but I left the readers of the *Evening News* to search for this grass before they could melt it in butter thickened with flour, and then stir in milk and cream with an egg yolk liaison at the last minute.

When I owned an aeroplane with Jamie Hamilton (we flew it on alternate weekends) Maynard invited me to Tilton and I flew down. I knew the fields round Charleston and Tilton well, but I had to select one where there were not any cattle and not too many trees. I spent some time flying round, incidentally scaring Roger Fry into driving into a gatepost, and finally landed in the field behind Charleston. I was pegging down the little Klemm, when a car drove up. Lydia got out and rushed towards me followed by Maynard and Sam Courtauld, who was my fellow-guest. Lydia flung her arms round my neck and turned to Sam.

'Is not Boony a hero?' she exclaimed, and getting only a faint acquiescence, repeated, 'Boony, you are my hero.' Sam Courtauld gave me a sympathetic smile.

What can I say about that weekend? We three men rejoiced in watching her, hearing her eager voice. And then, just as the sun recedes and all the colour changes – like that – a look of sadness, of doubt eclipsed her gay vitality. What was she thinking? Was she feeling lost in a strange country? She turned to Maynard, and a look from him restored her. There was the tough side, too. She kept that wonderful elastic body fit doing high kicks over the bar in her room at Tilton, holding her slippered toe and turning in a slow pirouette upon the point . . . No longer the great ballerina, she delighted us by her acting. But instead of 'Bravo!' I would have liked to call: 'Loppy – we love you.' After the applause of thousands in all the capitals, we three were the lucky few.

I have been asked about 'her non-acceptance by Bloomsbury'. Unless that is a polite euphemism for Vanessa's violent opposition to Maynard's marriage, I do not know what is meant. Clive Bell and Duncan Grant were charmed by her from the first moment. Vanessa always opposed the marriages of her friends, although she herself accepted the social convenience of being a married woman. But her opposition to Maynard's marriage was more violent and embittered than usual, because she had come to feel over the years that he was part of her household. Duncan was acutely distressed by Vanessa's hostility to the marriage, and when I once referred to it, wept and could not reply.

Thanks to Maynard's understanding and affection, he did not show resentment, and time, as always, healed the wound. The fact of Lydia's becoming a member of the Memoir Club helped. It also very soon became obvious that Lydia and Maynard were complementary. It was due to Duncan Grant that Maynard started his collection of pictures, but it was due to Lydia that he made ballet and opera a national concern, and that he got the Arts Theatre built in Cambridge. The Arts Council is his posthumous memorial.

One of my memories of Lydia is at parties in 46 Gordon Square, singing Victorian drawing-room ballads – set to music by Major Bartle Grant, Duncan's father. With what a pleading voice and pathetic expression did she utter the absurd lines:

> Oh, my earrings, my earrings:
> They have fallen down the well,
> And how to tell my Mirza
> I cannot, cannot tell.

Lydia's letters to Maynard

Polly Hill

During the years before Maynard's illness of 1937 many letters passed annually between Maynard and Lydia, since, during Full Term in Cambridge, he usually spent part of the week there, while she remained in Gordon Square in London, and daily letters were then the rule. The excerpts from Lydia's letters to Maynard, which I provide in this chapter, show her to be one of the most piquant, perspicacious, touching and humorous personalities of our time: I think there is no more effective way of conveying the true flavour of her magic than by citing them. (In doing so, I have taken the liberty of correcting some obvious slips, while retaining some of her characteristic, persistent, often intentional mis-spellings and un-grammatical phrases, which accurately convey the flavour of her impishness – though not the delights of her strong Russian accent.) The dates are tentative in some cases, most of the original envelopes being lost and the letters themselves being undated.

As a correspondent Lydia shared her husband's discretion, but was much more interesting and lively. From the beginning of their relationship, which pre-dated their marriage in 1925, Lydia realized the need to encourage Maynard's creativity and endeavoured to take a keen interest in his work. In the early years of her love for him she went so far as to comment on his economic and political writings, unintelligible though they were to her:

> 'Even I a non economic person see that deflation in the extreme just as bad as inflation in the extreme, also no real salvation for the unemployed, no free trade but 'preferences' all over, that will not improve the situation.'
>
> October 1923

North Pole is ascending on us. . . . I live with the fire as never before, reading *Monetary Reform* [Maynard's recently published book]. I arrive to capital levy and ended the chapter on the situation in France. I live to read financial literature with taste.

November 1923

I told them that I reached the 'quantity theory of money' moment and could not continue and yet would not follow your suggestion that all unintellectual readers may close their eyes for this especial chapter. I did not tell them but I feel that if I escape this chapter I am not an advanced person. How painful would to become such.

December 1923

My full admiration for your *Monetary Reform*; there is such fresh literary style of your own, zest of life in your constructive sentences and although Purchasing Power Parity or Forward Market in Exchanges are pure matters and more difficult to grasp for a usual person, there is always a holding interest. With 'alternative aims' I read it to the end with stimulus.

January 1924

Oh Maynardochka, do have more leisure and no overwork; when you come to London I shall be your jester and even inquire into 'Bank rate' or 'credit cycle', as for cotton I see that it stands up with 'vital tempo'.

November 1924

I am very glad you wrote about 'the Bank rate' as it is the most appropriate sphere to have your reflexions on it at the moment, while I had such nice heart-head functions as ever to be with you.

March 1925

Many of the earliest letters (in particular) include enormous black, effective deletion marks, for Lydia was a conscious and careful stylist, much interested in dictionaries and proper word usage:

Is there any resemblance between you and me. No! So different that it becomes attractive. I want to wrap up around you and give the *abundance* of my feeling. For this specially designed word I had to look into the dictionary. I did not know how this process spoke in English.

April 1922

Dobbie's Lydia is charming. [The artist Frank Dobson was sculpting her head.] She has not the hair yet, nor the last cover of the skin, but she is such as her mother nursed her in womb. (Dictionary also gives uterus but womb is such a beautiful word if I would be poetess I would use it in great many works.)

October 1923

When a friend saw a basket she was carrying on arrival in Paris to dance

... she thought perhaps there is a 'cadavre' in it, why should I carry such a big one to Paris, I replied 'shoes and dictionaries', both important elements in human nature.

April 1924

It is long time that I am spending in Paris ... I come after the theatre late, but I see glorious moon, and the world from the window appears such a *magnetiser*. This word is learned from dictionary, but it's application is more favourable than magic. I am filled with a forward outlook for your arrival.

June 1924

Innovatory and versatile, she invented many varieties of endearment to end her letters, which were reports on events and sensations rather than love-letters:

Maynard you are so brilliant I think sometimes I say things not so bright as you expect. Anyhow I try to develop my mind. Your fountain pen speaks such delightful things when I read it I have a smile inside and outside of me. ... Very tender at the same moment exotick kisses. L.

April 1922

I do have a stormy affection for you, 'Maynard' [which she pronounced 'May-nah'] crosses my mind early in the morning into late night. Lydia.

June 1922

I find in my Russian organ an article on Ricardo [the economist]. Very interesting, he was talented and with temperament of activity. But 'cut your losses and let your profits run' was not an idea of mine, after all. With a sad kiss. L.

October 1923

In the spacious inter-war days it was even enjoyable to walk in Bloomsbury, and bus rides were pleasant, the bus numbers being the same as today:

This afternoon your sister Margaret ... stayed till 7 o'clock, then I conducted her with the help of a police to Euston underworld, and after I do not know how I found myself in Mornington Crescent as I saw the tramways I decided it was almost in the country. I took one large road back strolled on and on, bought a Evening Standard to see if there was any humour in London's diary.

February 1924

The crossing of parallel lines if one looks from Euclids geometrical point of vue is absurd, but if it not Euclid it is truth, this is the idea of a revolutionary Russian writer, who breaks Euclid to pieces and strives towards Einstein. I see very little in it, because of ignorance, but you might see new forme in it. ... As it does not rain I like to have my stroll on the bus, this time again I'll take 73, because it is not as old as Euclid and I want to be a revolutionary, also, including kisses to you. L. P.S. I do write 'sometimes absurdity'.

November 1924

Dearest Lank [Maynard's current nickname, meaning 'lanky']: Today was the first rain of the year without wind or cross winds, I put on a makintoch and rambled without umbrella, with fresh waters dipping into my face, neck, etc., most exhhilirating. Elisabeth Ardens would be bankrupt if people knew that they walk with advantage in the rain, and I bought another moth-bag to celebrate what? I dont know; there is a force in my argument, inwardly, but no thought.

May 1936

The letters are very discreet: Lydia never criticized the various members of the Bloomsbury set, of whom she saw a great deal, especially when she was living at 41 Gordon Square before her marriage. (What she thought they thought of her is unknowable and uninteresting, for she lived her own life.) But sometimes she joked – mildly:

Why do I blab so much, I think I ought to be like Lytton [Strachey] when he is in society, but then there is no beard

attached to me, I do not possess such 'virtious property', also that
when your book is ready I will read it and be *very fond* of it.

                                                            November 1924

When I finished your letter last night Virginia [Woolf] came with
L. [Leonard] to offer a seat for 300 club, and besides to borrow
my wig that looks shingled to go to Mary's [Mary Hutchinson's]
party to night, she wants to be a la mode, Leonard hates all parties.

                                                            November 1924

After the theatre in Clive's [Clive Bell's] abode the old Bloomsbury gang with [Raymond] Mortimer, Valerie [Taylor] and me
as additions: Leonard, Virginia, Lytton, Vanessa [Bell], Duncan
[Grant], Valerie and Vita Sackville [West]; everyone was full of
good spirits, conversation in a loud voice, every member produced a laugh. I sat next to Lytton and strangely enough was not
afraid of him, Clive made a fool of himself trying to flirt with
me, so difficult to stop him, as he chose me as the 'victim' for the
evening. Apart from this incident, all was very pleasant. You
were missed, my long one, as you would produce so many crisp
phrases for the occasion. Tonight I will rest and take a bath as I
believe my feet are dirty.

                                                            November 1927

Lydia never bemoaned the little she saw of Maynard, who might
spend more than half of the week in Cambridge during Full Term,
and who was very much taken up with his financial, bibliophilic,
journalistic and allied activities when in London. Only once did she
express any disapproval – though, of course, she often reprimanded
him for working too hard: 'I simply cannot telephone to Osbert
[Sitwell]! I am sure you could change your memoir club for 46
[Gordon Square]: I dare say it is my will, but I do not show it often
and never spoil your engagements' (October 1933). Nor did she
complain of the somewhat tight financial rein on which Maynard
kept her, although he was so rich and extravagant (in certain direc-
tions) himself. In December 1934 she received a £20 fee from the
BBC; she invested this in a fur coat for £35, Maynard being
expected to pay the balance of £15. Of course, she was naturally
extravagant and very chic. Marks and Spencer was not her usual
level, but when she went there to buy chocolates for the staff at
Tilton, their Sussex farmhouse, she wrote, 'Marks and Spencer

attracts me, because so low, it is a sort of swarm of flies and it fascinates me to creep into it with the others, but I couldn't go there every day' (December 1934).

As I have mentioned in an earlier chapter, Maynard and Lydia shared a great love of Shakespeare, and of plays and poetry in general; at Tilton they often used to read aloud together. When alone Lydia sometimes sought to improve her mind: 'With all my activity the day was not a necessary one, I shall find my peace in Shakespeare reading' (May 1924). She regretted never having read Shakespeare in public: 'It is very sad never, never to achieve one's ideal in public in reciting Shakespeare, so I will go to the country of Bar-le-Duc and recite Moliere' (December 1936).

The earlier letters are much taken up with their common interest in the ballet – which, after all, had something in common with lecturing:

> I see how a composition creeps out into a forme out of your lectures; in a different and lesser degree it when I make exercises and then compose dance, of course your head is infinitely more elastic than my legs.
>
> June 1924

> She [Ninette de Valois] went to a lecture by a Douglasite [a supporter of Social Credit] and wants to have an answer from you, why cheap prices are not approved by the anti-Douglasites. I said 'higher prices create more employment' like a parrot, but I do not know why. I suppose that is a fact, and the other chimera.... Well, Lank, you see how well I am, that I write as early as birds make love in the spring. Your Loo-Poo.
>
> May 1933

I end with accounts of three functions that Lydia attended. The second excerpt, an account of an 'intellectual intercourse' meeting held at 3 Victoria Road, London, is from one of the longest letters she ever wrote to Maynard – her daily letters were mostly quite short:

> The audience the high breed of Mayfair.... So many women in the theatre were pregnangt one of them Lady Mosley [first wife of Sir Oswald Mosley] the daughter of Lord Curzon..She had a very big head gear but I was not taken in and looked on her stomach of 9 months instead. Your complete dog L.
>
> May 1924

The moment we arrived we were asked to drink coffee, being negligent to that kind of drink, we mounted on the other floor and were met by rather good looking lady with silver head, red scarf and a good deal of zeal on her, I showed the card and we both were taken Mrs Martineau and I for 2 Miss Keynes. We both protested and then I became famous. By some people I have been congratulated being married (again seeing it in Russian papers). The crowd looked 'bizarre' of course East and West were meeting each other, I advanced myself to Clare Sheridan, a handsome calculated vagabond, who was pleased to see anyone who knew her, I waited till she saw somebody else and tried to get into a situation with a chair near the pedestal, from which Susan Lawrence would be 1st to speak. She was an idealist, nice and mad, all for an idea, but life itself was dead in her. ... Then Clare was much more attractive as a speaker and as a woman, she was asked not mention politicks but who could resist not to drag in such an important item, especially coming from Russia. She and her brother by same circumstances in same places had to travel in bycycles, and all the Russians thought it was Churchill on bycycle with her. ... She was the success of the evening, of course she is a rascal. Then the third member was advertised, he had good intentions, but a face with features one did not notice ... and a hot potato in his mouth when he spoke, a quaker besides, no outer or inner force, but very good intentions. When we survived his speech, we ran it was so hot, perhaps 100 people all breathing at once; when we descended, 3 women addressed each other as 'camarades' so that element was searching for a taxi, like us, poor burgeois. It was really diverting and Mrs M. was very nice company.

December 1924

Dearest Lank: I went to the uncle Walter's lecture, [Sir Walter Langdon-Brown, a great gourmet and portentously fat] that is I was dragged by M.i.l. [Lydia's nickname for her mother-in-law] It was long, dry, but like Uncle W's head and his whole presence in a red gown, every hair was chizelled and curcumsised in fact he looked like a 'debutante'....

October 1936

The Economist's Wife

Austin Robinson

I never knew Lydia as well as did many of the other contributors to this book. Maynard had two lives. His London life of Tuesday to Friday; his Cambridge life of Saturday to Monday. I belonged strictly to his Cambridge life. I had no part, other than as an interested reader or very occasional onlooker, in his Bloomsbury life. From the time that I became his assistant editor of the *Economic Journal* in 1934, I was a small cog in his Cambridge life, usually seeing him on Sunday mornings in the bedroom of his set in King's College, lying in bed surrounded by all the Sunday papers, all the galleys of the *Journal*, manuscripts of articles, and everything else that was relevant or that he happened to be working at.

Lydia in those earlier days was part of his London life. It was only after Maynard took over in May 1937 the flat in St Edward's Passage, looking out over St Edward's churchyard onto the Arts Theatre, that the venue changed and my Sunday morning visit to Maynard at work in bed shifted from his set in King's to the flat.

It was at about this time that Maynard's heart began to give trouble and it became necessary for him to go slow and do less than his abundant energies and capacity for rapid work had made possible in the past. Thus, from 1937 onwards, my visits to Maynard were in slight danger of becoming a tussle in which I tried to relieve him of what I thought were quite unnecessary burdens, and he argued that he preferred to go on as usual. And here Lydia became the referee. When I arrived and was let in by her in her quilted dressing-gown she would tell me quickly how Maynard was and give me a ration of time. She seldom took any part in our discussions. On rare occasions she would encourage Maynard to let me take over something. On other occasions I would feel her unspoken discouragement to press Maynard further. When time was up, or she felt that Maynard was tiring, out she sent me.

From the time of the completion of the Arts Theatre in 1936 and Maynard's need to go slower, the dividing line between the London life and the Cambridge life had become a little less rigid and well defined, if only because Lydia was now more often in Cambridge. I had seen her dance for the only time, I regret to say, in my life in 1933, when the Camargo Society put on a special performance for the World Economic Conference and Lydia danced *Coppélia* with a magic that memory still treasures.

I first got to know Lydia better than on my editorial visits to Maynard when, in the autumn of 1944 and at less than twenty-four hours' notice, I was deputed to accompany them both by ship to Canada and Washington, where Maynard and I each had a part to play in negotiations with the American and Canadian governments about mutual aid during the expected four-year war (which mercifully never took place) against the Japanese after the coming defeat of Germany. Keynes and my then boss, Rab Sinclair, were the heads of the mission; I was heavily involved with Sinclair on the munitions side. The idea was that I should travel with Maynard and brief him on our side of the problems, about which he knew little.

We travelled first to Glasgow and there embarked on a returning troop-ship, the British-operated French liner *Île de France*, which was empty, apart from several thousand German prisoners behind barbed wire below decks, who, poor things, nourished on Goebbels' propaganda, expected hourly to be sent to the bottom. Above decks we nearly had the ship to ourselves and luxuriated in an unwonted diet of unlimited rich Canadian food, with infinite space for relaxing in deck-chairs. Maynard, alas, found it difficult to climb the stairs to the deck (two steps – rest – two steps – rest) and liked to work quietly in their large cabin. To leave him free, Lydia spent her time on deck, and much of the week or ten days that we were at sea – sailing alone, and diverted south of the Azores to avoid U-boat packs on our way to Halifax – she and I lazed, read and talked. From time to time we were joined by a young Wren officer attached to the ship for signals and decoding; having been at Girton, she had recognized all of us. Lydia, as we gossiped, told us of her early days in the St Petersburg Imperial Ballet School, of the martinets who trained them and the relentless training they received, of the youngsters being treated as pets by the Grand Dukes, of dancing there, of dancing later with Diaghilev's company. How I wish I had had just enough sense of what really mattered in life to have recorded for posterity a little of that endlesly rambling conversation!

This dream holiday had to come sooner or later to its end. (When we got back three months later Lydia was rewarded for her care of Maynard, who could not have travelled without her, by being told that she had incurred the severe displeasure of their Lordships of the Admiralty by travelling on a naval ship in wartime without the prior permission of the Board of Admiralty.) At Halifax we were hurried ashore to meet a reception committee before they began to unload the unhappy (though doubtless now much less frightened) German prisoners from below decks. But for Maynard, Lydia and myself a new and equally enjoyable programme was in store. The private saloon of the President of the Canadian National Railway had been sent down to Halifax for us. We were installed in all the luxury of this very comfortable mobile flat, with a saloon and balcony looking out from the rear of the train, our private bedrooms and, not least, a dining-room in which we were regaled at frequent intervals with wonderful meals by the incomparable steward, Romeo, and his wife. We pottered for a couple of days towards Montreal through maple forests, with the leaves just turning. At each stopping-place we were received by the mayor with a speech of welcome for Maynard and an armful of flowers and an enormous box of chocolates for Lydia. My memory of the journey is a confusion of blazing maples, long dishes of roast beef, graded from rare to well done, presented by Romeo, and helping Lydia to consume the avalanche of chocolates – very welcome to the deprived arrivals from England.

At Montreal Maynard and Lydia stayed over to discuss with Lord Cherwell. I had to hurry down to Washington. I saw comparatively little of them over the next few busy weeks, while we were engaged in our separate negotiations. But I was in the same hotel and from time to time breakfasted with them and heard a little of Maynard's frustrations. One memorable afternoon, however, when he was free, I drove out with them to Washington's home, Mount Vernon, and we talked nonsense and absorbed the beauties of that lovely house and its views.

About our return journey to England the less said the better. We travelled in the *Nieuw Amsterdam*, a vast, overcrowded troopship, with some fifteen thousand seasick American soldiers aboard. The passages below deck were stinking drains that one was forced to penetrate at intervals in search of food. Maynard nonetheless managed to write one of his most brilliant cabinet papers while lying on his bunk in his cabin. My only recollection of Lydia is of accompanying her to beard the captain (no-one less exalted could give the necessary order), to tell him that Maynard and Lydia had to be fed in their cabin and that if this was not done we could take no responsibility for his survival and would report to the Prime Minister just as soon as we landed. The necessary order was given. I think it was Lydia's furious eloquence rather than my explanations that won the day.

I have always thought that Lydia was the only possible wife for Maynard. I cannot imagine him married to a blue stocking, least of all to an economist blue stocking. If she were less than completely first-rate he would have despised her. If she had been first-rate he would have broken her heart. All first-rate economic theorists (I hasten to say that I have no claim to be one) have been egocentrics. They have put the pursuit of truth far above the pursuit of friendship. They have had no thoughts of wounds they might be inflicting. A retreat for any reason other than conviction has been cowardice. Mary Marshall, the ex-Newnham wife of the great Alfred Marshall, survived such a relationship only by retreating into utter self-abnegation and service to Alfred. She laughingly called herself his 'foolometer': Alfred would try his drafts out on her, and if she failed to understand them he rewrote them. But Maynard, with an inborn gift of clear exposition, needed no foolometer. What he needed, and found in Lydia, was a person as outstandingly professional as himself in an art in which he was intensely interested, but knew himself to be a layman.

If anyone had asked me five years ago what was Lydia's relationship to Maynard's economics, I would have said that there was 'absolutely none'. I had always supposed that she belonged completely to the leisure moments of his London life – that he deliberately kept her aloof from the strains, stresses and arguments of his economics, and found with her the relaxation that was necessary if he was to retain his sanity. I could not have been more wrong. When, a few years ago, Lydia had to be moved into a nursing home for more continuous care, there were found among her cherished hoards the daily letters which, without fail, Maynard had written to her whenever they were apart. There also survive her daily letters to him.

His absences from her, it must be remembered, were largely on Saturdays, Sundays and Mondays. As one reads, one finds oneself living an unending series of weekends, with all that went into them, from the early 1920s to the late 1930s; thereafter she was seldom apart from him.

What did he write about? I suspect that, like some of the politicians and generals whose diaries have been published, he used his letters to Lydia, as they have clearly used their diaries, as a safety valve from the irritations of the day. He is much more interested than I would have expected in the daily minor ups and downs of his health. We hear of his hours in the bursar's office in King's College. We see him at his regular Sunday lunch with his parents ('Fil' and 'Mil' to Lydia) and often with his brother or sister and their children at 6 Harvey Road. We learn the current gossip about the various Fellows of King's. Above all, we hear about the goings-on – and the intense boredom – of the three or four college and university meetings that he had to attend and of the incompetence of Provost Sheppard as a chairman – and, incidentally, as habitual speculator at Monte Carlo.

We hear constantly in the later years of long arguments with his close friends Ludwig Wittgenstein and Piero Sraffa. We naturally hear at length about the theatre and about plays produced and planned; George ('Dadie') Rylands constantly appears. But in the earlier 1920s he tells her of doings that I, knowing him well only later, had never imagined: riding with Macaulay, the bursar of King's, and stag-hunting with him on Exmoor. There was a streak of the Etonian Englishman in him, as well as of Bloomsbury.

Economics and economists appear only rarely in the letters. Nearly all his serious writing was done in London or at Tilton. He occasionally tells Lydia that he has had a clear day, usually in a vacation, and has made progress with something that he was writing. In October 1932 we find him telling her,

I have become completely absorbed in re-writing my life of Malthus and sit by the hour at my desk copying bits out and composing sentences and wanting to do nothing else with stacks of books round me. What a relief not to be writing arguments! What an easy and agreeable life fanciful writers must have.

Very occasionally he tells Lydia of arguments with other economists about proofs of his books. Of Dennis Robertson we hear
constantly as an actor, or as one with whom Maynard has dined and
has discussed plays and individual performances, but only on one or
two occasions does he appear as a critic:

> Are all the economists mad except Alexander [Lydia's name for
> Richard Kahn] and me? It seems to me so but it can't be true. I
> have just been having a hopeless debate with Dennis. His mind,
> though frightfully ingenious, seems to me to be maliciously per-
> verse. Again it is like arguing with a madman. But when I talk
> with Alexander it is all so quite different.

And in May 1936, after the publication of his book *The General
Theory of Employment, Interest and Money*:

> Hubert [Henderson] came to the Marshall Society yesterday with
> Dennis in the chair, to read his paper against my book. I was
> astonished at the violence of his emotion against it; he thinks it a
> poisonous book; yet when it came to the debate there was very
> little of the argument which he was really prepared to oppose. He
> came off badly in the debate with Joan [Robinson] and Alexander
> and myself barking round him. The undergraduates enjoyed the
> cockfight outrageously. One got the impression that he was not
> really interested in pure economic theory, but much disliked for
> emotional or political reasons some of the practical conclusions to
> which my arguments seem to point. As a theoretical attack there
> was almost nothing to answer.

Allowing for some exaggeration and simplification, I have learned
an immense amount both about Maynard and about Lydia from
reading one side of their correspondence: first, the vastly greater
need for support than I had ever imagined in Maynard, whom I had
believed to be the impregnable, rock-like optimist: his dependence
on her, not only for packing his clothes, choosing his suits and ties,
organising his household and countless small domestic matters, but
also for moral support and sympathy; second, I have learned that,
unknown to most of us, he let her share with him, much as his
mother had done at the time of the Treaty of Versailles, the strains
and stresses of the period when he was gestating the *General Theory*,
told her of his ups and downs, and relied on her strength. She gave

him something that no-one else could possibly give him, and without her he might never have done what he did.

One amusing trifle emerges from an earlier date. Most of us at some moment speculated about Lydia's age. On 13 November, 1931 Maynard teasingly writes to her, 'Well! I have been looking at the Radio Times. You are on every page! And they have found out your age and birthday, so that by cutting it out I shall know it too.' The *Radio Times*, like *Who's Who*, recorded her as having been born on 21 October, 1892. This book would have made a fitting celebration for her ninetieth birthday.

Maynard and Lydia Keynes

Isaiah Berlin

I first met Maynard Keynes when I was placed next to him at dinner at King's College, Cambridge, in the early 1930s, before reading a paper to the Moral Sciences Club. At first he did not speak to me. Then, he turned towards me at the last stage of dinner, when we were eating the sweet. He asked me, 'Why are you here? What are you doing?' I said, 'I am reading a paper to the Moral Sciences Club later this evening.' 'What about?' he asked. I said, 'Pleasure.' It sounded absolutely absurd as I said it. 'What?' he said. 'Pleasure,' I replied, and as I did so it sounded even more absurd the second time. He then said, 'Really. What a ridiculous subject. Now, what are we eating?' – he looked at the menu – 'We are eating "potage de something or other". Why don't you read about that? Just as good a subject.' Then a silence. Then 'What do you think of Whitehead?' I said that the early chapters of *Science and the Modern World* seemed interesting to me. Then – a much longer silence. Then 'I don't agree with you.' After which he turned away from me. I did not see him after that for some time.

The next occasion was at the Arts Theatre, Cambridge, in the second week of its opening in 1936, when Lydia Keynes was acting in *The Master Builder*, by Ibsen. Everyone came up to him and said how marvellous she was, and what a superb actress, and that they had hardly ever seen the part better played. I could not bring myself to speak such words because I thought he would see through them: I thought he saw through the others, too. She was wonderfully spontaneous and had great charm on the stage as well as off it. But she was not made to act Ibsen, and the whole thing was to me acutely embarrassing. I said nothing at all. Once again, I got rather a severe look from him.

After that, I met him four or five times in Washington during the war, when we had long conversations, which I found immensely enjoyable. He was charming to me, delightful to be with, indeed literally fascinating, and certainly the cleverest man I have ever met in my life. His intelligence seemed to me uncanny. He knew how one's sentences would end almost before one began them; his comments were sharp, illuminating, witty, and had an extraordinary – unconveyable – intellectual gaiety, sweep and brilliance. At a dinner in the British Embassy in Washington, I was introduced by someone as 'Professor Berlin'. I said, 'No, no, I am not a professor.' Keynes said, 'And neither am I, and as you may imagine people are always calling me that. When that happpens, I invariably say I reject the indignity without the emolument.' I once asked him for his impression of Lord Halifax, the Ambassador. By 1944, they seemed to me to be flirting with each other. Halifax had great charm when he chose to exercise it, and liked Keynes, but I did not know whether the feeling was mutual. I wondered about this and I asked him. He said, 'Well, I don't know whether I like him, or not, but I find his company agreeable. Not as agreeable as Bob Brand who was the principal representative of the British Treasury in Washington from 1943 is, but agreeable. I was particularly pleased when he said to me, "Lord Keynes, I wonder if you would help us. Would you look at a document about economic policy which my party may soon publish. I know that we do not hold the same views, you and I, but why I should like you to read it is because we don't want to talk rot."' I do not know whether Keynes ever did read the draft Conservative manifesto.

Lord Robbins told me a characteristic story about him. Sir Kingsley Wood, the Chancellor of the Exchequer, died suddenly from a heart attack in 1943. This happened to be at a time when there were informal meetings of the American and British financial experts in Washington. Keynes was head of the British Treasury delegation and Harry Dexter White the head of the American equivalent. Harry White got up at a lunch of the two delegations and said how very distressed his colleagues were at the news of the death of the Chancellor of the Exchequer and that they wished to convey their deep sympathy to the British delegation. Keynes rose to reply, and in his opening remarks said that he wished to thank Mr White for his words, which had greatly touched members of the British delegation, and then said something like this: 'The late Chancellor possessed one gift which I think that some of the highly intelligent and indeed brilliant people around this table might do well to note and perhaps even strive to emulate. No matter how dark, how tortuous, how complicated and how apparently incomprehensible an economic proposition seemed to him to be, he then had the gift of converting it with a few words into a platitude intelligible to the merest child. This is a great political gift, not to be despised, and some of us round this table could do well to cultivate it.' Robbins said, I think, that the Americans seemed rather shocked by this: such words when the corpse was hardly cold. It is probable that Keynes meant exactly what he said. The mixture of truth and irony, the wish to *épater* the solemn, somewhat humourless American officials, was very typical.

I first properly met Lydia Keynes at dinner in the British Embassy in Washington in November 1944. Maynard Keynes was there for the Stage II negotiations of the Lend-Lease agreement, and it was the night of the re-election of President Roosevelt for his fourth term of office. I was supposed to be an expert in American politics, which I was very far from being, but anyway I was summoned for this purpose, and asked to bring charts which some newspaper had printed as a supplement in order that we might follow the election results in the various States as they were announced on the radio after dinner. It was a small dinner party, so far as I can recollect, consisting of Lord and Lady Halifax, Lord and Lady Keynes, the Social Secretary, Miss Irene Boyle, Mr David Bowes-Lyon and myself. I sat next to Lydia Keynes and talked to her in Russian, which evidently pleased her, and she was in a very gay and agreeable mood. She told me about her three journeys in Russia with her husband, and how peculiar these experiences were, and of her curious conversations during one of them, in a sleeping car, with her famous brother, Fedor Lopukhov, the choreographer.

She also said how much she had enjoyed meeting the American Secretary of the Treasury, Mr Henry Morgenthau, who, she said was very fond of her husband, 'very fond of *Maynar'* ', as she called him; he hated all bankers, but approved of liberal economists and liked and admired Keynes. One day, when there was some sharp dispute about some monetary problem, she went to see the Secretary of the Treasury in his office, and reported that she had said to him, 'Mr Morgenthau, *Maynar'* cannot sleep at night. He says he wants sixpence from you: only sixpence more. Why, Mr Morgenthau, why cannot you give *Maynar'* sixpence? I do not know how much money you have, but sixpence is not very much.' And she assured me that Mr Morgenthau had yielded on the issue, and had given sixpence to Keynes, and had congratulated her on being one of the ablest and most skilful negotiators he had ever met in his life. Her intervention actually had effect. The story is confirmed in a letter from Keynes to Sir Richard Hopkins in the British Treasury, London, dated 6 November, 1944, in which he wrote, 'Speaking of Morgy, Lydia has certainly earned her passage money (let alone her maintenance of my good condition).'

In this rather happy mood we went upstairs after dinner, spread the various charts on our knees, and the election results began coming in. After we had heard that the State of Alabama had gone heavily for Mr Roosevelt, Lydia began to look bored by the proceedings, and suddenly said to me, 'Do you like Archie MacLeish?' (MacLeish was the Librarian of Congress and a poet.) Maynard said, 'Shoosh, Lydia, not now.' We went on listening to the results, and after ten or fifteen more, Lydia, who had now become even more restless, said, 'Do you like the President? Roosevelt? Rosie? Do you like Rosie? I like Rosie. Everybody here likes Rosie. Do you like Rosie, too?' 'Shoosh, Lydia, not now,' said Keynes again. After about another dozen results had come in, she spoke again. She was obviously getting very restive and could hold herself in no longer. She turned to me again, 'Do you like Lord Halifax?' The Ambassador was sitting about a yard from me at the time. I was speechless, and produced a neighing sound, I think. Nobody (save the radio) uttered a word. Keynes did not shoosh her this time, but stared straight in front of him with a faint smile on his lips and with his long fingers pointed together upwards. Lord Halifax looking faintly, very faintly, embarrassed, rose from his place, patted his little dachshund, called Frankie, and said, 'I don't think that Frankie is very interested in these goings on, you know. I don't think she is very politically minded. I am going to find out from Harry Hopkins [adviser to President Roosevelt] what the position is,' and he strode out of the room. He came back a few minutes later, and said, 'Harry says it's in the bag,' after which we left. I never met Keynes again. He died less than two years later. But I had several very enjoyable meetings with Lydia, in London, in Cambridge, in Sussex. She talked with great animation about Diaghilev, about the great ballerina Galina Ulanova, about her feelings about Bloomsbury. But I have no clear memories of that now.

Lydia Keynes

Malcolm MacDonald

One of my enthusiasms when I was an undergraduate at Oxford was the Russian Ballet. I had gained my first glimpse of it when, as a young boy, I saw the supreme dancer Anna Pavlova perform one evening in London. That was an unforgettably beautiful, almost magical sight. Through the next several years I went to boarding-school in Hampshire, and during my holidays I usually departed to Scotland, the Norfolk Broads or somewhere else away from Town; so I had little opportunity then to be dazzled by other theatrical stars in the capital.

Later I spent more of my vacations in London. As it happened, those years from 1918 to 1921 coincided with the renowned Diaghilev Ballet Company's earliest seasons there. They were glorious times for audiences who revelled in the grand art of ballet. In Diaghilev's team a remarkable group of geniuses was gathered together under the leadership of the temperamental but brilliant director himself. The principal musical composer was Stravinsky, the chief choreographer Leonide Massine, and among the designers of costumes, décor and scenery were Picasso, Matisse and Derain. As for the dancers, the ballerinas included Lopokova, Tchernicheva, Sokolova, Danilova and Karsavina, whilst the most prominent male performers were Massine, Idzikovsky and Woizikovsky.

Whenever the Diaghilev Company came to London I was one of their zealous devotees. I had little spare cash to spend on entertainments – or anything else – in those days; and I could not afford to sit in a box, among the stalls, or even amidst a circle of the theatre. Instead, I first stood for two or three hours in the queue of other impecunious enthusiasts on the pavement outside the gallery doors, and so qualified in due course to watch the show from 'the gods' within.

From the gallery's Olympian heights I became familiar with *The Sleeping Princess*, *The Three-cornered Hat*, *La Boutique Fantasque* and other enthralling ballets. Their music enchanted me, but what made me truly ecstatic was the dancing. I felt as if I could watch until Kingdom Come its every step, glide, leap, pirouette and other graceful movements enacted with such perfect skill. All my fanatical companions in the gallery evidently felt likewise, for we stayed tensely hushed and motionless – completely spellbound – throughout each scene; but when it ended no other part of the audience burst into such prolonged, thunderous applause.

The dancers appeared like some kind of divinities to me, even though I knew them to be mere mortals. They were artistes who achieved superlatively one of the most lovely of the arts. Among them my favourite masculine performer was Stanislas Idzikovsky, and my favourite female Lydia Lopokova.

At that time I was not acquainted with anyone who moved in distinguished theatrical circles; and so I had no opportunity to meet either my hero or my heroine. I never got nearer to them than the vast distance stretching between 'the gods' and the stage. From that remote, impassable point of separation I watched them night after night and for me they remained dream figures in a gorgeous hallucination occurring in the glare of the footlights.

Nor did I know in those days another celebrated personality who happened to be present every evening in the same playhouse. To me he was just a name printed now and then in the newspapers – and I was completely unaware of his existence in the theatre. He was John Maynard Keynes, the great, world-famous and indeed world-shaking authority on economics. He did not appear in the gleam of the footlights during the ballets; nor was he one of the shadowy figures sitting near me in the gallery. He was lost to my view in the darkness of the auditorium yawning like a chasm below me. Every night (I learned later) he occupied a seat in the stalls.

Keynes was a man of various distinguished attainments. The most potent economist of his generation, and perhaps of the century, he exerted an influence in national and international affairs more profound than that of almost any contemporary statesman. He also had several other claims to fame; and among them was his scholarly interest in the arts. His special passion was music, and he became an eminent patron of both opera and the ballet.

Yet his affection for the ballet was not the prime reason for his nightly attendance in the stalls during the Diaghilev Company's season in London. He had fallen in love with more than the music and dancing; he had given his heart to Lydia Lopokova. And that was little wonder! Her small, slim, lithe figure, poised on tiptoe in an elegant white ballet dress, with her face lit by the inspiration of dance, seemed angelic.

In fact Maynard Keynes was courting her. If I had known this at the time, I would perhaps have dropped something rather crushing on his head from my lofty seat in the gallery. But I was ignorant of the wooing, and so it continued without disturbance. Before long the attraction became mutual on both sides of the orchestra. Lydia fell in love with Maynard; and soon afterwards they became betrothed. Then she retired from the stage and the happy pair got married.

I met them in the flesh for the first time more than twenty years later, when I was the British High Commissioner in Canada. One day in 1944 Lord Keynes (as he had become) arrived in Ottawa to conduct some important financial negotiations with the Canadian Government; and his wife came with him.

I went to meet the distinguished visitors at the airport. On an early summer's morning I waited beside a runway to welcome them. Beside me stood a somewhat formal Canadian Minister of Finance, whilst at our backs were marshalled two rows of his and my officials. They were a parade of solemn-faced financial experts wearing neat black jackets and pin-striped trousers. The Keynes's aeroplane alighted, and we watched it as it taxied slowly towards us. At last it came to a halt twenty yards away, its propellers flipped round a few more times and then stayed still, and its noisy engines suddenly fell silent. An expectant hush enveloped the scene.

A ground-crew wheeled a high stairway to the aircraft's door so that the passengers could alight. As the entrance opened I advanced to greet Lord Keynes – but instead of him a female figure emerged on the platform at the head of the stairs. She looked at me and smiled. How well I remembered that charming and characterful, if rather peasant-like Slavonic face! For a few seconds she hesitated on her high perch – just as I had often seen her stand motionless until the audience's applause died down at her first entry on the stage in Diaghilev's programmes – and then she began to trip down the steps towards me. She no longer wore her neat white ballet dress and tights, but was sumptuously wrapped in a brown fur coat and hat. I thought I detected that her body was somewhat plumper than it had been when I last set eyes on it many years ago; but this did not matter. At once I knew that her personality possessed all its old magic, and that she was not so much Lady Keynes as Lydia Lopokova.

Since she and I had never met, I stepped forward to introduce myself politely to her. But she ran with out-stretched hands towards me, flung her arms round me in a warm embrace when we came together, and before I could say a word exclaimed aloud with a slightly Russian accent, 'Oh, my dear High Commissar, how are you? Last night I dreamed zat I was lying in bed, and zat you were lying in my arms.'

No doubt the Canadian Minister of Finance and our teams of advisers were rather startled by this unorthodox meeting; but with impeccable official decorum they betrayed no hint that they had noticed it. They pretended to be deaf and blind. So far as I was concerned, I hoped that in the hush of the early morning the whole population of Ottawa had overheard my greeting from the great ballerina.

Lord Keynes followed several paces behind her, and his and my exchanges of welcome was also cordial, if rather more conventional. I introduced the two visitors to the waiting Minister and our array of officials. We all chatted together for a while, and then jumped into motor-cars to drive into the city.

An hour later I went with my advisers to call on Keynes in the suite of rooms where he was staying in the Château Laurier Hotel. We were to hold a preliminary talk about the financial negoti-ations which he would start with the Canadian authorities that afternoon.

We sipped cups of coffee and chatted for a while prior to com-mencing serious business. The reason for this delay was that Keynes had misplaced the key to the official red box containing his secret documents and so could not get at the papers which he needed for our discussion. He thought he had given the key to his wife to keep with other precious objects in her handbag; but she declared that he had not done so, and that, in any case, it was not there. Whilst the rest of us conversed about the local weather, the latest war news and other items of topical interest she busied herself in their bedroom searching through the pockets of his trousers, her trinket boxes, various recesses in their suitcases and other likely places – but in vain. She kept passing in and out of the sitting-room where we talked, reporting to him one failure after another. She felt very concerned and uttered little exclamations like, 'Oh, dear Maynard, someone must have stolen ze key' or 'Perhaps you dropped it, Maynard, in ze aeroplane, and it's now on its way back to London.' He remained exceedingly calm in the face of what appeared to be a dangerous disappearance of a top-secret object, expressing the opinion that it would turn up somewhere in due course.

At length he decided to wait for the key no longer, remarking that he could probably remember everything that was written in the documents. We therefore repaired to a private study to start our conference. As he, my officials and I settled round a table, Lydia waved *au-revoir* to us and told Keynes she would go to have a bath and change of dress before a lunch party which the Prime Minister, Mr Mackenzie King, was to give later in their honour. She still wore her fur coat, for the crisis about the missing key had preoccupied her completely ever since their arrival.

We shut the door and started our discussion. Keynes told us the views of the British Government on the matter for negotiation, presenting the case with that brillance of argument for which he was famous. I explained to him the likely opinions of the Canadian Ministers; and we began to analyse the problems to which we must find solutions.

Whilst we were in the midst of considering a difficult point a knock sounded on the door.

Keynes called, 'Come in.'

The door opened, and into the room slipped Lydia Lopokova. She was no longer wrapped in furs; nor did she wear even a dress. For a moment I thought some whim had made her put on a ballet costume, for her long, shapely legs were as exposed as if she wore tights. Then I realized that they were naked, and also that the dramatic skirt of a ballerina's outfit was missing. In fact she wore nothing but a short white chemise (presumably with a pair of brief drawers below) which hung flimsily round her otherwise bare body. In that state of near nudity she stood in apologetic manner casting a half-guilty, half-mischievous look at Keynes as she said, 'Oh Maynard darling, I am so sorry. You did give me ze key; and I forgot zat

I hid it for safety between my little bosoms.' At that she clutched in her hands a ribbon hanging round her neck, and as he lifted it over her head raised from between her breasts – which so far as we could detect were not quite so small as she suggested – the lost article.

Keynes chuckled with laughter, remarked that he had said the treasure would turn up somewhere, and accepted the key from her. She blew him a kiss, turned in a ballerina's pirouette on her toes, glided through the door, and closed it behind her.

During the Keyneses' visit the summer temperature in Ottawa rose very high, reaching a few points above 100° F. The atmosphere was almost intolerably hot not only through daylight hours, but also in the middle of the nights.

One afternoon when I was drinking tea with Lydia and Maynard he described to me a sight which he alleged he had seen in the small, dark hours of that morning. Owing to the breathless heat in their bedroom he could not sleep, and lay uncomfortably conscious on his mattress. He heard Lydia tossing on her near-by bed, evidently also wide awake. Then the sounds of her restless movements ceased, and he became aware of her rising from her couch, quietly opening the door, and stepping into the corridor, where she switched on a light. He rose to see what she was doing, and to enquire whether he could help her. Looking into the passage-way, he observed her perspiring stark-naked figure hastening purposefully along it and then disappearing round a corner leading to their kitchen. Curious, he followed her, and reached the turning in time to see her slip into the kitchen and close its door behind her. He continued his inquisitive pursuit. When he pushed the kitchen door ajar and poked his head into the room he spied her opening the lid of a large ice-box, squeezing her body into the freezing interior, and shutting the lid 'like Alice in Wonderland disappearing down the White Rabbit's tunnel'.

Lydia laughed at his tale; but she did not either confirm or deny its veracity.

After that I often saw Maynard and Lydia, and we became great friends. Sometimes the three of us reminisced together about the earlier days when we were all so near and yet so far in a theatre in London – Lydia dancing on the stage, Maynard sitting in the stalls, and me perched in the gallery. Now and then we went to the ballet together; but we did not part at the theatre door and distribute ourselves in those separate places. We all sat side by side exchanging comments on the music, the dancing and the décor. Lydia's memories were particularly vivid on those occasions, and she often told fascinating stories about her own theatrical experiences, triumphs and sorrows.

She gave us, for instance, her version of the reason why the name of Tchaikovsky's ballet which should be called *The Sleeping Beauty* got changed to *The Sleeping Princess*. In the Diaghilev Company's performance of that classic she was cast to play the heroine's part; but Diaghilev felt bothered on a certain point, and mentioned it to her.

'Lydia,' he said, 'we musn't do anything that might arouse criticism of our production. We must maintain our standards of perfection. The critics might make derogatory remarks about my casting when you play the Sleeping Beauty, because your face is so plain that no one could say you're beautiful. So I think I'll change the title to *The Sleeping Princess*.

She and Maynard were perfect partners in life. They shared many cultural interests, and yet they were in some ways remarkably contrasting personalities. One part of him was the cool, superbly educated intellectual genius, whereas intellectually she was in some ways nearer to an untutored though intuitively wise little *gamine*. Another part of him was the warm artistic enthusiast, and there she came nearer to being his equal in knowledge whilst being also his superior in practice. Each was superlatively distinguished in his or her own main field of endeavour. At the same time they were both charming human beings – friendly, unassuming, intelligent, and unspoilt by their respective fames. Lydia was an entirely natural, uninhibited person who always said exactly what she thought – and her chief thought was that Maynard was the ideal man for whom she would give up everyone and everything else in life. On his side, he loved her very dearly.

In his latter years his health deteriorated; he suffered from a heart weakness which made it essential for him to be careful in all that he did. He never allowed this circumstance to interfere with his important work, prudently taking no unnecessary risk yet generously taking all other chances. She was constantly at his side to help him.

Thus, whenever he had to discuss highly confidential matters with guests at a meal which required that no servants should be present, she herself waited hand and foot on him and them.

I remember one such occasion in Washington when Lord Halifax (then our Ambassador in America), Maynard and I were conferring upon an important secret problem over lunch in the Keynes's hotel rooms. A waiter and butler had brought our foods and wine, put them on a sideboard, and then withdrawn. For the next two hours we sat engrossed in our conversation at the table whilst the great ballerina, Lopokova, played the part of our waitress, periodically flitting silently round us as she served our soup, entrée and sweets and kept our glasses filled with drinks. She never spoke a word until we were about to sip cups of coffee. Our talk was then nearly finished, and as she handed round a tray with milk and sugar Maynard suggested that she should join us for this refreshment.

She put a hand affectionately on his shoulder and said with mock sorrow, 'No, my darling! I used to be ze première ballerina but now I'm just ze second fiddle.'

A Visit to Lopokova in 1951

Cecil Beaton

Cecil Beaton first met Lydia Lopokova when he was a Cambridge under-graduate from 1922 to 1925, and again in the autumn of 1930, when he took photographs of her reciting, acting and dancing in the masque Beauty, Truth and Rarity *which was presented by Maynard Keynes at the Arts Theatre Club, London, in December 1930. He said that he became intimate with Lydia as a result of the photographs, and found her wonderful company, especially because she roared with laughter at everything, and at his 'own silly fantasy' in particular. He placed her 'very, very high, as a marvellous person to know, as a dancer, as a person who was highly trained in managing very well'.*

In July 1951 he was in Brighton for a few weeks at the opening of his play, The Gainsborough Girls, *at the Theatre Royal. The play received bad notices and was not transferred to London. Shortly after the opening, and depressed by the flop, Beaton decided to visit Lydia at her home at Tilton, near Firle village, twelve miles from Brighton. He had first seen her dance for the Diaghilev Company in 1923, and that year made an adverse comment in his diary on her portrait by Roger Fry. After the visit to Tilton, he persuaded her to go to London so that he could photograph her at her home in Gordon Square, but found that 'she loathed to be photo-graphed – but then she had left the stage, I suppose.' In conversation, he said that when he arrived at Tilton he found Lydia 'totally naked, picking raspberries down in the garden', but this was at a later visit than described in the ensuing account, which is an amalgam of Beaton's diary, as actually written, and what has already appeared in print in* The Strenuous Years, The Diaries of Cecil Beaton 1948–55 *(Weidenfeld and Nicolson, London, 1973).*

M.K.

One afternoon, in order to escape from the atmosphere of the theatre, I took a bus and went to Firle to call on that most stimulating and entertaining of all human beings – Lydia Lopokova the dancer. When I first discovered Diaghilev's ballet, the miniscule Lopokova was one of its wittiest adornments. Pert, chubby, with an unhealthy wax-doll quality, Diaghilev considered her downright plain. When he put on *The Sleeping Beauty* with various stars alternating in the main role, and it came to Lydia's turn to dance, he altered the posters to *The Sleeping Princess*. Lopokova could dance classical roles with exquisite grace, but in light roles, she had a staccato way of moving that was funny, original, and completely captivating.

The art of the actor and dancer dies with their performances; it is impossible later to judge their effect on the audiences of their time. My father used to try to convey to me the charms of the Victorian actresses, Connie Gilchrist and Nellie Farren, but their photographs, and even the Whistler portrait of the latter, give us little impression of the spell that they cast. All the pictorial documents of Lopokova are worthless: the photographs particularly misleading. Osbert Sitwell has tried in words, and with a certain success, to describe her quality, and he likened her waxen pallor to that of Christmas roses. But it is useless to try to conjure up Lopokova's contribution to that very original production of *The Good-humoured Ladies* with its Venetian night scene – surely Bakst's masterpiece of mysterious romanticism – except to say that, as the mischievous maid Mariuccia, she supplied a rorty, yet delicate humour that was an indispensable ingredient to an unforgettable and unique evening. When other ballerinas later danced her role they were too pretty and dainty: the ballet lost much of its strangeness as well as fun. Lopokova's indefinable marionette quality embellished *La Boutique Fantasque* and *Petrushka* and these ballets also were never the same without her. But her appearances were somewhat spasmodic. Once the London posters proclaimed 'Russian Dancer Vanishes'; Lopokova was nowhere to be found. After an interval she reappeared, with eyes even brighter periwinkles than before, having had a wonderful time with a stalwart high-ranking Army officer.

It was an equal surprise when it was announced that Lopokova had married Maynard Keynes, the economist and pivotal member of the Duncan Grant, Vanessa and Clive Bell, and Virginia and Leonard Woolf Bloomsbury group. The marriage was a success.

The Bloomsburys were continually amazed by Lydia's innocent *enfant terrible* frankness.

Among her fellow dancers Lydia had a reputation for directness of speech. At one time a certain elderly ballerina in the company was becoming so liberal with her favours that the young men in the *corps de ballet* were apt to arrive exhausted for rehearsals or the performances on stage. Something must be done about the situation. The elderly ballerina's husband must be told to control his wife: she was creating havoc; it was most reprehensible of her to behave like a nymphomaniac. Lydia was shocked at the idea of telling the husband. 'No – no! There is nothing wrong with poor Tania except that she has an irritable womb.'

The Keyneses divided their time between Bloomsbury, Sussex and Cambridge. Legion were the voices about her outspokenness and often embarrassing honesty. A certain well-known lady with a husband and large family was seen orbiting London's 'artistic' circles in the company of Osbert Sitwell. The gossip was that the two were enjoying a twilit romance. Suddenly the lady produced a baby. The church was crowded for the baptism. The baby lay in an elaborate Napoleonic crib in front of the altar. At the end of the ceremony Lydia tripped up the altar steps, peered into the crib, and in a surprised voice for all to hear, said: 'It doesn't *look* like Osbert!'

When Lydia accompanied Maynard to the White House for a large dinner given by Cordell Hull, she was heard, in a lull of conversation, to say to a neighbour: 'Two men – yes – I can see they've got something to take hold of. But two women – that's impossible. You can't have two insides having an affair!'

One day Lydia was alone in her Gordon Square house when a water-pipe burst. In vain did she telephone for a plumber. She then resorted to calling the Water Board. A crew of six young men, wearing high rubber boots, arrived to dam the flood. At the sight of the young men Lydia shouted: 'Oh, you're so beautiful! If only Diaghilev could see you!'

It was said that she was one of the most remarkably intelligent children that had never grown up. When, at last, I met Lydia she proved no disappointment. In fact, I doubt if anyone has had more the power to give me hiccups of laughter than this incredibly unselfconscious droll. I had certainly met her occasionally, but never had an opportunity of seeing much of her. So, when I was at Brighton I determined to visit her – and am glad I did. It was a rare and wonderful experience. I laughed inordinately. I was deeply amused and stimulated as I haven't been for a long time. It was a most wonderful antidote to the troubles in the theatre. She seemed, by her wisdom, to put a perspective on everything, to make one realize that one's troubles were only part of life, that failure was as necessary as success. She calmed me by saying it always takes three weeks to get over bad Press notices.

After suffering from a bad heart for ten years, Maynard died leaving Lopokova his remarkable collection of pictures and, if little cash in hand, three places in which to live.

When my bus deposited me near her house on the Downs near Lewes, Lydia rushed out to meet me wearing a mercerized silk skirt of cream leaf pattern, cocoa-coloured stockings, woollen socks, straw boots, an apron, and about three different sweaters over a silk blouse. Her head was tied in a maize-coloured handkerchief: a pale grey, shiny face without make-up, but freckled and sunburnt at back of neck.

Tilton House proved to be typical of the Bloomsbury taste when the Omega workshop ordained that nothing brighter than terracotta could be used among the clay, oatmeal and slate colours of their domineering palettes. But Lydia's own personality was very apparent, for everywhere was a mess of all the things she was interested in: yellow snapshots, bits cut out of the newspaper – how to stop snoring, a review of Roy Harrod's book on Maynard. The chimneypieces, the occasional tables, sideboards, even the piano, were all stacked with tins of food, cardboard boxes of provisions, matches, serried jars of pickles; everything on view. Surprising it was among all this litter to discover, skied high on the walls, a marvellous collection of Modiglianis, Cézannes, Seurats and Picassos. 'Oh, they don't belong to me,' said Lydia. 'They were Maynard's, and they're only loaned until death.' What other woman would disclaim ownership in this modest way? But such humility is typical of Lydia; the impression she creates on the world means absolutely nothing to her. When Maynard flew to Washington during the war to confer about the economic situation, Lydia accompanied him. On arrival they posed on the gangway for the Press photographers; Lydia, grinning, was almost hidden behind a large paper bag prominently marked 'Sennet, Fishmonger, Cambridge'.

The widow chuckled, and exclaimed in her thick Russian accent: 'I have to ask the trustees for every half-crown, and for a hand-basin

for my bedroom, but I don't really want for anything. I live well. I
drink wine with my meals; I have here a garden with peas in it, the
rooms in Gordon Square, and a flat at Cambridge. When Maynard
died I thought I could never live without him, and I suffered a lot.
But now I never think of him.' She was utterly absorbed by her new
life. 'I go into the raspberry canes and I imagine I'm in the jungle,
and I bend my body and it gives me such a feeling of freedom; and
I picked these peas for our lunch.' ('Will you have sausages or cold
ham?' She rushed off and shouted to a hidden servant; 'He wants
ham!') 'Yes, I'm blissfully happy here. I have a married couple
whom I gave this nice home to, and in return they do the cooking
for me. I can't cook. Oh, it's too much of a bore – too messy! But
sometimes I try to experiment – and the other day I ate a squirrel! It
tastes rather like a bird – it lives on nuts and apples – and it's delicious,
and next time I'll eat half a dozen! But I always make my own bed;
I like that, it gives a rhythm to life. And I go for walks, and I read
a bit, and the days aren't long enough; twenty-four hours aren't
long enough at this time of the year.'

Lopokova once had the historical experience of sharing a sleeping
compartment on a train from Madrid to Paris with a large, fattish
lady 'obviously made for men's delight'. Lydia said: 'We were very
polite, and I agreed to take the upper berth; it was easier for me to
climb up.' But at the frontier the lady was not allowed into
France, and Lopokova did not know until later that she had been
travelling with the spy Mata Hari.

Her descriptions of people are quite remarkable.

Fred Ashton – 'I'll write him a letter one day but I can't tell him
now I don't like his new ballet. He must go away from Sadler's
Wells; he's stale.'
Ninette de Valois – 'I hate important men, but important women
are impossible and she's become important!'
Constant Lambert – 'There's a genius there; it's rich and talented in
spite of all that drink. I like it.'
Dick Buckle – 'He hasn't got a penny in the world and he arrives
here in a Rolls-Royce. I like that.'
Margot Fonteyn – 'She's pure, and fine. She's got true quality.'

During my visit Lydia, looking like Widow Twankey, danced
the 'Valse des Fleurs' of the *Casse-Noisette*. She did imitations of the
way that Michael Somes moves, leaning slightly forward as if sand

was falling out of his behind, and proved in a thousand different ways that there are no disadvantages to old age when one is as completely lacking in selfconsciousness, is as interested in as many aspects of life as she continues to be, and is able to laugh as much as ever. She is one of the very remarkable women of our day.

Tea at Tilton

Henrietta Couper

née Garnett   m① Burgo Partridge
② *[handwritten annotations]*

Even before I became friends with Lydia, she had already figured in my life. By then – 1955 – Maynard had been dead for nine years, and she was living at Tilton. Tilton is down the lane, obscured by trees, and so not quite visible from Charleston, the house in which my grandparents lived (Vanessa Bell and Duncan Grant). I had already met Lydia once or twice, when she very occasionally came to supper at Charleston. Then I was still too small to be allowed to join the grown-ups for dinner. But sometimes I had glimpsed her, sitting upright and tiny, and always muffled up in a great many clothes, when her farm manager, Logan Thompson, drove her into Lewes or Eastbourne to have lunch on her cook's day off.

My grandparents hardly ever went to Eastbourne. They were snooty about it. They only used Lewes. It may seem strange today, but the fact that Lydia frequented Eastbourne made her seem to me a creature of mysterious and fascinating habits.

Both my grandparents were painters. During the school holidays, my elder sister Amaryllis and I used to stay at Charleston frequently. Then Nessa and Duncan would bribe us to sit for them as models, and during these hours, when we tried to sit still, they would endeavour to make us fidget less by telling us stories of their youth. It was in this way that I learned that Lydia was Russian, had danced for Diaghilev, had been ravishingly pretty, *not really*, had vanished for a short spell under circumstances tinged with mystery and scandal, and that she had eventually married Maynard Keynes.

In the studio at Charleston, Duncan had a beautiful, small silver travelling clock, by which he used to tell when it was time for us children to have our rests between sittings. On its back was engraved Lydia's name and lines from a poem by Sir John Suckling beginning,

'But, Oh, she dances such a way.' The clock had been presented to Lydia in 1914 by a theatrical company in the United States which had mounted a play called *The Young Idea*, in which Lydia had acted. It was definitely not Duncan's clock, and to Amaryllis and me it seemed exceedingly fishy that Duncan should have acquired it.

If Nessa was snooty about Eastbourne, she was also more than a little snooty about Lydia, and dismissed references to her with a tolerant but superior laugh. Lydia may have been very pretty and a good dancer, but it was clear that Nessa found her a little trying and thought her somewhat silly. On the other hand, it was not in Duncan's character to make such judgements about members of the human race.

One afternoon, when I was about seven years old, Amaryllis and I had gone out for a walk with Clive Bell (my grandmother's husband). We had walked further than we had intended, and we were anxious not to be late back for tea. Clive suggested that we should take a short cut through Tilton Wood, then steal unseen through Lydia's garden. But he emphasized that we should be very stealthy, because Lydia often sunbathed naked in between her red-currant bushes and she would not like us to see her. So when we reached her garden, we dropped on to all fours and crawled very quietly around the edges of her flower beds: Clive in front, and us two following him. At one point he stiffened, then proceeded to crawl on most gingerly. Amaryllis and I just caught sight of someone very small and brown, like a walnut kernel, camouflaged by currant leaves. I do not know if she was aware of our invasion, for of course I never referred to it after, nor did she.

One summer's afternoon, when I was ten years old, I took it into my head to call on Lydia. I went up to the house and knocked on her door. After what seemed to me to be a very long time (during which I became extremely nervous, and longed to run away, but did not dare to), the door was opened and I was led into the drawing-room and asked to wait for her Ladyship.

The drawing-room at Tilton was one of the strangest rooms I had ever been in. It was crammed with an excessive amount of very ugly furniture. From the walls, suspended by chains and hung ludicrously high, were a great many impressively fine pictures. Although it was a sunny day, a fire was burning and the room was stuffy. There was a great deal of thick, soft upholstery, all in hideous colours, and the curtains were thick and ugly too. I sat staring about me. After a while, Lydia came into the room.

She was tiny. Although I was only ten (and even now, I am not a tall person), I was taller than her. She was wearing a surprising amount of clothes for such a warm day, and around her head were bound a great quantity of scarves. She looked rather like an old tea-cosy, except for her feet, which were delicate and beautiful, and for her hands, which were very graceful.

We took to one another like ducks to water. I dare say it seems strange that a little English girl and an old Russian woman should strike up such a friendship. But we did. We shared much in common. Lydia had a very engaging, child-like streak in her; I was far from being grown-up. She loved to chatter; I adored to listen and to ask her questions. Sometimes we laughed and giggled over the absurdities of life; sometimes we were on the verge of tears.

On this first visit, she offered me a glass of sweet Sauterne and a marron glacé. She talked to me about the ballet, the Mariinsky Theatre, Petipa, and about what it was like in Russia when she was young. I sat and sipped my wine, and I listened to her.

She told me that when she was ten years old, she had gone for an audition to the Imperial Ballet School. Her mother had given her some especially pretty white silk open-work socks for the occasion. The audition took place in a very large room, entirely empty except for a dais on which the examiners sat. Lydia was asked to take off her pretty socks and her shoes, and to run barefoot the length of the hall towards the examiners, and then back again to where she had statrted from. That was all the audition consisted of. It was very simple, she said, to judge the natural grace and dancing potential of a child from the way in which it ran.

When I left, I noticed a large number of tiny boots, slippers and shoes standing in a row in the hall. Lydia told me that she had most of her shoes hand-made for her, and that she only bought ready-made shoes from Russell and Bromley. She advised me to be particular about my own shoes. Feet, she said, had to endure one's entire weight, and therefore one should be kind to them. Then she covered my face with short and dry little kisses, and told me to come again.

After that first visit, I always went to see Lydia whenever I was staying at Charleston. Life at Tilton went on: the changes were barely perceptible. At one time, Lydia had a wall constructed inside her house, so that her cook – whom she disliked, but whom it never occurred to her to sack – would not drive her mad by her proximity. The cook also had a part-time job in the local lunatic asylum in Eastbourne. It was rumoured that she was blind to the distinction between cooking for the lunatics of Eastbourne and cooking for Lady Keynes.

Occasionally, as I grew older, I would sometimes sit in the lane between Tilton and Charleston and scribble down the chatter I had enjoyed with Lydia. I wish I had kept more of these jottings. One which I did keep is the following extract from an account I wrote of the last visit I paid to Lydia at Tilton. The date was 1 May 1975. By then, Lydia was in her eighties. Logan Thompson still managed the farm. Mrs Whiter was the housekeeper. Ruby Weller did the house-work for Lydia and in my opinion, Lydia was lucky that Ruby did.

I had met Ruby in the farmyard as I was walking up to Tilton. She clasped my hands.

'Shall I come up to the house with you? Her Ladyship's expecting you, but her memory comes and goes.'

'How is she?' I asked.

'She's a bit vague, poor dear. It's her mind that wanders up and down, and since she was ill she doesn't remember all that much. Still, you can't help being fond of her, can you?'

We walked slowly to the house. We continued to pass the time of day, Ruby in her thick stockings, her apron, her worn slippers. We trod over the cattle grid, and then onto the sweep of gravel in front of the house.

The last daffodils had been bent by the wind and were nodding their battered trumpets down to the polyanthus and the frilly young yellow snapdragons.

'She can't get out much now,' said Ruby. 'Sad, isn't it? She was always out before, sunbathing and that. But sometimes Logan takes her out on fine days in the Land Rover. They drive up to Bo-Peep; sometimes to Mad Misery.'

Ruby opened the front door for me, and I went inside.

Tilton had scarcely changed since my first visit to Lydia. But I was aware of something more peculiarly foreign about the atmo-sphere within the house. It evoked an environment I was already familiar with, through Lydia and also through literature, but it was an atmosphere of far away and long ago: *Dream Tales and Prose Poems, A House of Gentlefolk.*

Lydia and Logan were sitting opposite one another in sturdy armchairs in the hall, beneath an over-hanging electric element. They gave me the impression that they spent much of their lives sitting silently in these chairs. Several times, as the afternoon faded towards evening, Lydia would say, 'Ah, but that would make the time pass more quickly.'

She was more shrivelled and more shrunken. Her head was wrapped, as always, in several scarves; her tiny feet were thrust into a pair of short orange rubber boots. She wore a dark-green nylon jacket, buttoned to her chin, which made her look even more Russian than ever.

I had brought a bunch of flowers for her from the walled garden at Charleston. She was pleased by them. She took them from me eagerly, seized them in one small fist, then flung them down abruptly upon the table beside her armchair. We exchanged several kisses. Logan levered himself from his chair: his leg had grown gammy.

As usual, I was offered a glass of Sauterne, and, as usual, I accepted it. As usual, too, the conversation rattled swiftly to the subject of ballet.

'... it was a good school, my dear. We were taught. They do not teach you now. Not like that. And the food was good; that is so important.'

'But surely they didn't allow you to grow fat?' I asked.

'If you were going to get fat, you would get fat anyway. But if you did get fat, you were dished. Dished for the Dance. Limbs and bones must be seen for the Dance.

'At night, I dream of the faces of my teachers. Petipa had an old face, but his ankles continued to be interesting. It was an excellent school. They had technique, you know. And technique they do not have here in London now. They never had good teaching in London. And now ... they do not know. But Diaghilev was a great man to work with. He was a good man. He was a creator. Yes, I liked to work with him very much.

'Nijinsky – he was potty. They took him away. He finished badly. His soul had holes in it. But when he danced, then his holes were healed. Then he became alive, and he was not unhappy any more. I liked to work with Nijinsky.'

Lydia spread her hands upon her knees, and then she leaned forwards to fish a packet of cigarettes from an enormous handbag by her feet. She smoked slowly, with extreme and touching grace.

Outside, the sun still shone. In the hall, where we sat, the furniture was hideous, and it dwarfed Lydia utterly.

'I do not like the winters now,' she said. 'Do you know that I am very old? More than eighty. I cannot count any longer. But yes, poor Nijinsky, he was potty. But that did not matter, because he was a very great dancer. Now, Isadora Duncan did not know about technique. But she used her hands like swans. Before Isadora, no one ever used hands. Before her, the Russians just had fists. But Isadora showed us how to use our hands. And because of Isadora, the dance was extended, and that was wonderful for all of us. There is soul in the fingers when they are used. But beware! Hands can betray you, you know, if they are used improperly. A dancer dies quickly, quickly. After forty, it is all over. Then only mime is left for the aged dancer, and yes – well there are character parts. It is the bones that alter. The body alters. It develops a difference. Then you cannot, should not, dance as a young dancer any longer. Surgery exists for the face. But that is vulgar. And in the Theatre, there can be no lies. Everything shows, no matter how good your technique. And to have wrinkles is to be noble. We all of us grow old; what matters is how you age. It is the hands that are the first to show the signs of age. Veins come between the fingers, here and here. It is an insult to show veins in the theatre. A dancer may not have veins. But the veins come; age comes. We all grow old, very old, and then we die.'

'I was out in Tilton Wood with Clive,' said Logan, speaking for the first time. 'Clive was the one I knew best in the family at Charleston. Been shooting. I said to him, "You know Tilton Wood'll be a suburb of Eastbourne one of these days, Clive." And he turned to me and he said, "I think you're right, Logan," he said "But thank God I'll be dead by then!"'

Logan slapped his right thigh and he roared with laughter.

'And by God, he was right!' He bellowed again.

After a pause, during which we all three recovered our breaths, Lydia asked me, 'How are Nessa and dear Duncan?'

'Mrs Bell is dead, Madam,' said Logan.

He was mildly annoyed with Lydia for losing her memory.

'Nessa dead? Ah well, she had to die. Dear Duncan. We all love him. There is nothing more to be said about him. We love him and that is enough.'

'We had a good time in Spain,' she said. 'The Spanish people loved us. Massine tried to dance the Spanish dances. They are very complicated, so very difficult. Particularly for Russian dancers. But Massine figured the Spanish dances well. He has the looks; black eyes, like a cat. Massine lives in Italy now. I think he has a good post teaching. We do not correspond; we were never intimate enough to afford the stamps and the envelopes.'

'But poor Karsavina. She is old now. She is very old. She is older than I am. And she is poor. That is terrible. I love Karsavina. She had beauty and poetry. To work with Karsavina was to be happy. A good spirit. But it is awful to have to hunt for food.'

'There's that Benevolent Society that Madame Rambert ...', Logan tried to interrupt.

Lydia cut him short. 'Yes, Yes. And Mim, she is clever. But she is the same and yet not the same as Ninette de Valois. I am less fond of Ninette, but Marie was a good teacher. She invented a good school for the little English girls. Ninette will always be successful. Ninette was never a great dancer, but she was good to have in the company. She never put a foot wrong.'

There was an irrepressible gaiety about Lydia. From time to time, she waved her hands in the air, and then she laughed like a young girl.

'I am fond of Lord Gage, but he is the worst landlord in the whole of England. Look at the drive, with its holes, where I am battered. No repairs at all. He came and sat in the chair where you sit now, Henrietta. I do not remember if he talked. Is Leonard [Woolf] dead?'

'He died a few years ago,' I said.

'That is a pity. He was a good man. Well, we are none of us Christians. Soon, we shall all be dead.'

I kissed Lydia goodbye. Logan shook my hand. She asked me to come again, but that visit turned out to be the last occasion I met her. Shutting the door behind me, I saw Lydia and Logan still sitting, face to face in silence, as they had been upon my arrival.

I walked back along the flinty lane to Charleston. I walked slowly, and, as I did so, I thought how queer it was that, at tea with Lydia, there was never any tea.

Portraits of Lopokova

Milo Keynes

Lydia Lopokova's personality, on stage and off, in characterization and repose, in speech and in motion, was unusually individual. No wonder that the London public fell in love with her when she appeared with the Russian Ballet in 1918! No wonder that artists were eager to draw and paint her, as they had portrayed Pavlova and Karsavina! Many portraits in oils, drawings and sketches were made of her between 1917 and 1933, not to mention a bronze bust, an etching, caricatures and a representation in mosaic. The following account, although doubtless incomplete, records all the likenesses of Lydia (apart from photographs) that I have succeeded in locating or that have come to my attention.

The earliest drawings of Lydia were done in Rome in 1917, when she was twenty-five years old. The Diaghilev company arrived there from America in late March, and Lydia immediately started to rehearse the role of Mariuccia in Massine's ballet *The Good-humoured Ladies*, which was to be performed in April. Cocteau and Picasso were also in Rome, preparing *Parade*, a ballet to music by Satie and with choreography also by Massine, in which Lydia was the female acrobat; this was to be performed in Paris in May. Picasso made several quick drawings of Lydia in green ink. At least one of these shows her with Diaghilev. Another, which shows her dancing with Massine, was kept on the mantelpiece of the drawing-room at Tilton after Picasso sent it to her, signed and inscribed, in 1958. Picasso's present was a substitute for his later drawing, done in 1919, showing Lydia dancing the Can-Can with Massine in *La Boutique Fantasque*, which he had wanted to give her but had mislaid. During his stay in London in 1919 Picasso made a sensitive pencil drawing of Lydia

seated in a chair and at least two ink drawings of her, shown dancing
the Can-Can with Massine. On his return to Paris at the end of the
year he sent her a New Year's card (actually part of the back of a
menu), drawn from memory in ink. This is, perhaps, his best likeness
of Lydia as a dancer.

In London, in 1918, Elizabeth Polunin made a pastel drawing of
Lydia as Mariuccia. She was the English wife of Vladimir Polunin
(1880-1957), who had arrived in England, originally from Russia,
just before the First World War. Polunin became Diaghilev's principal scene painter in London, working with Derain on *La Boutique
Fantasque* (June 1919) and with Picasso on *The Three-cornered Hat*
(July 1919).

In 1919 Lydia allowed the future Dame Laura Knight, RA (1877-
1970) to use her dressing-room at the London Coliseum as a studio;
she also introduced her to Cecchetti and his dancing academy, as she
thought the classes might provide her with subject-matter. Indeed,
Cecchetti found the resulting sketches so accurate that he used them
for correcting the postures of his pupils. Laura Knight made
numerous drawings and oil paintings of subjects from the ballet and
in 1920 published a portfolio, *Twenty-one Drawings of the Russian
Ballet, whose contents were mainly sketches of Karsavina and
Lopokova. In an issue of the Dancing World* (1922) Cyril Beaumont
reviewed an exhibition in which seven oil paintings and seven
drawings by Laura Knight were on view: one of the oils showed
Lopokova dressed in the costume of the Can-Can dancer from *La
Boutique Fantasque* and standing before her dressing-table, lightly
powdering her arms before going on stage. In another Lopokova
was shown resting in an armchair in her dressing-room, wearing the
pantaloons and fur cap of the Ballerina in *Petrushka*, while her dresser
is putting finishing touches to the skirt she wears in *Les Sylphides*.
On the wall hangs the Ballerina's skirt, which the dancer will put on
the moment the dresser is free to help her. Laura Knight painted two
other oils of Lydia: one shows her standing in front of a mirror,
dressed for the Can-Can, while her dresser adjusts the back of her
costume; the other shows her leaping across the stage, arms out-
stretched, in *Les Sylphides*, with members of the corps de ballet
behind her. The Keynes family possesses a drawing (1921) of Lydia
sitting with crossed legs in her dressing-room, wearing the costume
of the Lilac Fairy from *The Sleeping Princess*. This gift, inscribed 'To
Lydia from Laura', is very lively. In another charming pencil draw-

ing by Laura Knight Lydia is sitting at a table covered with tea things, listening to some music. The artist also made a pen and wash drawing, very dashing in outline, of Lydia and Massine dancing in the Can-Can from *La Boutique Fantasque*.

The frontispiece of Cyril Beaumont's *The Art of Lydia Lopokova* (1920) is a most successful portrait of Lydia, in sanguine, by Glyn Philpot, RA (1884–1937).

On 16 July 1921 Lydia received the following letter:

Dear Madame Lopokova,

It was a great joy to have you at my party the other night. I hope you were amused. Polunine [sic] encourages me to hope that you will pose for me some time. I believe you are going away shortly but are returning in the autumn. I shall look forward with greatest excitement to painting a portrait of one I admire so greatly.

Gratefully yours,
Augustus John

John's diary records four sittings for the portrait: on 27 and 30 July and 1 and 2 August. A pencil study (in the National Museum of Wales) shows Lydia standing, with one arm resting on a pillar; the figure seems somewhat elongated, but is graceful. The study is more successful than the oil, which was never finished, as, according to Lydia, she was too frightened to go to the last sitting. John depicts Lydia in costume and shoes, with one foot pointed awkwardly forward, suggesting an anatomical deformity. The picture was sold in 1962, when the contents of John's studio were dispersed, and the present owner wrote to Lydia about it; she replied, expressing her delight that she 'had turned out to be so expensive'.

In a letter to Vanessa Bell, dated 23 September, 1918, Duncan Grant wrote,

We had an old-fashioned ballet from Tchaikovsky [sic] Prince Igor which I always enjoy. Everyone says 'Good-humoured Ladies' is best. Ottoline [Morrell] then took us into the passage and introduced us to Diaghilev ... We then trapsed [sic] round to meet the artistes by the back door and were ushered into a not very large dressing room where we were introduced to a little creature in a kimono no bigger than a Lap – Madame Lopokovua [sic] – the principal ballerina. She was absolutely charming with–

out any sort of sham feeling and perfect manners and very pretty and intelligent looking painted still with blue eyelids. She has an old Italian husband who is a perfect darling.

Was Maynard Keynes with Duncan Grant that evening? He is said to have met Lydia for the first time at a party on 10 October. He had certainly been with Duncan Grant and Vanessa Bell in London at the height of the Russian Ballet season during the previous weeks, according to a letter to his mother, dated 13 October.

Duncan Grant (1885–1978) designed the set and costumes for a Massine ballet, *Togo, the Noble Savage*, to music by Milhaud, which formed part of a 'jazzaganza', entitled *You'd be surprised*, produced in 1923; Lydia danced in it in the role of the wife of a Mexican gentleman. He also designed the backcloth and costumes for a ballet, *The Postman* (1925), in which Lydia also appeared. But, despite his close friendship with Maynard Keynes, Grant only painted Lydia rarely. (This is also true of Vanessa Bell and Roger Fry, who also knew Keynes well.) In 1922 Grant designed a dress for Lydia in the style of Ingres's Mlle Rivière, and both he and Fry painted her that year in this dress at the same sittings. Grant's painting is the best portrait of Lydia, signed and dated 1923, and is now at King's College, Cambridge. Also in 1922 Lydia danced at Covent Garden, as 'L'Ecossaise' and, wearing a kilt, in a *pas seul* Scotch reel, with choreography by Massine and music by Percy Grainger. Grant, who knew several Scottish dances, had advised Massine on the choreography. He made a drawing of Lydia in the part, as well as an oil, and Lydia wrote to Maynard, 'Vanessa gave me the drawing by Duncan of me – I look like a Scottish whirlwind – so much activity and not only in the legs, everywhere.' There are two watercolours by Grant of Lydia, shown dancing on stage, and five drawings of her (all dating from about 1922) were found in his studio after his death. There is also an oil (head and shoulders) in his estate, painted in the early 1940s, showing Lydia in a pink dress.

Vanessa Bell (1879–1961) is known to have painted a three-quarter length portrait of Lydia which I have been unable to trace. It represents her sitting, holding a flower, and was exhibited at a London Group exhibition in April 1923 and reproduced in *Vogue*. J. Alton wrote about it in the *New Statesman*: '... most delightful: a wonderful presentment of the vivacious and childlike little dancer'. Bloomsbury used to have theatrical evenings, and at one of them, in

1926, Maynard and Lydia danced the 'Keynes-Keynes', a version of the Can-Can from *La Boutique Fantasque*. This was repeated at subsequent parties, and Vanessa Bell made a cartoon labelled 'Recollection of a party at 46. G.S.' [46 Gordon Square]. The cartoon, which used to hang at the top of the stairs at Tilton, was shown there as a sort of backcloth at a 'theatrical event' in September 1927. In 1942 Vanessa Bell painted an oil of the Memoir Club, whose members included all those who could be said to belong to the Bloomsbury Group, as well as some outsiders. Founded in 1920, it met at irregular intervals for its members to read papers, until 1964, when Clive Bell died. In the oil, in which Vanessa Bell obviously intended to record the membership, eleven living and three dead members appear; Maynard and Lydia are both well shown in this group portrait.

The portrait (dated 1922) of Lydia by Roger Fry (1866-1934), which is now in Canada, was seen by the young Cecil Beaton at a one-man exhibition at the Independent Gallery, London. In an unpublished diary he wrote on 16 April 1923:

> The thing of Lopokova was ridiculous – there are 2 things I can say in favour of it – one is that although he has painted them the wrong shape, he has got the idea of her eyebrows very cleverly – they are a beautiful line of pale brown and the other clever thing is the modelling of the painting of the face. Lopokova has such a lovely smoothe [sic] buttery face – and Roger Fry has indicated this by putting the paint on very thickly and smoothly – otherwise I should have no idea of whom the portrait was meant to be: the eyes were the wrong shape and there was no life in them. The face was egg shaped and not round – the mouth was a bad imitation of Lily Elsie's and the nose, instead of pointing up – pointed down – the colour was disgusting. Biscuits, strawberry ice pinks, parma violet mauves and vivid yellow – it was exactly like a chocolate box cover, and very badly ordinary composition [sic].

At the sale of the Degas collection in Paris in 1918 Maynard bought a Cézanne, two paintings by Delacroix and an Ingres drawing. After taking this crucial step as a collector of paintings, Maynard, in the immediate post-war years and advised by Vanessa Bell and Duncan Grant, added a Seurat, a Matisse and a Derain, as well as pictures by British artists. One of these was an oil, *The Bar Parlour*, by Walter Sickert, RA (1860-1942), which Keynes bought in 1922

– a particularly helpful time from the artist's point of view. For Sickert had only recently returned from Dieppe, distraught at the death of his second wife – 'For two years I did not wish to live,' he told Virginia Woolf – and very short of money. The sale of his picture gave him great and practical encouragement, and he was very grateful. In November 1924 he handed over to Lydia a portrait of her as a present to Maynard. The oil, which is painted in sombre colours and rather thin pigment, is a profile of Lydia's head and shoulders. It has never been a favourite portrait in the family and was never hung in a prominent position at Tilton.

In 1925 Maynard Keynes and Samuel Courtauld started the London Artists' Association, which was to act as an agent for its members, help them financially, provide business management for them and mount exhibitions of their paintings. It lasted until 1935, having suffered a severe setback in 1931, when Vanessa Bell, Duncan Grant and Keith Baynes resigned. (The terms that Agnews had offered them (somewhat surprisingly) were too tempting to resist.) Just before this Lydia had opened a one-man exhibition by Keith Baynes (1887–1977) at the Reid and Lefevre Gallery, London, which was widely covered by the press and was very successful as a result. Her opening remarks were as follows:

> I do not feel appropriate to this occasion. If Mr Baynes was a dancer, I could tell you if he had a good instep. If I were Mr Baynes himself, I could tell you which of the pictures are the best. If I were Mr Baynes's dog, I could bark. If I were my husband, I could tell you to cure unemployment by buying pictures. For if you buy a savings certificate instead of buying a picture, Mr Baynes will go on the dole and the Government will use your savings to pay Mr Baynes his dole. So, it will all come to the same thing in the end – except that *you* will have no picture!'

The dachshund George received almost as much attention from the newspapers as Baynes himself.

Ambrose McEvoy, ARA (1878–1927) painted a full-length portrait (now cut down) of Lydia in the last year of his life; it was exhibited posthumously at the Royal Academy winter exhibition in 1928. The picture was bought from McEvoy's widow in 1959 by a member of the Keynes family.

One result of running the London Artists' Association, was that Maynard Keynes got to know and to help struggling artists, either by buying their pictures at exhibitions mounted by the Association or by commissioning works from them. A particularly happy commission of this kind was the double portrait (now at the National Portrait Gallery, London) of Maynard and Lydia by William Roberts (1895–1980), painted in 1932. The picture is off-key, but has a certain intimacy; it is an expressive work, although, in comparison with the painting of the faces, the sitters' hands, which are shown holding unlit cigarettes, are rendered with striking artificiality.

Other portraits of Lydia, drawn over the years by various artists, should be mentioned. The earliest is an etching by the American, Troy Kinney (reproduced in *The Sketch*, 1924), of Lydia and Nijinsky dancing in *Les Sylphides* in New York in 1917. This was one of the last times that Nijinsky danced with Lydia and for the Diaghilev Company. Adrian Allinson painted a watercolour of Lydia, shown in the ballet *Cleopatra*, in 1918. There is an ink and wash drawing of Lydia and Massine in *La Boutique Fantasque* (1919) by John Nash, done for a magazine called *Land and Water*. In 1920 Randolph Schwabe (1885–1948), later principal of the Slade School of Art, made a perceptive pencil drawing, heightened by watercolour, of Lydia as Columbine in *Le Carnaval*. This was reproduced on the cover of Cyril Beaumont's *The Art of Lydia Lopokova*. He also made a sensitive drawing of her in her dressing-room, shown at his memorial exhibition in 1951. Nikolai Legat drew a coloured caricature of Lydia in his ballet, *The Postman*, in 1925. Ethelbert White drew Massine with Lydia as the Miller and his wife, in *The Three-cornered Hat*, and also Lydia in Massine's first ballet, *The Midnight Sun*. In 1928 Cecil Beaton (1904–80) made a line drawing for *Vogue* entitled 'Lydia Lopokova (Mrs Maynard Keynes) sits in a box at His Majesty's and watches Nikitina, Dubrovska, Tchernicheva and Lifar dancing in Stravinsky's *Apollon Musagète*'. He showed great pleasure in producing it for examination in the last year of his life, and it is reproduced in Richard Buckle's *Diaghilev* (1979).

Frank Dobson (1888–1963), whose importance as a sculptor has recently been acknowledged, made a fine bronze bust of Lydia in 1924. One copy of the bronze belongs to the Keynes family, and one was bought for the Arts Council in 1949. Lydia was a founder member of the Arts Council until 31 December 1949, but there is no record that she ever attended any meetings, and certainly she never served on any of its committees.

Finally, Lydia was one of those who acted as models for the mosaics created by Boris Anrep (1885–1969) for the floors of the entrance to the National Gallery, London. Anrep, a Russian by birth, was sent to school in England; later he studied at St Petersburg University, where in due course he became a professor of law. In time he gave up this post and travelled in Russia, the Near East and Italy to study mosaics. In 1908 he worked in Paris, and in 1910 in Edinburgh. Eventually he settled in London, where Augustus John gave him his first commission. He became a friend of Roger Fry and made the selection of Russian works for the second Post-Impressionist exhibition mounted by Fry in 1912. He continued to work in England, but moved to Paris after his English wife, Helen, had left him in 1926 to live with Roger Fry. In 1923 Anrep had completed a mosaic for the floor of the William Blake Room at the Tate Gallery. In 1926 he began the three mosaics for the floors of the entrance area of the National Gallery, which were paid for by public subscription, Samuel Courtauld being one of the principal donors. The mosaic for the west vestibule, *The Labours of Life*, was finished in 1928; that for the east vestibule, *The Pleasure of Life*, in 1929. Money then ran out, but in 1933, after fresh funds had been raised, the third mosaic (for the half-landing), entitled *The Awakening of the Muses*, was completed. In this work Sir Osbert Sitwell was the model for Apollo, the God of Music; Virginia Woolf for Clio, the Muse of History; Greta Garbo for Melpomene, the Muse of Tragedy, and Lydia Lopokova for Terpsichore, the Muse of Lyric Poetry and Dancing – an appropriate identification and a good and presumably enduring likeness. (The fourth mosaic, for the north vestibule, entitled *The Modern Virtues*, was finished in 1952; Margot Fonteyn was the model for Delectation.)

This account of portraits of Lydia testifies to the fascination which her elusive personality exercised over a wide diversity of artists – a fascination which is the counterpart of the enthusiastic delight with which countless audiences greeted the performances and impersonations of the Prima Ballerina.

Appendces

This account of Anna Pavlova by Lydia Lopokova has never been published before in this form. It has been compiled from scripts written by her at different times in the 1930s, for a public address or for broadcast introductions to programmes of Russian music presented by the BBC.

MK

Pavlova

Lydia Lopokova

The first time I saw Anna Pavlova was on the Imperial stage of St Petersburg, not so very long after the 1906 Revolution, in her thrilling success of *Giselle*, an old fashioned French ballet. She had worked up through the ranks to gain the much prized title of Prima Ballerina of the Imperial Theatre in the great days of Olga Preobrazhenskaia, Matilda Kshesinskaia and Vera Trefilova. I had just finished at the Imperial School and now belonged to the corps de ballet. After *Giselle*, she danced several of the new pieces with which Fokin was renewing the life of the ballet. I remember her in *Les Sylphides* and *Le Pavillon d'Armide* in the days when Adeline Genée and the Empire Ballet still ruled.

It was not long after Fokin made the Polovtsian dances in *Prince Igor* that he began his romantic ballets – *Les Sylphides, Carnaval* and *Le Spectre de la Rose*. The rest of us always associated this great new movement of his with the visit of Isadora Duncan to St Petersburg, though Fokin himself would never quite agree that her influence on him was so great as we thought. We had always been taught to hold our bodies tight and stiff, in precise positions. The visit of Isadora Duncan and her girls, with their wavy, flowing rhythmical movements, opened to us a new world. We girls exchanged chocolates and kisses with Isadora's little troupe, while the master of the ballet was receiving from Isadora herself the stimulus to combine the new elasticity with the old precision – which was the foundation of the later Fokin choreography. At the time *Les Sylphides* marked one of the greatest revolutions in the art of the ballet, as remote from the precisions of Petipa as Massine's staccato dances later on.

Then, about 1909, Pavlova came to the West, the very first of the great Russian dancers to leave the Imperial stage, and began to tour the globe. For many years I was never so unlucky as to arrive in a capital where I could not see her, captivating all by her beauty, her mystery and her aroma of motion. She was always a star, more brilliant shining alone than as part of a great ensemble. She prepared the way in Western Europe and the United States for Serge Diaghilev's Ballet, and she even danced with it for a moment. But this was not her métier. She was happier in solitary glory, even if that meant a lesser art. Lovers of the ballet are divided between those whose enthusiasm is for the brilliant union of the arts which spread from Diaghilev, Fokin, Bakst, Stravinsky and Nijinsky, and those who are carried away by 'La mort de la cygne', the fluttering wings of Pavlova's swan.

When Pavlova made her first conquest of London, it was in dancing Glazunov's *L'Automne Bacchanale* with Mordkin at the Palace Theatre in 1910. I remember her in *Bacchanale* in Russia, though there the ballet was called *The Seasons*. Pavlova represented autumn and wore long tarlatan skirts, wine-coloured, with golden leaves around her hair. Later, I also danced to this same music in Diaghilev's ballet *Cleopatra*, staged by Fokin. Here I wore a white Grecian tunic with green spots, but nobody remembers me in it.

At rehearsal, Pavlova would wear a dark blue taffeta blouse and a black taffeta skirt, black lisle stockings with lace-work in them, and black patent-leather shoes with English heels – not French heels.

As a full ballerina she was allowed *not* to dress at the first rehearsal, if it was a character dance such as *Bacchanale*, in which I can still hear her rustling skirts as she pirouetted in a line across the stage. But it is in *The Dying Swan* which she danced at almost every performance for many years that we can recall her most easily. It was like a religious exercise of the ballet. Thousands saw it, and everyone was spellbound. She was 'the delight of all and the phoenix of creation'. Not an earthly swan, for how ugly can swans be, with their long necks and short legs, for Pavlova's swan was a most harmonious, ethereal spirit, floating in a dreamland. Yet, a dancer can leave nothing behind her, and even music will not help us to see her again and to feel what she could give us, nor the best words.

I have said I first remember Pavlova in St Petersburg when I had finished at the Imperial School. With other young dancers we then used to have a class with Cecchetti early in the morning, and that is where I began to know her in the practice room. The great Madame would always begin her exercises at eight o'clock, and after her we stepped into our tights. Her class lasted until nine o'clock, and by half-past nine she would be gone, and then we girls used to go to her dressing-room, where she had an enormous basket of Italian ballet shoes and eau-de-Cologne. We poor youngsters would get a pair of shoes for four performances and for practising, too, and they would be soon worn out and soft so that we could scarcely stand on our toes. Being satin, the shoes wore out quickly, although we mended them. A ballet dancer with her needle mending her shoes is a familiar sight behind the scenes. And the shoes were expensive, and Anna Pavlova had that wonderful basket of shoes. She was then a full ballerina and rich and had dozens of slightly worn-out shoes which she used for practice. So, sometimes we put our dirty old shoes at the bottom of the basket and took out better ones, though not the very new ones of course, as that would have been too noticeable. It seemed nothing could have been naughtier. And then the Maestro Cecchetti would ask who had been meddling with the basket of shoes? 'Oh, no, Maestro,' we said – the four of us – 'we know nothing about it.' I do not really know if it was bad, but we did it. Pavlova never said anything about it, but perhaps she *also* knew.

When we had been dancing three or four months Anna Pavlova would say that Monsieur, a great balletomane, had come to the ballet last night and thought we had made great progress and this judgement was very important to us. Madame could be jealous as a cat to those who would pretend to be her rivals. But to us she was grace and kindness. She could be a demon, but she was also an angel with wings. When the revolution came she was grandly generous. From her cosmopolitan gains she sent sums of money to Leningrad to increase the little income of the old ballerinas who had retired on fixed pensions – for all but the very exceptional must retire at last. And in the famine, the troupe in Leningrad were fed by her bounty through the Quakers and the American Red Cross.

I danced the Fokin ballet *Carnaval* many and many a time. I remember how badly I danced it at Montevideo in South America, only on half-toes. We had been a month on the boat and too seasick to practise. My toes got out of order – I had no breath and no toes, but perhaps as the women in Montevideo were veiled, they did not see. Pavlova came to see us and sent flowers. She always sent me flowers when I danced badly! It seemed that she did not like you nearly so well when you were at the top of your form. Perhaps I should not say that, but she was also *very* generous, of course.

She always said, as soon as she finished school, 'I will go away, and travel the whole world, and have my troupe.' And it was not long before the swan took wings, and her unending pilgrimage began round the world, driven by the Muse and her nature and the love of fame, until she had carried the Ballet to the ends of the earth and had become herself the symbol, the Muse of Ballet, as she will always remain. She travelled for many years and was the first to carry successfully something so difficult so widely. Fred Ashton was born in Peru, saw Anna Pavlova there and was inspired by the Muse. Bobbie Helpmann was born in Australia, saw Pavlova there and was inspired by the Muse. They are examples. Diaghilev led a new movement of culture in the great capitals of the world. Anna Pavlova carried the Muse of the Ballet as a Holy Saint of Beauty to high and low, to everyone in the world. We must commemorate her great memory – her art, her beauty, her caprices, her indomitable nature.

Memories of the Russian Ballet

Lydia Lopokova

In several of her introductions to programmes of Russian ballet music, broadcast between 1934 and 1938 by the BBC, Lydia Lopokova spoke of Diaghilev's Company. The following text, not previously published, has been compiled from these comments.

M. K.

Last time I spoke to you on Russian ballet, I told you of my life at the Imperial School in Theatre Street [this explains the title, *Theatre Street*, of Tamara Karsavina's autobiography] and how strictly we were brought up as little nuns. But the good Victorian conventions ruled our elders as well, and it was two famous occasions when they were broken that happened to lead to the Diaghilev Russian Ballet and its invasion of Paris and London from 1911 in full name.

When I was at school, the Prince Volkonsky, who died a few weeks ago in New York, was appointed Court Director of the Imperial Theatres by the Tsar, and he brought Serge Diaghilev into the world of ballet by making him his secretary. Volkonsky was a great gentleman and of fine taste, but he was not the man to control the wilful Matilda Kshesinskaia, who was then at the height of her fame as the Ballerina Assoluta of the Imperial Stage, Kshesinskaia, who afterwards married the Grand Duke Sergei★ and rose to the greatest power of any dancer on the Russian stage, Kshesinskaia, who came from Paris last year out of her retirement to appear once more at the gala at Covent Garden and to show us that beauty and dignity and an unrivalled command of the stage and the audience are still hers.

It was the rule in those days that female dancers must wear their ballet skirts just long enough to fall below the knee – of the length that I wore in *La Boutique Fantasque* – and indeed it is a most becoming length. Even this was a concession. When Taglioni danced

★ Actually, she became his mistress, not his wife.

before Queen Victoria, her skirts were half-way to the ankles, like the skirts worn today in *Les Sylphides*. But skirts coming only half-way to the knee, such as all ballerinas now wear in the classical ballets, which show completely the perfection of the leg and of the technique, were strictly forbidden, as belonging only to the music hall. Now, Kshesinskaia broke this rule; and it was then that Diaghilev started to organize concerts of Russian music in Western Europe. But there was also another rule. Male dancers must wear little trunks over their tights, and tights continuing unbroken to the waist, like Romeo's I mean, which are usually worn today, were not allowed.

Soon after Kshesinskaia's *faux pas*, the famous Nijinsky danced the romantic ballet *Giselle* in full tights without those little trunks. The former Tsarina, the Empress Marie, the sister of your Queen Alexandra, sitting in her box was deeply shocked. And for that breach of discipline he, the greatest male dancer of our generation, was dismissed outright from the Imperial company. It was this second trunk murder, so to speak, which determined Diaghilev to form a permanent company of his own, instead of borrowing the Imperial artists for a short summer tour in the holiday months. It is hard today to believe that the pure, romantic *Giselle*, in which Nijinsky was the ethereal lover pursuing the ghost of the demented maiden through the moonlit glades, could be the cause of a scandal. Some of you may know this ballet of a hundred years ago, for the Camargo Society revived it with Spesivtseva at the Savoy Theatre and since then the Vic-Wells and the Markova-Dolin Ballet have given many performances.

In the beginning, Diaghilev did not want to make Massine a dancer. He never encouraged him to become *premier danseur*, as there was a slight defect in his body, bandy legs just above the ankles, which he skilfully hides with a particular kind of trousers. You very seldom see Massine dancing in tights. For example, he danced *Les Sylphides* very seldom. Diaghilev was very much against it.

So, when *La Boutique Fantasque* was first conceived, Idzikovsky was chosen as the male Can-Can dancer. But somehow, one way or another, Idzikovsky was never allowed to rehearse, and Woizikovsky used to rehearse in Massine's place, and in the end it was Massine who danced in those long trousers, and it is one of his magnificent parts. All his life Diaghilev was searching for a Greek god's body, and he could not forgive that defect in Massine. When he was angry,

Diaghilev used to say, 'He has a pair of handsome eyes and bandy legs.' *La Boutique Fantasque*, with music strung together from enchanting fragments by Rossini, was the first ballet by Massine in which his genius reached its full expression and showed him in his gay youthfulness. We appeared together in its first performances as the Can-Can dancers. In his later work with Diaghilev, Massine may have seemed to have got into toils and entanglements, lacerating and imprisoning the bodies of his dancers, from which he could not find an escape for himself or for them, but in this ballet he found an escape into the world of unimprisoned emotion.

In the last war we of the Russian Ballet spent a good deal of time in Spain. The country was not at war and we thought to take advantage of a neutral country. We were successful enough in Madrid and Barcelona, but the small towns in Spain did not flock to see us, and we had only just enough money to pay our hotel bills. The soles of Diaghilev's shoes were worn out, but when his rich friends in Paris offered to keep him, he would not leave us; so we all stuck together and in the end arrived in England for the long season at the Coliseum, which was the foundation of Diaghilev's vogue in this country. That time in Spain had a big influence on the development of the ballet. For Massine and Diaghilev were going round to every little place where Spanish dancing was to be seen, where the Spaniards sipped manzanilla, listening to the guitar.

Meanwhile Massine himself was learning Spanish dances and Spanish movements. Picasso, the Spaniard, spent much of his time with us. He married one of our dancers. Manuel de Falla was with us. We sipped in the flavours of Spain. In Seville, where the choir boys dance a ballet before the high altar, the organist priest fell in love with us, allowed us in by ourselves to the dim cathedral and played Bach on the organ. The Spaniards loved us for all that was least Spanish in what we could show. But we gathered more than we gave, and out of this period came much in the ballets which may not be easily identified as Spanish. The ancestry of one ballet of that period is clear enough – *Le Tricorne* [*The Three-cornered Hat*]. Here Massine danced in tight black-trousered legs *à l'espagnole*, which was so much better for him than tights.

The Good-humoured Ladies is the best of Massine's ballets in his first year as a choreograph, in which eighteenth century Venice came to life. He made it in Rome in 1917, and Diaghilev used to take him to Naples to see the Neopolitan comedies. You see that influence in the scene of the table with forks and knives and the beautiful, grotesque waiter. But the movements of the dancers' bodies were something quite new in this ballet, different both from classical and from character dancing. Massine took the posturings from the eighteenth century figurines in porcelain and china. So, when the critics called me 'a dainty rogue in porcelain' – words which always make me cross and I thought silly – there was some truth in it. The movements were so new that at the rehearsals our bodies began to ache as never before. The knee was always bent and the arms akimbo – the limbs never in a straight line. Gradually our bodies got used to it – one acquired a shape for such things. But more trouble began with the general rehearsal. There is very vigorous dancing in this ballet, and they gave us heavy padded costumes with farthingales. It was *torture*. We felt like rugby football players dressed as eskimos pretending to be the most elegant and dainty females of the eighteenth century. It is easy to forget how we airý fairies sweat and blow and gasp flat on our backs the moment we reach the wings. I had a dance in *The Good-humoured Ladies* which was the equal to run a mile in four minutes.

But one can get used to so many things. We even got used to those costumes, though the false nose they made me wear I couldn't get used to, and after a few performances when the directors got less strict I was allowed to leave it behind. Eleonora Duse came to see us when we first danced this ballet at the Constanza Theatre in Rome. She watched us from the wings, very sweet and sad, and thanked us on the stage afterwards. So, I kissed her hand and then saw that the imprint of my painted lips had spoiled her glove, and was so distressed. But she replied beautifully, 'Ah, I will keep this glove among my treasures.'

The Midnight Sun will always be interesting in the history of the ballet because it was Massine's first. It was composed in Italy in 1916 with much help from Diaghilev and the artist Larionov. It was before the full influence of Spanish dancing and French painting on Massine, and was still very Russian. It had something of the plains and their humility, and was picturesque with quaint Russian colours. I rehearsed it with Massine in Lisbon and danced the first performance at the Coliseum. But in Rimsky-Korsakov's strong original music there was no suitable dance for me. So Diaghilev introduced a number from Rimsky's opera *The Snow Maiden*. The dance of the maiden is really the aria of the Shepherd from that opera. It is a dance of a maiden's emotion, but also the dance of a goat or a lamb or a half wit – with irrepressible jerks.

One of the best music-drama compositions that ever existed is Stravinsky's *Petrushka*. Nowadays we might call it Pirandellian – this theme of dolls and men interchangeable. The scenario, as well as the costumes and the set, was invented by Benois, the artist; and I have always thought that he played the biggest part in the composition. Stravinsky never planned it as a ballet. He was composing it as a pianoforte concerto for a virtuoso performer. Diaghilev heard it – all the little group heard it – and pleaded with Stravinsky, 'Why not turn it into a ballet?' So, all the little group working together, Diaghilev, Benois, Fokin, Stravinsky – there never was a ballet so much of team work as *Petrushka* – created out of the pianoforte concerto this peculiar Russian folklore drama. Its rich earthy atmosphere of the Russian holiday crowd, carefree and doomed, gay and tragic. Reality and symbolism perfectly blended, half-obvious, half-hidden and unfathomable, to which every spectator can give his own meaning. Man has a soul, the music tells, but his soul too is sawdust. His creator and his tormentor are one.

I have danced the part of the doll so many times that I have forgotten when I began it. But I remember well the last time. It was after I had half-retired from the ballet and was not in full practice. After midnight Diaghilev rang me up on a trunk call from Paris. He had no one for the part on the next night. Would I come from London and do it? So arriving an hour or two before the performance, unrehearsed, I did my best, not too well, for the last time. Big Serge and the company crowded round kissing me, saying that I was a good sport, and I felt gay and tremulous in the sweet comradeship of the old lot in which I was brought up and made.

It was chiefly with Massine I danced this ballet, and only seldom with Nijinsky. Massine mimed the part [the Moor] with his hands, stiff and hanging – in Massine's mime the hands are very important. Nijinsky moved more with his whole body. Massine's was an intellectual creation, Nijinsky's of inward bodily genius, only half-conscious. But both were grand creations. In the light of Vaslav Nijinsky's misfortunes afterwards, Petrushka has come to seem the symbol of his personality, the imprisoned genius in the docile body of the puppet struggling to become human and falling back again, as in the death scene of Petrushka, which he mimed with such sensitive insight.

Les Sylphides was built up from the piano pieces of Chopin by Fokin when he first came under the influence of the flowing movements of Isadora Duncan, and is the beginning of the modern school of ballet after Tchaikovsky. It was in *Les Sylphides* that Diaghilev gave me my first big part, saying that if I could succeed, he would give me *Carnaval* in the place of Karsavina who was away. Well, it was to that music that I danced myself out of the nameless ranks of the corps de ballet, for I was one of the four principal dancers who are posed in front of the coryphées to render the variations. Never shall I forget how, when the performance was over, the great, generous big Serge came up to me and gave me a present of three hundred francs, and with what sweet content I slipped off next morning to buy a new hat and coat and some false curls, not looking at all like one of those high and mighty ballerinas which the world sometimes imagines they should look like.

Fokin's famous ballet *Carnaval*, is one of the few creations of a ballet which was an improvisation and yet survives. He was asked to design something quickly for a charity performance, and in a single day it was done, with only three rehearsals, so perfectly was Schumann's music fitted for interpretation by ballet to express the eternal challenge of youth to age, that is to say, to the dull, stupid old pedants and professors. It is not as important choreographically as *Les Sylphides*, not nearly, but yet still, and still, it lives. It is a combination of very good things; not least of the good things is the Schumann music. It is a safe item in the repertory, and you can always open a programme with it. It has an extremely good introduction. But unless there is style in the dancers, it loses enormously. Nijinsky was the Harlequin and I was the Columbine at Diaghilev's first performance of it, which was in Paris. In those days all the dancers except Columbine wore masks, which had its piquancy. But afterwards, the masks were given up. I wore a long dress with short pants underneath, and when the leg went up it was very pretty. I danced it many and many a time.

One of the greatest ballets of the classical repertory is Tchaikovsky's *The Sleeping Beauty*. Diaghilev and Sir Oswald Stoll gave it a magnificent revival at the Alhambra Theatre in 1921 when it was renamed *The Sleeping Princess*. The wicked Diaghilev always laughed at my nose – he would have liked to make my face quite perfect and meaningless. So, when he decided that I should be one of his team of four, 'We can't', he said, 'call it *The Sleeping Beauty*.

We must call it *The Sleeping Princess*,' and so it was announced all through the season. A fortune was spent on the costumes and scenery designed by Bakst – and a fortune lost. It was splendid entertainment, and to say that it was the most wonderful feast of decor as well as of dancing London has ever seen would hardly be an exaggeration.

Those were still the times when the first ballerina could not be expected to dance every evening, so Diaghilev had a team of four, Trefilova, Egorova, Spesivtseva and myself, who alternated the principal roles. I shall never forget the first night when I danced the Lilac Fairy the machinery failed; when I waved my wand and cast my spell, nothing happened, and nothing rose from the stage to cover us. There we remained in full view of the audience, the whole illusion destroyed, and the beautiful climax lost. It was before the days when all the suburbs were balletomaniac, and my husband, who was courting me in those days, would sit alone in an empty row of stalls. Diaghilev never fully recovered from the financial blow of that season.

Asked for three sentences on Diaghilev, I would say, first, that he was the most absolute and the most beloved of tyrants; second, that his reign was the most splendid in the history of the ballet. As for the third sentence, Diaghilev would not have allowed me to add it.

Serge Diaghilev (1872–1929)

Lydia Lopokova

This obituary appeared in The Nation and Athenaeum *on 31 August 1929.*

M. K.

It is hard to realize that Diaghilev is dead. He leaves a big empty space which it is impossible to fill. For he was a Life-Force, something extraordinary, which made the world more vital and moving than it can be when he is gone.

Twenty years ago a few Russians came together to propagate the arts of their country in Paris and Western Europe – Diaghilev, Benois, Bakst, Stravinsky and Fokin. The talents of this little group of friends laid the foundations, but Diaghilev soon assumed the supreme directorship, with Nijinsky and Karsavina as his leading artists. Apart from Stravinsky, who wrote, I think, no less than seven ballets, and lately Prokofiev, he came gradually to depend more on French, Spanish, Italian, and occasionally English, than on Russian collaborators for music and décor. But from his first performance in Paris in 1909 to his last in Covent Garden in 1929, he carried the burden – uninterrupted even by the war – of choosing, displaying and financing as remarkable a combination of work by the greatest artists of the day as any age has known. He has formed the tastes of our generation. He has furnished the capitals of the world for twenty years with splendid and lavish spectacles. I think that when we look back in later years it may seem that the Ballets Russes of Diaghilev will stand out as the representative artistic achievement of this epoch.

Perhaps it is worth while to make a list of some of the artists whom Diaghilev employed during their life-time:

Musicians – Rimsky-Korsakov, Liadov (his own master), Glazunov, Tcherepnin, Stravinsky, Prokofiev, Debussy, Ravel, Poulenc, Auric, Milhaud, Falla, Rieti, Respighi, Tomasini, Strauss, Hindemith, Lambert, Berners.

Painters – Matisse, Braque, Derain, Laurencin, Utrillo, Gris, Roualt, Miro, Picasso, Benois, Bakst, Golovin, Goncharova, Larionov, Yakulov, Pruna, Chirico.

Choreographers – Fokin, Nijinsky, Massine, Nijinska, Balanchine.

Dancers – Pavlova, Karsavina, Trefilova, Spesivtseva, Lopokova, Egorova, Tchernicheva, Sokolova, Nemchinova, Danilova, Dubrovska, Nikitina, Bolm, Woizikovsky, Idzikovsky, Vladimirov, Slavinsky, Vilzak, Lifar, Dolin (besides the choreographs above); and Maestro and Madame Cecchetti.

I try to recollect the qualities which made all this possible – apart from the taste and knowledge, which was, of course, at the bottom of everything I put first of all his *authority*, which did not always stop short of ruthlessness. It needed an Ivan the Terrible or Catherine the Great to drive this mad, egotistical and capricious crowd! He bluffed, scourged and tyrannized over that list of impossible persons which is printed above; and it was necessary.

Next there was his energy. He never did anything himself indeed; there must always be a staff to carry out the orders. But he was not a lazy person. For example, he would stay for many hours in the theatre without food before a new production, until all was in order.

Next, his courage. He would not yield to the opinion of anyone where it was contrary to what he believed himself. At the worst moments of the war, with no money, no contracts and no passports, when his rich friends were urging him to leave the dancers and come quietly to Paris, he would sit with us for hours in the Park at Madrid and then say, 'No, I can't do it.' There were times after 1914 when his best artists deserted him; but he always came up out of the pit and resurrected himself with a new triumph.

Next, there was his combination of a lavish willingness to spend money to produce the effects he desired, with a remarkable financial prudence. There were certain financial risks which he would never take upon himself – someone else must first be found who could carry them for him. Before 1914, when money came more easily, he was naturally generous. But afterwards he became extremely economical, and by this means he produced many score of costly spectacles and dragged a company of fifty or sixty persons about the world for twenty years. Recently the good patronage of English audiences made things easier again. Formerly he would always mock the English, but lately he appreciated and was grateful for their support and had begun to say that London, no longer Paris, was the best centre. Indeed, the love of the English for ballet has been greater than that of any other people outside Russia, and I think that the galleries of the English theatres both understand and discriminate good ballet from bad better than any other audience.

Then there was the cunning with which he knew how to combine the excellent with the fashionable, the beautiful with the chic, and revolutionary art with the atmosphere of the old regime. Perhaps this corresponded to something in his own nature. In spite of his love for the *dernier cri* and the emancipation of his taste, no one could ever have called Diaghilev a 'high-brow'. He was an orthodox believer, and devoted slave of Emperors and Kings. Indeed, he was a convinced snob, and it was not only thoughts of the box office which made him so spry and contented when the King of Spain, the Duke of Connaught, or even the Aga Khan was in the theatre! He was superstitious; charms, potions, love-philtres were not entirely outside his mentality.

He was remarkable in his foresight of what gifts could be developed in a dancer. He knew better than anyone whom to cast for what part, and had an instinct what line of body would be suitable. Although he had experimented in other arts, he loved the ballet chiefly. When I would tell him that I had ambitions for the drama, he would answer: 'To say with words is nothing. Do it with your body. I want the movements. They are much stronger.'

And lastly, as the force without which, I think, the rest could not have been enough, there was the personal motive of his successive attachments to Nijinsky, Massine and Lifar. It was his unceasing preoccupation to educate, inspire and develop the natural talents of these dancers and choreographers to the utmost limit of their possibilities. It would be half true to say that all this energy was exercised, the great Opera Houses of the world rented, and the most famous musicians and artists commissioned in order that a splendid ensemble might be created for their setting off, that glory should surround their triumphs and the most perfect opportunities be offered for their self-expression.

In trying to give a true portrait I have written a few words which may look hard. But they are not meant so. He had a big nature, and faults which might not be forgiven in others were in him part of a grand naturalness. He took a great deal out of life, because he was so determined to be and to do what he chose. No one could be more full of charm and kind mockery and affection, when life so moved him. I drop a wreath of tender and grateful feelings on the tomb of Big Serge.

We Russians – You English

Mrs Maynard Keynes

This article appeared in the Daily Chronicle *of 13 March 1929*
M. K.

I am so used by now to English customs (and climate) that I almost (not quite) take milk with my tea. I begin to forget Imperial Petrograd, where I was brought up in the Tsar's boarding school which he kept as a part of his gigantic Court for the children of the ballet. But twice since the Bolsheviks' revolution I have been back to Red Leningrad.

The glory is gone. Yet I am not sure that it is so much changed as you might suppose. Even my old school survives so that the proletariat may feel themselves as good as Romanovs. They danced in the famine of 1921-2 with the temperature of the theatre below zero, and a cabbage and a herring's head to eat, but they danced on. You can still buy the delicious cakes at Gourmet's Restaurant on the Nevsky (for the famous pre-war pastrycooks have been nationalized!) – that is if you have enough money. But, above all, you can still talk – which is the only thing a Russian really cares about. Which brings me to the greatest contrast of all I feel between English life and eternal Russia. The English are not exactly dumb – I do not say that. They even make after-dinner speeches. But they do not talk as we do in the train, in the tram, in the café, eagerly, endlessly, uproariously, just for its own sake. Very often we are unreasonable, we talk nonsense, we exaggerate and we lie. One remembers the heroine of *The Cherry Orchard* and the old Chekhov world; their conversation was their only outlet. When I ask an English lady to lunch she begins to put on her gloves – what a horrid, rude unsocial, by-the-clock custom that is! How I hate to see it! – almost as soon as we leave the table. But when I ask Russian friends, they arrive, it is true, an hour late, but they stay on to tea, and to dinner if there is any encouragement, and will think it natural to spend the night on the drawing-room sofa.

Can you imagine such habits in England? The servants would be shocked – it would be against their principles. But the Russians have no principles – it is only a question if the conversation is good and flowing and disinclined to come to a terminus. Being so conversational, we naturally drink more tea, very weak tea, but always fresh, poured down the larynx with two drops of lemon, just enough to readjust that organ to a fresh starting point of words. *Conversation gives life fullness and variety, and is one of the best creations of the human mind.* The English can smile, I know, delightfully. There is the Prince's smile and Mr Baldwin's smile, if he were to take the pipe out, and Mr Bernard Shaw boasts that he can outsmile Mussolini, since, he says, it comes to him more naturally. But the English middle classes – perhaps the working man and the charladies have more capabilities in this direction – can't sit round as we do for hours and hours talking, talking – about nothing at all – yet making of it something delightful, a sort of art of life.

But there is something else, of quite a different kind, which always strikes me. Everyone in England seems to have a small income, even if it is only a few pounds a year, from an investment or a legacy. But, on the other hand, everyone subscribes to something – the English are so good – to some church or cause or fund. I found it funny – does that show a bad heart? – when I discovered that every respectable person in England pays five shillings to convert the Jews, five shillings to end war, five shillings to a cats' home, five shillings to teach birth-control to miners, five shillings to illegitimate mothers in villages and five shillings to translate the Bible into Papuan. I do not take my husband seriously when he draws the cheques for his subscriptions. No one in Russia has ever subscribed to any thing since the world began. They would think you mad if you suggested it. But we have a much greater expense to make up for this little economy. We support our families. The criminal classes support their families. The most outrageous Communist supports his wife's brother-in-law's aunt. For when I say family, I mean anyone anyhow connected by blood or marriage.

I have an old friend in the Russian ballet, a great dancer. One half of his income he gambles away, besides pawning his wife's furs; with the other half he supports his parents, his child by his first wife, his second wife's parents and his second wife's child by her first husband. And this is the literal truth. But he does not subscribe to a hospital or to anti-vaccination or to provide for the widows of cabmen. And that, I suppose, is how he manages to afford it. Perhaps it is that we in Russia support our relations while we are alive, but you in England, with your legacies, do it after you are dead. So this is how we live in Russia, talking, drinking tea, supporting a hundred relations, though we do not find it necessary to write up what I find on the portal of every church in England *that a man may not marry his grandmother*.

Twelfth Night at the Old Vic

Virginia Woolf

This review of the production of Shakespeare's play in which Lydia Lopokova acted the part of Olivia appeared in the New Statesman and Nation *on 30 September 1933. It was reprinted posthumously in* The Death of the Moth and other Essays (*Hogarth Press, 1945*).

M. K.

Shakespeareans are divided, it is well known, into three classes; those who prefer to read Shakespeare in the book; those who prefer to see him acted on the stage; and those who run perpetually from book to stage gathering plunder. Certainly there is a good deal to be said for reading *Twelfth Night* in the book if the book can be read in a garden, with no sound but the thud of an apple falling to the earth, or of the wind ruffling the branches of the trees. For one thing there is time – time not only to hear 'the sweet sound that breathes upon a bank of violets' but to unfold the implications of that very subtle speech as the Duke winds into the nature of love. There is time, too, to make a note in the margin; time to wonder at queer jingles like 'that live in her; when liver, brain, and heart' ... 'and of a foolish knight that you brought in one night' and to ask oneself whether it

was from them that was born the lovely, 'And what should I do in
Illyria? My brother he is in Elysium.' For Shakespeare is writing, it
seems, not with the whole of his mind mobilized and under control
but with feelers left flying that sport and play with words so that the
trail of a chance word is caught and followed recklessly. From the
echo of one word is born another word, for which reason, perhaps,
the play seems as we read it to tremble perpetually on the brink of
music. They are always calling for songs in *Twelfth Night*, 'O fellow
come, the song we had last night.' Yet Shakespeare was not so
deeply in love with words but that he could turn and laugh at them.
'They that do dally with words do quickly make them wanton.'
There is a roar of laughter and out burst Sir Toby, Sir Andrew,
Maria. Words on their lips are things that have meaning; that rush
and leap out with a whole character packed in a little phrase. When
Sir Andrew says 'I was adored once,' we feel that we hold him in
the hollow of our hands; a novelist would have taken three volumes
to bring us to that pitch of intimacy. And Viola, Malvolio, Olivia,
the Duke – the mind so brims and spills over with all that we know
and guess about them as they move in and out among the lights and
shadows of the mind's stage that we ask why should we imprison
them within the bodies of real men and women? Why exchange this
garden for the theatre? The answer is that Shakespeare wrote for the
stage and presumably with reason. Since they are acting *Twelfth
Night* at the Old Vic, let us compare the two versions.

Many apples might fall without being heard in the Waterloo
Road, and as for the shadows, the electric light has consumed them
all. The first impression upon entering the Old Vic is overwhelm-
ingly positive and definite. We seem to have issued out from the
shadows of the garden upon the bridge of the Parthenon. The
metaphor is mixed, but then so is the scenery. The columns of the
bridge somehow suggest an Atlantic liner and the austere splendours
of a classical temple in combination. But the body is almost as
upsetting as the scenery. The actual persons of Malvolio, Sir Toby,
Olivia and the rest expand our visionary characters out of all recognition. At first we are inclined to resent it. You are not Malvolio; or
Sir Toby either, we want to tell them; but merely imposters. We sit
gaping at the ruins of the play, at the travesty of the play. And then
by degrees this same body or rather all these bodies together, take
our play and remodel it between them. The play gains immensely
in robustness, in solidity. The printed word is changed out of all

recognition when it is heard by other people. We watch it strike upon this man or woman; we see them laugh or shrug their shoulders, or turn aside to hide their faces. The word is given a body as well as a soul. Then again as the actors pause, or topple over a barrel, or stretch their hands out, the flatness of the print is broken up as by crevasses or precipices; all the proportions are changed. Perhaps the most impressive effect in the play is achieved by the long pause which Sebastian and Viola make as they stand looking at each other in a silent ecstasy of recognition. The reader's eye may have slipped over that moment entirely. Here we are made to pause and think about it; and are reminded that Shakespeare wrote for the body and for the mind simultaneously.

But now that the actors have done their proper work of solidifying and intensifying our impressions, we begin to criticize them more minutely and to compare their version with our own. We make Mr Quartermaine's Malvolio stand beside our Malvolio. And to tell the truth, wherever the fault may lie, they have very little in common. Mr Quatermaine's Malvolio is a splendid gentleman, courteous, considerate, well bred; a man of parts and humour who has no quarrel with the world. He has never felt a twinge of vanity or a moment's envy in his life. If Sir Toby and Maria fool him he sees through it, we may be sure, and only suffers it as a fine gentleman puts up with the games of foolish children. Our Malvolio, on the other hand, was a fantastic complex creature, twitching with vanity, tortured by ambition. There was cruelty in his teasing, and a hint of tragedy in his defeat; his final threat had a momentary terror in it. But when Mr Quartermaine says 'I'll be revenged on the whole pack of you,' we feel merely that the powers of the law will be soon and effectively invoked. What, then, becomes of Olivia's 'He hath been most notoriously abused'? Then there is Olivia. Madame Lopokova has by nature that rare quality which is neither to be had for the asking nor to be subdued by the will – the genius of personality. She has only to float on to the stage and everything round her suffers, not a sea change, but a change into light, into gaiety; the birds sing, the sheep are garlanded, the air rings with melody and human beings dance towards each other on the tips of their toes possessed of an exquisite friendliness, sympathy and delight. But our Olivia was a stately lady; of sombre complexion, slow moving and of few sympathies. She could not love the Duke nor change her feeling. Madame Lopokova loves everybody. She is always changing. Her hands, her face, her feet, the whole of her body, are always quivering in sympathy with the moment. She could make the moment, as she proved when she walked down the stairs with Sebastian, one of intense and moving beauty; but she was not our Olivia. Compared with her the comic group, Sir Toby, Sir Andrew, Maria, the fool were more than ordinarily English. Coarse, humorous, robust, they trolled out their words, they rolled over their barrels; they acted magnificently. No reader, one may make bold to say, could outpace Miss Seyler's Maria, with its quickness, its inventiveness, its merriment; nor add anything to the humours of Mr Livesey's Sir Toby. And Miss Jeans as Viola was satisfactory; and Mr Hare as Antonio was admirable; and Mr Morland's clown was a good clown. What, then, was lacking in the play as a whole? Perhaps that it was not a whole. The fault may lie partly with Shakespeare. It is easier to act his comedy than his poetry, one may suppose, for when he wrote as a poet he was apt to write too quick for the human tongue. The prodigality of his metaphors can be flashed over by the eye, but the speaking voice falters in the middle. Hence the comedy was out of proportion to the rest. Then, perhaps, the actors were too highly charged with individuality or too incongruously cast. They broke the play up into separate pieces – now we were in the groves of Arcady, now in some inn at Blackfriars. The mind in reading spins a web from scene to scene, compounds a background from apples falling, and the toll of a church bell, and an owl's fantastic flight which keeps the play together. Here that continuity was sacrificed. We left the theatre possessed of many brilliant fragments but without the sense of all things conspiring and combining together which may be the satisfying culmination of a less brilliant performance. Nevertheless, the play has served its purpose. It has made us compare our Malvolio with Mr Quartermaine's; Our Olivia with Madame Lopokova's; our reading of the whole play with Mr Guthrie's; and since they all differ, back we must go to Shakespeare. We must read *Twelfth Night* again. Mr Guthrie has made that necessary and whetted our appetite for the *Cherry Orchard*, *Measure for Measure* and *Henry the Eighth* that are still to come.

This review was written only with reluctance and at Lydia Lopokova's request. The earliest of Virginia Woolf's letters in which she mentions Lydia acting in *Twelfth Night* is dated 31 July 1933: 'Lydia is now going on the stage, as Rosalind or Ophelia: though she speaks English like a parrokeet.' Then, on 3 September: '... while Lydia sits mumbling the part of Olivia in 12th night which she is to act at the Old Vic.' On 10 September: 'Lydia makes me write about 12th Night. Must go to London to Old Vic. Must write journalism.' On 19 September, to Quentin Bell:

> ... have you read the mornings paper on Lydia? The D.T. [*Daily Telegraph*] is scathing.* My god; what shall I say? I think the only possible line to take is how very exciting it is to see Shakespr mauled; of course one might make play with the idea that the Elizabethans were just as unintelligible; and throw in a hint about opposites being the same thing as equalities – if you take my meaning. Either the worst, or the best – that sort of remark, Well. Pity me.

In a letter to Lady Ottoline Morrell dated 7 October, Virginia Woolf wrote, 'Oh how I hated writing that tough little article! Poor dear Lydia asked me to do it – she attached great value to her acting – she wants to be an actress – and the whole thing was a dismal farce, and she is out of the Cherry Orchard in consequence. But never will I write about a friend again. They may wear the stones out on their knees before I go through that agony.'

On 27 December she wrote to Hugh Walpole, 'Lydia wants to act but cant.' There is, however, a reversal of her bad opinion of Lydia's acting in a letter to Quentin Bell dated 8 March 1934:

> Also there was Lydia's Dolls House, which was a triumphant success, much to our surprise. Dear Old Maynard was – this is exactly true – streaming tears; and I kissed him in the stalls between the acts; really she was a marvel, not only a light leaf in the wind, but edged, profound, and her English was exactly what Ibsen meant – it gave the right aroma. So shes in the 7th Heaven and runs about kissing and crying. Whether it means business I dont know.

---

* W.A. Darlington had written, 'Lydia Lopokova makes her bow ... as the most humourless female in literature. ... What possessed anybody to give the part of Olivia to her?'

Lydia Lopokova

Cyril W. Beaumont

This appreciation of Lydia Lopokova was published in The Art of Lydia Lopokova *by C. W. Beaumont in 1920.*

M.K.

If ever anyone was destined for the dance it is surely Lydia Lopokova, for the gods who were present at her birth bestowed their gifts unsparingly. She has a compact and beautifully proportioned body, rounded limbs, plump cheeks, a charming air of innocent surprise. Yet she reminds one irresistibly of a bird, perhaps one of those canaries she loves so well.

One is impressed even more by her extraordinary vitality and youth. She dances with an *élan* and *joie de vivre* that render one speechless with admiration. And then she possesses that supreme gift of being able to achieve the most complicated *pas* as if it were the merest bagatelle. The spectator is not for one moment conscious of the effort entailed by such a movement or the hours of study that brought forth such a facility of gesture. Everything seems spontaneous, a happy inspiration, and here is revealed the true artist, for the highest form of art is surely that which conceals the labour that produced it.

Her personality is extraordinarily complex. She has the dignity, the repose and exquisite grace that contemporary writers attributed to Taglioni; the fascination, archness and twinkling steps of Grisi and the power to execute the wonderful leaps and bounds that were the glory of Cerrito.

Here is no dancer, no mime who merely changes her dress. Every role is separate and distinct. It is almost impossible to believe that the same heart beats in the breast of the angular marionette-like figure of the Ballerina in *Petrushka* as in the dare-devil dancer of the Can-Can in *La Boutique Fantasque* – white limbs flashing in a foam of lace and ribbon.

Whether she be the frenzied Bacchante of *Cleopatra*, the pert Mariuccia of *The Good-humoured Ladies*, or the chaste vision that floats like a cloud in *Les Sylphides*, she gives her being, her soul, to the realization of her creation. And yet all is fresh, unmarred by time, as if but just composed.

Will you share with me my memories?

Here is the burning Egyptian desert, crested with gleaming pyramids shadowed by the sharp outline of a sombre temple. Couched upon a *lectus* is Cleopatra, cold, statuesque as some marble Sphinx, dispelling the spectre of her thoughts with the wine-cup and the rhythm of the dance. Rose petals are whirled into the air to fall fluttering like so many pink butterflies. The Bacchantes sweep in to the crash and jungle of cymbals and tambourines. A lithe figure, clad only in a flowing *chiton* - arms flung aloft, head thrown back, golden tresses streaming in the wind - leaps, bounds, dances with all the grace and agility of a Mænad.

It is night. Let us tread this *allée* lined with massive clumps of giant yews, lightly flecked with the wan rays of the moon. It is peopled with vague memories of pavanes and minuets, of courtly bows and graces, of Arnould, of Guimard. Sweet melodies caress the ear and through the trees glide a band of sylphs. Here is one so sad that the heart yearns with sympathy, one who floats so gracefully, so regardless of the laws of gravitation, as to seem a cloud poised on two feet, while her long white arms ripple and undulate - a wind-borne ribbon.

Venice, with its twisting canals, its flat roofs, its towering *campanili*. It is the hour of Carnival, the air is scented with *billets-doux*. Enter the lady of good humour, Mariuccia; pert, winsome, seducing everyone with her gay chatter, bright eyes and merry laughter. She is an eager party to every fun and frolic; she is the spirit of mischief. How she flirts with Leonardo and Battista! Can you forget the joy of that tomboy pas de trois, the coquettish elbowing of each in turn? Then the uproarious fun at the supper-table set to the music of clashing knives and forks, the dances, the kisses, the naughty whispering into the speaking-trumpet of the amorous old Marquis! Is she not adorable, this little minx?

Now, sorrowful again in *Papillons* - a primrose butterfly whose fragile wings are broken by the clumsy Pierrot. Then her recovery and last glance over her shoulder at the poor fool enslaved in her toils, as she departs, leaning on her lover's arm. Do you not remember that smile, half amused, then saddened, as his face betrays the anguish of his broken heart?

I see her in *Carnaval*, that innocent, irresponsible, roguish little person, the swish of whose silken petticoat suffices to set all hearts a-flutter. How delightfully she coquets with the fussy Pantaloon, luring him on with enticing smile and shaded glance until just as he feels his conquest to be complete, he is dismissed with a push into the wings. Then the pas de deux of the *Renaissance*, the dainty tip-toeing with Harlequin. She beckons him to her side. Can you forget that prettily tilted chin, that coyly raised finger? I am always re-minded of one of those demure china shepherdesses awakened to life.

The scene changes. I see a dense forest, the overladen branches of whose trees twist and curl in the most fantastic shapes. Every breeze whispers of magic and witchcraft. There are mysterious rustlings, the shrill long-drawn cry of an unknown creature calling to another, while the earth dimly echoes with the dull, methodical tapping of gnomes working underground. All is dark save for one tree, which stands apart from the rest and gleams with an orange radiance. The air is filled with the tremulous beating of the wings of a bird soaring in circular flight and to the golden tree darts the glowing Bird of Fire. How gaily she plays amid the glittering leaves. Then that moment of terror when she is caught in the strong embrace of the prince. Do you remember those pleading eyes, half filled with tears, the quivering of her breast, the pitiful fluttering of her arms? But when her liberty is regained, how she flits with little, short steps into the depths of the forest, in the joy of her regained freedom.

Again the same being, but this time a puppet, a creature of sawdust and painted wood. Can it be that this toy Ballerina, with glassy eyes and vermilion cheeks, is she who only a few minutes since, disported in the enchanted glade of Fairy-land? I see her swift feet pattering in her little box, the automatic dance in the snow, her disdain for Petrushka, her entrance into the gorgeous apartment of the Moor, the dainty dance with the toy trumpet. Then, dazzled by his splendid costume, she falls, a by no means unwilling victim, to the wicked advances of the sensual Moor.

Yet again I see her as a Polovtsian maiden in *Prince Igor*, her body animated from head to toe - her feet leaping and stamping, her arms shaking, with so savage a ferocity that one's blood turns to fire. There she stands, a vivid symbol of war, silhouetted against the red glow of camp-fires, while the earth rocks under the frenzied lashing of bows, the rhythmic thud of countless feet, and the air quivers to the shrill blare of horns, the reverberating crash of cymbals, the pulsating throb of lustily beaten drums.

And lastly in *La Boutique Fantasque* – who can forget the audacity, the verve, the *délire des jambes* of the can-can performed by the little lady in the frou-frou skirts of the Third Empire? It is amazing to see this quiet figure, stiff, inanimate as a china doll until – bang goes the drum and she is transformed into a Bacchanalian fury. Her body bends and sways as though fashioned of indiarubber, her foot leaps above her head, writhes, twists, turns, revolves amid a sea of foaming lace and ribbon. It is an astounding performance, yet in her hands it is a thing of delirious joy, revealing not a trace of the vulgarity that it might obtain were it performed by a lesser artist.

I cannot believe that there will ever be another dancer like Lopo-kova who has the gift of being elf, sylph, bacchante at will. Who can forget those wonderful *grands jetés* of the mazurka in *Les Sylphides*, those dazzling *entrechats* in *Petrushka*, those breathless *ronds de jambe* in *La Boutique Fantasque*? Her body resembles some exquisite mechanism in the delicate sensibility, the acute precision of its movements. Only in the very greatest dancers does the body become so completely the slave of the spirit. But when she dances one is no longer conscious of the body's painful response to the mandates of the mind. There is some cunning alchemy by which matter and spirit are so incorporated, so fused together that they seem indivisible. Doubtless, something of this perfect balance is derived from the careful technical training she received from Maestro Cecchetti.

As a mime, her extraordinary youth and vitality, her buoyant personality fit her for the art of comedy rather than that of drama. Who can forget the dainty coquetry of her Columbine in *Carnaval*, the piquant artlessness of her Mariuccia in *The Good-humoured Ladies*, the *naiveté* of her Ballerina in *Petrushka*, the pleasant naughtiness of her Can-Can Dancer in *La Boutique Fantasque*?

And her arms – was it not Noverre who remarked in his *Lettres sur la Danse* that 'peu d'artistes sont distingués par un beau style de bras'? Again, Blasis, in his *Code de Terpischore*, states that of all the movements of the dance, the most difficult is the correct deportment of the arms. Her arms are more expressive than the spoken word. 'Her gestures have a language, her hands a mouth and her fingers a voice.'

No one who has not seen her fresh from the fall of the curtain can imagine how completely her soul enters into the body of her creation. For many minutes she still lives whither her role has led her. To visit her after *Carnaval* is to see a young girl alive with fun and overflowing with good spirits as if she had just returned from some long-promised children's party. I recall the first night of the revival of *Les Sylphides*. Her dressing-room was crowded with friends eager to voice her praise. Then she came, fairy-like in white muslin, her hair wreathed about with forget-me-nots, her countenance still reflecting the sadness of Chopin's music and in her hands a little posy of wild flowers – pale, sweet, fragile as some chaste Victorian bride.

But hush, you are to see the theatre in darkness, the footlights glow green, and threading his way through the white faces of the orchestra, appears the thin silhouette of M. Defosse. He climbs into his seat – three metallic taps as his baton strikes the iron frame of his desk – his arms swing into view – the overture has begun. The curtain leaps upwards, to carry with it our thoughts, our woes, our cares. We have no knowledge of the outside world, of age, of time, of space – Lopokova dances.

Index